FROM POPE JOHN PAUL II TO BENEDICT XVI

FROM Pope John Paul II

An Inside Look at the End of an Era, the Beginning

EDITED BY SISTER MARY ANN WALSH, RSM

TO Benedict XVI

of a New One, and the Future of the Church

WITH REPORTING BY CATHOLIC NEWS SERVICE

A SHEED & WARD BOOK

ROWMAN & LITTLEFIELD PUBLISHERS, INC.
Lanham • Boulder • New York • Toronto • Oxford

A SHEED & WARD BOOK
ROWMAN & LITTLEFIELD PUBLISHERS, INC.

Published in the United States of America
by Rowman & Littlefield Publishers, Inc.
A wholly owned subsidary of The Rowman & Littlefield Publishing Group, Inc.
4501 Forbes Boulevard, Suite 200, Lanham, Maryland 20706
www.rowmanlittlefield.com

PO Box 317
Oxford
OX2 9RU, UK

British Library Cataloguing in Publication Information Available

Library of Congress Cataloging-in-Publication Data
From Pope John Paul II to Benedict XVI : an inside look at the end of an era, the beginning of a new one, and the future of the church / edited by Mary Ann Walsh ; with reporting by Catholic News Service.
    p. cm.
  "A Sheed & Ward book."
  Includes bibliographical references and index.
  ISBN 1-58051-202-X (cloth : alk. paper)
  1. Benedict XVI, Pope, 1927- 2. John Paul II, Pope, 1920- —Death and burial.
I. Walsh, Mary Ann, Sister, RSM. II. Catholic News Service.

BX1378.6.F76 2005
282'.092'245634—dc22

                                                                                    2005023458

Printed in the United States of America

♾ The paper used in this publication meets the minimum requirements of American National Standard for Information Sciences—Permanence of Paper for Printed Library Materials, ANSI/NISO Z39.48-1992.

CONTENTS

ACKNOWLEDGMENTS

M ANY people assisted in the development of this book, including the United States Conference of Catholic Bishops' Department of Communications, directed by Msgr. Francis J. Maniscalco. Special thanks to Tony Spence, Catholic News Service director and editor in chief; CNS Rome bureau chief John Thavis; CNS Rome correspondents Cindy Wooden and Carol Glatz; CNS photography editor Nancy Wiechec; Tony DeFeo, former CNS graphic artist; intern Zachary Dunham; and Mary Esslinger, associate editor, Origins. Thanks also to Sister Amy Hoey, RSM, colleague and critical reader; Sherri Watkins and Alecia Maniatis, of the USCCB Office of Media Relations, and Jeremy Langford, former editor at Sheed & Ward, who saw the significance of this book. Thanks too to Cardinal William H. Keeler of Baltimore, whose sense of history inspired him to bring home from the conclave mementos pictured here.

Others who contributed to the book include CNS staff Julie Asher, Agostino Bono, Bessie Briscoe, Jerry Filteau, Barb Fraze, Nancy Hartnagel, James Lackey, Katherine Nuss, Nancy Frazier O'Brien, Mark Pattison, Cassandra Shieh, Stephen Steele, Patricia Zapor and Carol Zimmermann, and CNS correspondents and reporters Benedicta Cipolla (Rome), Tess Crebbin (Germany), Sarah Delaney (Rome), Eleni E. Dimmler (Rome), Barbara J. Fraser (Rome), and Jonathan Luxmoore (Poland and Rome). The editors also acknowledge the contributions of CNS clients and stringers throughout the world.

INTRODUCTION

PRIVILEGE doesn't often come my way, but it certainly did in April 2005 when I was in Rome during the papal transition after the death of John Paul II. Being there made me part of the experience, which included celebrating the funeral of a pope who had led the church for more than 26 years and the election of Benedict XVI as the 264th successor of St. Peter.

As deputy director for media relations for the United States Conference of Catholic Bishops, I served as liaison between the U.S. bishops and the media. Sometimes my role involved setting up a press conference, at other times, explaining church teaching. Usually I was behind the scenes; occasionally, I appeared on camera, speaking to the world via CNN.

Even if my job had been handing out bottles of water to the people on the streets as one of Rome's many volunteers during those days, it would have been worth it just to be there at that moment. For Rome, in April 2005 in the year of Our Lord, was a graced place, the center of a worldwide religious experience that brought out the best in everyone.

Media work is frantic by nature, but Rome has a way of imposing meditative moments upon everyone. Standing in line, even while surrounded by cell phones, can leave you open to a word from God.

My first such moment was waiting for admission to the burial site of John Paul II, the day after he was entombed in the grotto beneath St. Peter's Basilica. Queued with journalists for a visit before the public was admitted, I thought about the Apostles' Creed. Since my arrival two days after John Paul's death, the lines into the basilica had seemed endless. There was time to think, and St. Peter's always makes me think of the creed. A sense of the great events that have occurred in this holy place in past centuries permeates the air. And I always wonder about the figures great and small who have walked on these stones or glided across this marble in an earlier age.

When I reached the pope's tomb, I prayed the Apostles' Creed and offered a prayer that the Lord would grant him eternal peace. It was a small gesture, but at least it was something I could do for the late leader of the Church. With the words, "Compassionate Lord Jesus, grant him rest in peace," I offered the prayer I say for any deceased person I call to mind. There's something humbling about the fact that Catholics pray the same prayer and hold the same funeral rites whether the deceased is John Paul II or John Doe the 10,000th. In the Catholic tradition, popes and paupers all get the same sendoff to their eternal reward.

I thought of the great paradox of life: Each one of us is unique yet at the same time we're all equal in the eyes of God. Once I interviewed the pastoral theologian Father Henri Nouwen, who told me each of us is "God's favorite child." When I asked how this could be, Father Nouwen said that it was my inability to imagine that led me to limit the Lord. God can have more than one favorite child, he said. So here I was at John Paul's tomb, one favorite child praying for another.

I smiled at the late pope's prime real estate—near the bones of St. Peter himself and close to the only two women buried under the basilica, 15th-century Queen Charlotte of Cyprus and 17th-century Queen Christina of Sweden. Blessed John XXIII had been there until he was moved up into the basilica following his beatification. He had been placed in a sarcophagus above the ground; John Paul lay under the floor.

Souvenir hunting is part of Rome, especially at historic moments. One morning I found myself waiting in line for 90 minutes to get *sede vacante* stamps. The stamps bore the image of a half-closed umbrella, the symbol of the church when there is no pope. As I stood in line at the Vatican post office, I prayed the rosary. It felt right as I stood among locals posting their mail and tourists seeking remembrances of the papal transition. Anything else seemed unworthy of this moment. The stamps would soon be worthless for postage but priceless in reminding me of a certain emptiness, a betwixt and between feeling, that marks the absence of a leader.

A most profound sense of expectation filled me in St. Peter's Basilica at the Mass that opened the conclave. As a temporarily accredited member of the Vatican press corps, I had a wonderful, though uncomfortable position on scaffolding about 9 feet above the congregation.

After climbing the narrow rungs of a perpendicular ladder, I found a place where I could see well. There was time to look about and study the well-known and not-so-well-known churchmen, dignitaries and people from the neighborhood gathering in the basilica; but I found myself mesmerized by a figure below and across from me, my favorite statue in the basilica—the 13th-century bronze sculpture of a seated Peter, his right hand in blessing, his left hand holding the keys to the kingdom of heaven. His right foot juts out, and so many people have kissed or touched the toes that they have been worn away. I was awed by the fact that the cardinals were about to enter the conclave to elect Peter's successor.

Journalists often leave Mass to write their stories after the homily, but I couldn't get myself to leave. The church universal was united in prayer throughout the world, and I wanted to be as close to that as possible.

Once the conclave was under way on Monday, a new period of anxious waiting overtook me because as media liaison I had to organize a press conference about the new pope upon his election. The main difficulty lay in not knowing when the election would take place or which cardinals would be present. To compose myself, on Tuesday morning I slipped into the chapel of North American College after the seminarians had gone to class. Alone in the dark with just a flickering sanctuary lamp in the distance, I prayed, "Lord of reporters and technicians, if this press conference is to happen, it's up to You." A small measure of confidence came over me that let me rest in the unknown. I e-mailed the media with tentative plans, and I waited in peace. That night some cardinals met individually with the media, just hours after the election. On Wednesday morning all seven cardinals heading archdioceses in the United States appeared at a formal press conference at North American College and all felt right with the world.

Like tens of thousands of others, I'll always remember the moments that followed the appearance of white smoke rising from the chimney of the Sistine Chapel. Crowds began pouring into the street. The bells of the basilica started to peal, a sure sign a new pope had been elected. A cardinal came on to the balcony and announced his name: Joseph Cardinal Ratzinger. The people cheered. Mindful of the polarization in contemporary society and even in the church, a spontaneous wish for the new pope came to my lips, "Bring us together," I pleaded. "Bring us together."

Reflecting the incisive work of an outstanding team of reporters from Catholic News Service, led by its Rome bureau chief John Thavis, and including photographs by CNS photo editor Nancy Wiechec, *From Pope John Paul II to Benedict XVI* captures the moments of the church during the days of mourning, waiting, rejoicing, and looking forward. It serves as a keepsake of a vital time in the church's life, while inviting everyday Catholics into deeper reflection about and understanding of the witness of the church today. It recalls a worldwide event whose participants ranged from world leaders to street sweepers, from Christ-centered nuns in monasteries to people who wonder if there is a God at all. It reveals the power of the church's timeless rituals and liturgy that remind us there is a life beyond the one we know on earth. At the same time, it does not try to interpret what happened, for the events—the outpouring of millions of people into the streets of Rome, the worldwide wake via television, the proclamations of the people calling "Sainthood now!" for John Paul II, and the rapid election of Pope Benedict XVI to succeed him—speak for themselves.

SISTER MARY ANN WALSH, RSM

CHAPTER 1

A Giant Dies

S T. PETER'S Square is a gathering place. It's where friends meet at an Egyptian obelisk, tourists stand awed before the encircling Bernini colonnade, world leaders pause to observe the dome designed by Michelangelo for St. Peter's Basilica, and ordinary people wait for a glimpse of the vicar of Christ on earth.

In April 2005, it became home to the world as thousands assembled in person and millions more via television to show their solidarity with the ailing Pope John Paul II.

The piazza, as the square is known in Italy, became the stage for a human drama unknown in previous history.

The story began to unfold March 30, when the pope made a poignant appearance at his apartment window to greet pilgrims in St. Peter's Square and tried in vain to speak to them. After four minutes, he was wheeled from view, and the curtains of his apartment window were drawn—for the last time, as it turned out.

For more than a decade, the pope had suffered from a neurological disorder believed to be Parkinson's disease. As the pope's health failed in early 2005, many of his close aides said his physical decline, never hidden from public view, offered a remarkable Christian witness of suffering.

The crowd in the square that day sensed the closing of a historic papacy of more than 26 years, the third longest in history.

The 84-year-old Polish pontiff had been hospitalized twice for spasms of the larynx, and in late February he had undergone a tracheotomy to make breathing less difficult. Doctors inserted a nasogastric tube to aid nutrition on March 30.

On the evening of the next day, March 31, the pope showed signs

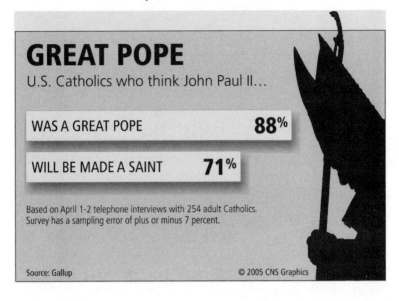

GREAT POPE
U.S. Catholics who think John Paul II...

| WAS A GREAT POPE | 88% |
| WILL BE MADE A SAINT | 71% |

Based on April 1-2 telephone interviews with 254 adult Catholics.
Survey has a sampling error of plus or minus 7 percent.

Source: Gallup   © 2005 CNS Graphics

of a urinary tract infection, and developed a high fever and septic shock, which brought on heart failure. He was treated immediately with antibiotics and respiratory equipment that had been installed in the papal apartment, and his condition stabilized temporarily. But it was clear the pope's condition was deteriorating.

That day the pope received the "holy viaticum," a reference to the Eucharist given when a person is approaching death, the Vatican said. It was the pope who decided to be treated at the Vatican instead of returning to the hospital, said Vatican spokesman Joaquin Navarro-Valls.

Cardinal Mario Francesco Pompedda, who visited the dying pope, described the scene in the pope's bedroom: Assisted by several doctors and his personal staff, the pontiff lay serenely on a bed in the middle of his room, comforted by cushions, occasionally opening his eyes in greeting to the handful of visitors allowed inside.

As word of the pope's failing health spread, tens of thousands of faithful streamed to St. Peter's Square, some staying all night in quiet and prayerful vigils, aware that there was little hope for his recovery. Journalists who tried to enter the square were turned away unless they were coming to pray. The world's media arrived in unprecedented force, surrounding the Vatican with broadcasting trucks and film crews. A supplementary press office was prepared for the thousands of reporters who arrived for the pope's funeral and the conclave.

The Vatican's Web site was overloaded soon after the pope's situation took a turn for the worse, and the Vatican switchboard was jammed. E-mail messages also poured in, offering prayers and condolences.

On the following day, April 1, the crowd continued to grow. Archbishop Angelo Comastri, the pope's vicar for Vatican City, spoke to the assembled people and recalled that when Pope John Paul II made his first public appearance after his election in 1978, he said, "Do not be afraid. Throw open the doors to Christ."

"This evening or tonight Christ will throw open his doors to the pope," said the vicar.

Leading the recitation of the rosary in St. Peter's Square at 9 p.m. that night, Archbishop Comastri said, "When one's father is suffering, his children suffer and when he is dying, his children gather around him."

The recitation of the rosary, he said, was an expression of Catholics' love for the pope and their desire to be with him at the end of his life.

In his honor, the Marian prayer followed the mysteries of light, five reflections on Jesus' life that Pope John Paul added to the traditional rosary prayers in 2002.

Polish Cardinal Zenon Grocholewski, prefect of the Congregation for Catholic Education, spoke to reporters near St. Peter's as the rosary was about to begin.

"Christ will provide for the church," the cardinal said, "and let us hope that he will find a successor as strong as Pope John Paul II. He was truly a strong man, and I think it will be difficult to find someone with the kind of strength he demonstrated."

Before the rosary began, Mario Pascarelli, 70, of Rome, brought his grandchildren and some of their friends to the square.

"This is a moment they must live," he said.

Asked what he will remember most about Pope John Paul, Pascarelli said with feeling, "Everything. Everything, everything, everything, from the very first moment he spoke [after his Oct. 16, 1978, election] and asked that we correct his Italian."

Pascarelli's daughter, Flavia, said she dropped everything as soon as she heard the pope was in critical condition.

"I had to come," she said. "I work. I dropped everything. My job. My house is a mess. But I had to come. I felt it inside."

Larissa Khomitska, 58, of Lviv, Ukraine, said what she will most remember is the pope's 2001 trip to her country.

She said that as a foreigner who has lived in Italy for five years she would miss the Polish pope's presence in a special way.

"It is a loss for us foreigners. He was here for us somehow," she said.

Paolo Orianna Salucci, 16, of Rome, said of Pope John Paul, "He was close to young people, who were always inspired by his goodness."

"I think the pope has been the cement of our times," Salucci said after a pause.

The crowd gradually diminished throughout the night, although a core group of about 200 young people spent the night in the square praying, singing and every once in a while breaking into the chant, "*Giovanni Paolo Secondo*," (John Paul II).

Vatican spokesman Navarro-Valls said that on April 2, the pope was told the young people were there, and "he seemed to be referring to them when, in his words and repeated several times, he seemed to have said the following sentence: 'I have looked for you. Now you have come to me. And I thank you.'"

Every once in a while, Vatican police tried to convince the youth to stop chanting, thinking it disturbed the atmosphere of deep prayer that had reigned over the square.

One of the chanters, a 24-year-old woman from Monterotondo, Italy, said, "It was not lack of respect at all.

"The pope was always so close to us; he shared our enthusiasm," said Laura, who would give only her first name.

Antonio Gentile, 26, from Naples, said he came to the square because Pope John Paul "was the pope all my life."

"He came from a humble family and was practically an orphan" after his mother died when he was almost 9 and his father died when he was 20, Gentile said.

"Now he's dying, and he has no family around him," the young man said. "I thought I would come here like a relative—not as a grandson, but more like a distant cousin."

Remigiusz Tkaczyk, 32, a Pole who works in Rome, and his friends spent the night in the square standing near a Polish flag surrounded by votive candles.

"We were here praying that the cross of our pope comes to an end," he said.

"He showed us the way to live," Tkaczyk said. "Without him, churches would be empty. He filled the churches with young people. Others just complain about what we do wrong or yell at us. He tried to understand us and just show us another way to live."

Conscious and alert the day before his death, the pope was able to concelebrate Mass in his papal apartment, the Vatican said. He began slipping in and out of consciousness the morning of April 2.

In the hours before his death, prayers went up on the pope's behalf from all over the world, from China to the pope's native Poland, from Christians and non-Christians. Rabbi Riccardo di Segni, the chief rabbi of Rome, came to St. Peter's Square to pray, saying he wanted to offer "a sign of participation" with the church.

U.S. Cardinal Edmund C. Szoka led a candlelight prayer service in the packed square.

"Like children, we draw close around our beloved Holy Father, who taught us how to follow Jesus and how to love and serve the church and the people," Cardinal Szoka said.

"This is the gift we present to him as he prepares to take his last journey. May the Madonna present him to her Son and obtain for him, through her intercession, the reward promised to the faithful servants of the Gospel," the cardinal said.

The pope's death was announced in St. Peter's Square after the prayer service. Many in the crowd wept, and after long applause the square was enveloped in silent prayer. The bells of St. Peter's Basilica tolled a steady death knell.

"Dear brothers and sisters, at 9:37 this evening our most beloved Holy Father John Paul II returned to the house of the Father. Let us pray for him," Archbishop Leonardo Sandri, a top official of the Vatican's Secretariat of State, told the crowd.

Navarro-Valls, the Vatican spokesman, later said, "The Holy Father's final hours were marked by the uninterrupted prayer of all those who were assisting him in his pious death and by the choral participation in prayer of the thousands of faithful who, for many hours, had been gathered in St. Peter's Square."

The spokesman said those at the pope's bedside at the moment of his death included his personal secretaries, Archbishop Stanislaw Dziwisz and Msgr. Mieczyslaw Mokrzycki; Cardinal Marian Jaworski, the Latin-rite archbishop of Lviv, Ukraine, and a longtime personal friend of the pope; Polish Archbishop Stanislaw Rylko, president of the Pontifical Council for the Laity; and Father Tadeusz Styczen, a former student of the pope's and director of the John Paul II Institute at Lublin University in Poland.

Also present were the three nuns who cared for the pope's apartment, the pope's personal physician and two other doctors and two nurses, the spokesman said.

About 90 minutes before the pope died, Navarro-Valls said, the cardinals and priests at the pope's bedside began celebrating the Mass for Divine Mercy Sunday. During the course of the Mass, he said, the pope received Communion and the anointing of the sick.

Father Stanley Pondo of Indianapolis, who was in the square when the pope's death was announced, said the pope's death left him "sad and happy."

"John Paul II has been the pope my whole adult life. He's been my inspiration. I didn't enter the seminary until I was in my 30s and it was partly because of his influence. . . . I'm happy because I'm sure he's in heaven now," he said.

Father Pablo Gadenz of Trenton, N.J., said, "We all feel like orphans now, but it's a time of grace, a time of faith. The Holy Spirit will guide the cardinals to choose a worthy successor, so we pray for whoever that might be."

In St. Peter's Square, with the crowd estimated at 100,000 people, another public prayer service began at midnight and was led by Archbishop Paolo Sardi, an official in the Vatican Secretariat of State, who said, "This is a holy night of vigil and prayer in memory of our beloved Pope John Paul."

When the pope died, Vatican Radio interrupted regular programming, and the radio's program director, Jesuit Father Federico Lombardi, celebrated Mass in Latin.

The home page of the Vatican Web site was changed, the usual drawing of St. Peter's Basilica replaced with the emblem used when the papacy is vacant: two crossed keys under a partially closed *umbracullum* (umbrella or canopy).

The Italian Parliament lowered its flag to half-staff.

In Warsaw, Poland's capital, the pope's death was marked by the tolling of church bells and the sounding of air-raid sirens. On Polish TV, several commentators were in tears as they announced the death.

On April 3, Vatican officials, Italy's president and top politicians, ambassadors to the Vatican, cardinals, bishops and even a dozen journalists were led into the Clementine Hall of the Apostolic Palace to pay their last respects.

The ceremony followed a Mass attended by some 70,000 people in St. Peter's Square.

Cardinal Angelo Sodano, who had served as the pope's secretary of state, celebrated the memorial liturgy.

The cardinal said Pope John Paul had spent his entire papacy promoting the "civilization of love" against the forces of hatred in the world and had called the church to be a "house of mercy, to welcome all those who need help, forgiveness and love."

At the end of the Mass, a Vatican official read the message the pope had prepared for the midday recitation of the *Regina Coeli*, a Marian prayer prayed in the Easter season.

"To humanity, which sometimes seems lost and dominated by the power of evil, selfishness and fear, the risen Lord offers the gift of his love, which forgives, reconciles and opens the spirit to hope once again," the pope had written.

The same day the Vatican published the information contained on the official death certificate signed by Dr. Renato Buzzonetti, the pope's personal physician and head of the Vatican health service.

The cause of death was listed as "septic shock and irreversible cardiocirculatory collapse."

POPE JOHN PAUL's body was brought to St. Peter's Basilica for public viewing and prayer Monday afternoon, April 4. It was carried by 12 laymen, the *sediari* who once carried popes on their thrones through the crowds, a practice Pope John Paul never followed, even when he could no longer walk.

The ceremony for the transfer of the body from the Apostolic Palace to the basilica began with the cardinals present in Rome and top Vatican officials chanting in Latin: "I am the resurrection and the life; whoever believes in me, even though he dies, he will live."

Cardinal Eduardo Martinez Somalo, the camerlengo, or chamberlain of the Holy Roman Church, sprinkled the body with holy water while those assembled sang, "In the company of the saints I will go to the house of God."

He then said, "Dearest brothers and sisters, with great emotion we will accompany the mortal remains of the Roman pontiff John Paul II into the Vatican basilica where he often exercised his ministry as bishop of the church in Rome and pastor of the universal church."

"While we leave this house, we thank the Lord for the innumerable gifts which, through his servant Pope John Paul, he has lavished on the Christian people," the cardinal said.

He also prayed that the merciful God would grant the pope eternal rest "in the kingdom of heaven and give comfort of supernatural hope to the pontifical family, to the holy people who live in Rome and to all the faithful throughout the world."

The cardinals and priests formed a procession, singing Psalm 23: "The Lord is my shepherd, there is nothing I shall want."

The pallbearers were preceded and flanked by members of the Swiss Guard.

The Polish nuns who cooked and cleaned for the Polish-born pope, his valet, his personal physician, his personal secretaries and his press spokesman followed the body.

The entire service and procession were broadcast live on television and shown on large screens set up in St. Peter's Square and along the main avenue leading toward it. Tens of thousands of people were already lined up to enter the basilica to pay homage to the pope.

After chanting other psalms, members of the procession sang Mary's Magnificat: "My soul proclaims the greatness of the Lord; my spirit rejoices in God my savior."

The procession went down the broad Noble Stairway, through

several frescoed rooms on the first floor of the Apostolic Palace, down the Royal Stairway and through the Bronze Doors. It went into the center of St. Peter's Square, where thousands of people were waiting, then into the basilica through the central doors.

Pope John Paul's body was carried into the basilica accompanied by the chanting of the litany of saints and a series of invocations to Christ, including: "You who rose from the dead, have mercy on him. You who ascended into heaven, have mercy on him. You who will come to judge the living and the dead, have mercy on him."

The prayers in the basilica were not only for Pope John Paul, but for all humanity, that it would be freed from hunger and war.

"Give the whole world justice and peace," the assembly prayed. "Comfort and enlighten your holy church; send new workers into your vineyard; protect the bishops and all the ministers of the Gospel."

Once the pope's body was laid before the main altar in St. Peter's, Cardinal Martinez Somalo again blessed it with holy water and with incense. Then the cardinal pulled out a handkerchief and wiped the tears from his eyes.

The Sistine Chapel choir sang: "Come, saints of God; run, angels of the Lord; receive his soul and present it before the throne of the Most High."

"Eternal rest grant unto him, O Lord, and let perpetual light shine upon him," they prayed.

The service included a brief Liturgy of the Word with a reading from St. John's Gospel, quoting Jesus' prayer that God would welcome his disciples.

"I made known to them your name and I will make it known, that the love with which you loved me may be in them and I in them," the Gospel says.

The ceremony ended with the Canticle of Simeon: "Now, master, you may let your servant go in peace, according to your word, for my eyes have seen your salvation, which you have prepared in the sight of all the peoples."

The cardinals and priests present paid homage to the pope's body before leaving the basilica.

When the public was let in, a nun read Psalm 23 while a man

sang a modern version of the refrain, "The Lord is my shepherd, there is nothing I shall want."

Songs and prayers, including the recitation of the rosary, were scheduled to take place throughout the night.

Once inside, ushers kept the crowd moving. While a genuflection was allowed, those who knelt to pray were helped up and asked to keep moving out of courtesy to the thousands of people behind them.

As darkness fell, the faithful and the curious kept streaming to the Vatican. Carmen Borgbonaci, 53, and her sister Maria Hilda, 55, came from Valletta, Malta, and went straight from the airport to St. Peter's Square, getting in line at noon.

Asked how long they were willing to wait, Borgbonaci said, "All night. We've brought sleeping bags and water and cake."

Maria Grazia Galasso, 57, came with her husband from Viterbo, an hour north of Rome, ready to spend the night in line if necessary.

"We have our coats and half a liter of water. We'll be fine," they said after four hours of waiting and at least another five to go.

"It will be difficult for another pope to equal him," Galasso said.

An elderly Italian man begged the Carabinieri, Italian military police, to let him pass to the front of the line.

"I have a foot with gangrene" and a weak heart, he said. After he produced proof that the Italian government recognizes him as disabled, they found a place for him to sit.

The police said people with handicaps were able to use a special entrance to St. Peter's Basilica, but had to wait until 9 p.m. like everyone else.

An elderly Italian woman, shaking and in tears, pleaded with the police near the front of the line, "Please let me in. Please. I was here when he was elected."

An officer in the Carabinieri finally let her through to a bench near the front of the line.

He then turned to his men and said, "Please do not send these people to me. I can't take it."

The pope's death ended a history-making pontificate, one that dramatically changed the church and left its mark on the world. Many observers consider Pope John Paul an unparalleled protagonist in the political and spiritual events that shaped the modern age, from the end of the Cold War to the start of the third millennium.

For the church, the pope's death set in motion a period of official mourning and reflection that culminated in the election of his successor.

Cardinals made their way to Rome to participate in the April 8 funeral and the papal conclave or election, scheduled to begin April 18, 16 days after the pope's death. Among the 183 cardinals, the 117 cardinals under the age of 80 were eligible to vote in the closed-door conclave, and 115 did.

A youthful 58 when elected in 1978, the pope experienced health problems early. He was shot and almost killed in 1981 and spent several months in the hospital being treated for abdominal wounds and a blood infection. In later years, he suffered a dislocated shoulder, a broken thigh bone, arthritis of the knee and an appendectomy. He stopped walking in public in 2003 and stopped celebrating public liturgies in 2004.

In later years, the pope spoke with increasing frequency about his age, his failing health and death. He was determined to stay at the helm of the church, but also said he was prepared to be called to the next life.

"It is wonderful to be able to give oneself to the very end for the sake of the kingdom of God. At the same time, I find great peace in thinking of the time when the Lord will call me: from life to life," he said in a 1999 letter written to the world's elderly.

The pope continued: "And so I often find myself saying, with no trace of melancholy, a prayer recited by priests after the celebration of the Eucharist: '*In hora mortis meae voca me, et iube me venire ad te*' (at the hour of my death, call me and bid me come to you). This is the prayer of Christian hope," he said.

The city of Rome announced plans to deal with the flood of visitors to Rome in the days after the pope's death. A special bus line ran directly to the Vatican from the train station, and officials set up tents around the Vatican to provide assistance to pilgrims.

During the last years of his pontificate, Pope John Paul II revealed an aspect of his personal life that he did not want history to overlook.

In autobiographical books and in selected talks, the pontiff emphasized that what kept him going was not the power of the papacy but the spiritual strength that flowed from his priestly vocation.

"With the passing of time, the most important and beautiful thing for me is that I have been a priest for more than 50 years, because every day I can celebrate Holy Mass!" he told some 300,000 young people in Italy in 1997.

While many writers have recounted the pope's early life as a semi-political pilgrimage under Nazi occupation and communist domination in Poland, the pope himself remembered those years as a crucial time of spiritual formation.

In his 1996 book, *A Gift and Mystery*, he recalled how the sense of being called to the priesthood filled him with joy, but it also cut him off from acquaintances and other interests. In one of the most moving passages he ever wrote as pope, he said he still felt a debt to friends who suffered "on the great altar of history" during World War II, while he studied in a clandestine seminary.

Karol Wojtyla, the future pope, lived an unusually varied life before his priestly ordination. As a teen, he split stone at a quarry, wrote poetry and supported a network that smuggled Jews to safety during the German occupation of Poland. As a young priest, he was a favorite with students at Lublin University who flocked to his classes and joined him on camping, hiking and canoeing trips. As the second-youngest cardinal ever named by the Vatican, he ran an informal office and celebrated holidays with Krakow actors.

It should have been no surprise that he would redefine the traditional role and demeanor of the papacy by traveling extensively, continuing to enjoy outdoor activities and taking on a wide range of political and moral issues.

As a high school student in his hometown of Wadowice, in southern Poland, Wojtyla impressed classmates by the intense way he would pray in church, a habit of deep meditation that remained with him for life.

"Even as a boy he was exceptional," said Rafat Tatka, a neighbor who knew the young boy as Lolek, a nickname that translates as Chuck.

The Nazi takeover of Poland in September 1939 meant an official end to all religious training and cultural activities, but Wojtyla attended an underground university in Krakow and helped set up a clandestine theater group that performed in stores and homes.

In addition to the quarry, he worked in a chemical factory—experiences that provided material for his poetry and papal writings on labor. He participated in daily Mass, spiritual exercises, Marian devotion and Bible study.

Friends said that when his father died in 1941, Karol knelt for 12 hours in prayer at his father's bedside. Soon after, he withdrew from the theatrical group and began studying for the priesthood, a decision that surprised many of his friends, who tried to convince him his talent lay in the theater.

He studied in a clandestine seminary operated in Cardinal Adam Sapieha's Krakow residence in defiance of Nazi orders forbidding religious education. The archbishop saw him as a future church leader. Yet the young man who wrote poems and a doctoral dissertation on the mysticism of St. John of the Cross was attracted to monastic contemplation. Twice during these years he tried to join the Discalced Carmelites but was turned away with the advice: "You are destined for greater things."

He was ordained Nov. 1, 1946, just as the communist regime replaced the Germans at the end of the war.

Father Wojtyla was sent to study at Rome's Angelicum University, where he earned a doctorate in ethics. Back in Poland in 1948, the young priest was assigned to the rural village of Niegowic for a year before returning to Krakow.

There, at St. Florian Parish, he devoted much of his attention to young people—teaching, playing soccer and inviting university students to his house for discussions.

After earning a second doctorate in moral theology, Father Wojtyla began teaching at Lublin University in 1953, commuting by train from his Krakow parish. He published more than 100 articles and several books on ethics and other subjects, and at age 36, became a full professor at the Institute of Ethics in Lublin.

Father Wojtyla's interest in outdoor activities remained strong, and younger companions called him "the eternal teenager." Groups of students regularly joined him for hiking, skiing, bicycling, camping and kayaking, accompanied by prayer, outdoor Masses and theological discussions.

Father Wojtyla was on a kayaking trip in 1958 when, at age 38, he was named an auxiliary bishop of Krakow—the youngest bishop in Poland's history. He continued to live a simple life, shunning the trappings that came with his position. For instance, he only left his Krakow apartment for the more luxurious bishop's residence after friends moved his belongings one day when he was out of town.

In 1964, shortly before the end of the Second Vatican Council, he was named archbishop of Krakow. Just three years later, at the age of 47, he became a cardinal. But he continued his open approach in Krakow, seeing visitors without appointments and holding seminars at the cardinal's residence for actors, workers, students, priests and nuns.

In 1976, after touring several U.S. cities and attending the International Eucharistic Congress in Philadelphia, Cardinal Wojtyla attended a conference of Polish-Americans at St. Mary's College in Orchard Lake, Mich. True to form, having sat through a string of indoor meetings, one afternoon he canceled a session to go canoeing.

After the pope's death hundreds of thousands of people filled St. Peter's Square and the surrounding streets, waiting to pay homage to Pope John Paul II. The solemn, prayerful pomp of the ceremonial transfer of the pope's body from the Apostolic Palace to St. Peter's Basilica April 4 was replaced by informality and expressions of simple piety as the public lined up to view the pope's body.

Hundreds of police officers from the Vatican, Italy and every imaginable branch of the Italian military, as well as Red Cross workers and civil protection volunteers, patrolled the area, keeping order, handing out water and helping those who tired of waiting in line for hours.

They also had to open and close barricades to give people access to the portable toilets.

While a few people gave up, most seemed content to wait, chatting with friends, reminiscing about the pope, praying the rosary or talking on their mobile phones.

Rocco Conserva, 58, of Rome was in line at 3 p.m. even though Italian television and radio stations already were reporting the basilica would not open until after 8 p.m., rather than 6 p.m. as originally announced.

He said he would wait "as long as it takes" to see Pope John Paul.

"I have seen five popes in my lifetime," Conserva said. "I loved

Pope John XXIII very much. He was the good pope. But this pope
was universal so he was my pope . . . he belonged to all of us."

CARDINAL ADAM J. MAIDA

Archbishop of Detroit

WHENEVER I think of the late Holy Father, Pope John
Paul II, a flood of memories comes to my mind and heart,
and my soul is filled with deep gratitude to God for the
great blessing he was to our church and our world. It was clear to me
that he was truly in love with the Lord Jesus and his body, the
Church. He was truly a holy man. He lived what he preached. The
manner in which he integrated his spirituality with his humanity was
indeed a model for all of us. This was especially evident in the way
he radiated his love for God's people through his warm smile and his
intense look whenever he greeted anyone—a dignitary of great importance or a humble peasant; in his eyes, as in God's eyes, we were
all good, beautiful and significant.

It was not a surprise, therefore, when people from all over the
world, of all ages and station in life, flocked to Rome to offer their respect and gratitude for his Petrine ministry.

One of the greatest lessons I learned from our Holy Father was his
appreciation for the intimate and necessary connection between
faith and culture. As he often explained, a Gospel that has not yet
permeated the culture is a Gospel that has not been adequately proclaimed. I had many conversations with our Holy Father in the language we shared, Polish. As he saw it, Christianity and Gospel values
were an intricate part of the Polish ethnic heritage and could not be
separated. He understood that at the heart of every culture was the
intuition of faith in Almighty God, the inspiration and energy that
gives life in poetry, art, and drama, the strength of the spirit that connects people as they communicate their deepest joys and sorrows and
grapple with the deep questions of life and its meaning, suffering and
death. Like everyone else, I was in awe of the way Pope John Paul II
not only learned to speak the languages of most nations he visited,

but more importantly, how he truly got into the mind and spirit of their particular social and cultural heritage. He was a father to everyone!

I was privileged to discuss with him the creation of the Pope John Paul II Cultural Center in Washington, which stands as a visible testament and legacy of the connection of faith and culture. The center is a source of catechetical evangelical outreach and a forum for intellectual discussion and debate on the issues of our day, the very kind of thing that was so compelling in our late Holy Father's speeches and 14 encyclicals.

As a diocesan bishop, I know how much time and energy it takes to relate to people of all ages and backgrounds, particularly the young. And even to his dying breath, our Holy Father had a special resonance with young people. I recall vividly how many youth came from all over the world to pray for him and pay their last respects as his body lay in state. In particular, I recall the experience of Denver, Colo., during the World Youth Day events, when our Holy Father took his usual expression about not being afraid and turned it around. He told the young people, *"Be proud of the Gospel!"* More important than his words, his very attitude of joy, hope and courage inspired me, as it did the young people that day, to be a missionary of the new evangelization.

Finally, I had the opportunity over the last few months of the Holy Father's life to see him and to talk with him, and to witness his very obvious physical limitations. And yet, precisely in his weakness, his true strength of character was shining forth more than ever. I will continue to treasure in my heart the sacredness of those last encounters when I could truly see the face of Christ shining through him. What a gift and blessing he has been to our church and the whole human family!

CHAPTER 2

Funeral

THE FIRST papal funeral of 26 years drew unprecedented crowds. The Vatican estimated that more than 3 million people descended on Rome in the week following John Paul's death to pay their respects to the late pontiff. They had come to laud the Polish pope who had revolutionized the papacy. He "raised the bar," said Cardinal Theodore E. McCarrick of Washington, as he recounted John Paul II's accomplishments at a press conference at the North American College. The once athletic pope had captivated the world's imagination both in his prime as the skiing, mountain-climbing pope and in his decline, when he continued to meet with large assemblies despite the frailties of illness and old age.

His wake drew millions to view his body and the media broadcast it into homes all around the globe. It stood as a tribute to a man more popular than even his admirers had imagined.

The last mourners had not yet filed out of St. Peter's Basilica late April 7 when people began converging on the streets and parks outside the Vatican walls to participate in the funeral Mass.

They wrapped themselves in sleeping bags, pitched tents or simply resigned themselves to standing throughout the chilly night.

When asked why they were there, many gave the same answer: "He was our pope."

Shortly after 7 a.m. the next day, their long vigil was rewarded, and the crowd began streaming into St. Peter's Square for the 10 a.m. funeral Mass.

Although the mood was somewhat brighter than it had been in the preceding days, when long lines of mourners waited to file past the pope's body, it was still subdued. Many people prayed, and a few wept.

"Since his death, we have felt first sadness, then serenity. This is a day of joy for us, because we are celebrating resurrection," said Pedro Paul of Caracas, Venezuela.

"The pope didn't have a mother or father, but he had us," said Eustolia Valladolid of Guadalajara, Mexico, who spent the night just outside the Vatican with her daughter, son-in-law and 7-month-old granddaughter. Her eyes filled with tears as she said: "He was a spiritual guide for people. His advice was very important for families."

Death seemed to have reinforced Pope John Paul's special bond with the young people who flocked to the plaza, many of them carrying their country's flags.

"When he was young, he lived a life like ours—he was involved in sports and theater," said a man who identified himself only as Paul, a graduate student. "We can identify with his first 25 years. He told us it wasn't easy to be our age, but that we shouldn't be afraid, that if we make mistakes, we should pick up and go on."

Pope John Paul was the only pontiff many of these young people had known, and they saw age and illness transform him.

"He showed us how to accept pain and old age, not as a defect, but as a stage of life," said Vicente Zucaria, a student from Bogota, Colombia.

"He challenged young people to live a radical way of life that this generation was ready to embrace," said Kevin O'Connor, who traveled from Peoria, Ill., to attend the funeral. "He empowered us to change the world."

Hundreds of police officers, some standing shoulder to shoulder, controlled entry to the square, but there were no disturbances. Even Rome's omnipresent pickpockets seemed to have given up their trade in the square for the occasion.

"People have been very good-humored," said Michael Pierce, 47, of Scotland, who was in Rome on business. "They have been very gentle, patient. That's the mood of the crowd."

The lines seemed endless, and so did the outpouring of affection for Pope John Paul II.

All day and all night they came to St. Peter's Basilica to say good-

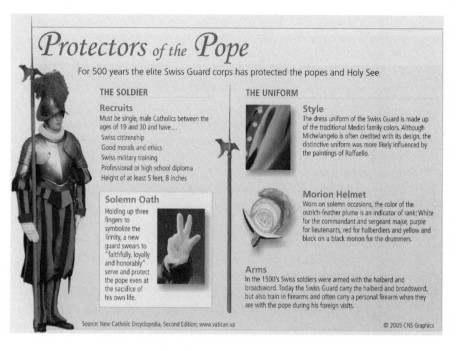

Protectors *of the* Pope

For 500 years the elite Swiss Guard corps has protected the popes and Holy See

THE SOLDIER

Recruits
Must be single, male Catholics between the ages of 19 and 30 and have...
Swiss citizenship
Good morals and ethics
Swiss military training
Professional or high school diploma
Height of at least 5 feet, 8 inches

Solemn Oath
Holding up three fingers to symbolize the Trinity, a new guard swears to "faithfully, loyally and honorably" serve and protect the pope even at the sacrifice of his own life.

THE UNIFORM

Style
The dress uniform of the Swiss Guard is made up of the traditional Medici family colors. Although Michelangelo is often credited with its design, the distinctive uniform was more likely influenced by the paintings of Raffaello.

Morion Helmet
Worn on solemn occasions, the color of the ostrich-feather plume is an indicator of rank: White for the commandant and sergeant major, purple for lieutenants, red for halberdiers and yellow and black on a black morion for the drummers.

Arms
In the 1500's Swiss soldiers were armed with the halberd and broadsword. Today the Swiss Guard carry the halberd and broadsword, but also train in firearms and often carry a personal firearm when they are with the pope during his foreign visits.

Source: New Catholic Encyclopedia, Second Edition; www.vatican.va

© 2005 CNS Graphics

bye to the late pope, whose body lay on a damask-covered bier in front of the main altar.

No one remembered seeing such a big a crowd at the Vatican, and it just kept growing, hour by hour and day by day.

"He was like a father to us. This is like saying farewell to a relative," said 26-year-old Laura Errante. She stood for several hours in a slow-moving wall of people that stretched for more than half a mile down the main avenue in front of the basilica.

"What I liked about John Paul was that he could be spontaneous, and he knew how to communicate. This crowd is the proof that he knew how to touch the hearts of the young," she said.

On the second day of the public viewing, the crowd was full of young people, many of whom had attended the World Youth Day celebrations initiated by Pope John Paul early in his pontificate.

As they prepared to pay their last respects, they sang World Youth Day songs and helped create an almost cheerful air outside the basilica. Once inside, the mood turned more somber.

Francesco Molinari, 18, called the pope "a myth," one of the highest terms of praise among Italian youths.

"I grew up with this pope. He connected with young people because he was able to transmit hope to them," he said.

Molinari and 51 other Boy Scouts took a seven-hour bus trip from southern Italy, then stood in line for several more hours before entering the basilica. He recalled that at a big meeting of scouts at the Vatican in October 2004, the pope, despite his frailty, had come down unexpectedly to see them.

"He made a big effort to greet us, and now we're returning the favor. It's the least we can do," he said.

Another group of young people held up a sign that read: "You looked for us and we came to you," an adaptation of a phrase the pope was said to have uttered on his deathbed about young people.

One of the homemade banners held above the sea of people read, "A white angel has gone up to heaven."

Despite the huge crowds, the public viewing continued without major problems. Traffic in Rome had to be rerouted, the subway lines were packed even tighter than usual, and the portable toilets filled quickly.

On average, people were spending between three and four hours in line. During the chilly night of April 4, a few people who became ill were treated in first-aid tents. Parents with children in strollers were allowed to stand in a safety corridor.

Cardinals just arriving in Rome went to the head of the line and were allowed to kneel at length before the pope.

Italian Cardinal Tarcisio Bertone of Genoa joined the crowd for a few minutes early April 5, blessing babies, shaking hands and thanking people for waiting so long.

"The pope did so much for the world. It is an extraordinary day with all these people giving back to the pope the love he gave them," the cardinal said.

The basilica was kept open day and night, with a break for cleaning between 2 a.m. and 5 a.m. But on the first night, the doors were closed at 3 a.m. and opened 20 minutes early to accommodate the crowd.

Giant TV screens set up alongside the line showed retrospective films about the late pope, as well as pro-life videos, charity requests and even appeals for organ donation.

As the faithful moved inside the basilica and toward the pope's body, they heard prayers and songs in various languages, sung in turn by visiting choirs. Masses were celebrated on the hour in the chapel directly behind the main altar.

The crowds were kept moving as they flowed past the dead pope. Some crossed themselves, and those who dropped to their knees were quickly helped up and moved on. Despite rules against cameras, many took photos of the pontiff.

After people saw the pope, they said the wait was worth it.

Vittoria Chironi, 58, took a six-hour train ride from northern Italy, then waited four hours before passing by the pope's body.

"I would have waited even if it had been another eight hours," Chironi said. "I had hoped to come and see him when he was still alive, but I failed in that. I had to come and see him now."

Federica Uggias, 17, said he had come to say "not goodbye, just *ciao*."

"I hope that whoever follows him will unite so many different kinds of people as much as he did," he said. "He was the only pope to mobilize all the world."

In the area closest to St. Peter's, police waved metal detectors over the people entering the square, while Interpol agents hovered on the fringes of the crowd.

A hush fell over the square when the entrance procession for the Mass started with 164 concelebrants from among the world's 183 cardinals. Another 500 bishops and 3,000 priests, wearing red stoles, also participated.

As images of the simple wooden coffin bearing the pope's body appeared on the giant screens on either side of the basilica, the crowd burst into sustained applause.

The prayers and readings echoed from huge loudspeakers set up along the broad avenue leading from the basilica to the Tiber River. Hundreds of people who had spent the night sleeping on the pavement sat or stood quietly, while police officers, street sweepers and volunteer public safety workers turned toward the altar in silence.

Compared to the days before the funeral, when the line of mourners waiting to view the pope's body snaked around the Vatican walls and over the river, snarling auto and pedestrian traffic, the side streets seemed eerily empty.

Not everyone who came to the funeral was able to get close. Scaffolding several stories high, set up for television crews, blocked the view for bystanders at the end of the avenue. One TV cameraman good-naturedly snapped photos with cameras that people passed up to him, giving them at least one unimpeded view to take home.

Among those shut out was Jason Pittelli, 26, of Toronto, who was in Cape Town, South Africa, on a round-the-world trip when the pope died. He spent $2,000 to reach Rome by the night before the funeral, flying first to London because Rome's airspace was closed for security.

"I planned to wake up at 6 a.m. and head to St. Peter's, but I slept through the alarm. I can't even see the TV screens," he said. Still, he said, he did not regret the journey. "It's better to be here, regardless."

Many people outside the Vatican walls could not even hear the loudspeakers but followed the liturgy on the radio, heads bowed and hands clasped. Some had come to mourn the pope, while others were drawn by the historical significance of the moment. Many were not Catholic.

"He was a great man. He touched people," said Alison Mitchell of Glasgow, Scotland, who was in Rome with her husband, Robbie, to celebrate their 14th wedding anniversary. The couple, members of the Church of Scotland, recalled the pope's 1982 visit to their homeland.

"There was much more of an ecumenical movement afterward," Robbie Mitchell said. His wife added: "A Catholic sister came to our church after his visit. Before, that would have been heresy."

The congregation in the square was eclectic: street sweepers who had cleaned the square earlier that morning; kings, queens, presidents—including U.S. President George W. Bush. Cabinet ministers and ambassadors representing more than 140 nations sat off to one side of the pope's casket. Other political dignitaries included King Juan Carlos and Queen Sofia of Spain, Britain's Prince Charles and Prime Minister Tony Blair, Ukrainian President Viktor Yushchenko, Canadian Prime Minister Paul Martin, Iranian President Mohammad Khatami, Zimbabwe's President Robert Mugabe and U.N. Secretary-General Kofi Annan.

Across from them sat representatives of the Orthodox, Oriental Orthodox, Anglican, Protestant and U.S. evangelical communities.

Jewish and Muslim organizations sent delegations. Buddhists, Sikhs and Hindus attended too. Among the U.S. delegates from other Christian churches were Ted Haggard, president of the National Association of Evangelicals; John A. Graham of the Billy Graham Evangelistic Association; and the Rev. Jesse Jackson.

Everyone was at his best—even the man selected to lead the pope's funeral services, Cardinal Joseph Ratzinger, dean of the College of Cardinals. Known most for his scholarship and academic skills, Cardinal Ratzinger brought a pastoral presence to the moment that had seldom been seen publicly before. His words and demeanor bespoke "shepherd." As he sat in the presider's chair at the altar in the square, the handsome, white-haired elder even looked as if he could be pope.

He spoke in human, not metaphysical, terms and his words drew applause.

Pope John Paul II "offered his life for his flock and for the entire human family," Cardinal Ratzinger told hundreds of thousands of people gathered at the April 8 funeral Mass.

Cardinal Ratzinger highlighted stages of Pope John Paul II's life. He described how the once-vigorous priest who camped with young people in his native Poland grew frail and weak in old age, giving a witness of "suffering and silence."

"Our pope—and we all know this—never wanted to make his own life secure, to keep it for himself; he wanted to give of himself unreservedly, to the very last moment, to Christ and thus also to us," Cardinal Ratzinger said.

Cardinal Ratzinger said the words *follow me*—the words of the risen Christ to St. Peter—were the thread running through the pope's life.

"As a young student, Karol Wojtyla was thrilled by literature, the theater and poetry. Working in a chemical plant, surrounded and threatened by the Nazi terror, he heard the voice of the Lord: Follow me," Cardinal Ratzinger said.

As a young priest he came to love the academic world and pastoral work among the young, Cardinal Ratzinger said. When he was called to be a bishop, it was probably not a welcome appointment, the cardinal said.

"All this must have seemed to him like losing his very self," Cardinal Ratzinger said, but the future pope accepted the appointment, remembering the words, "Follow me."

As a bishop, he was able to use his talents and his special love of words, poetry and literature to give new vitality and new urgency to the preaching of the Gospel, Cardinal Ratzinger said.

When called to the papacy, he accepted because he loved the Lord, the cardinal said.

"The love of Christ was the dominant force in the life of our beloved Holy Father. Anyone who ever saw him pray, who ever heard him preach, knows that," he said.

In a reflection on Pope John Paul's last, difficult years, when he could no longer stand or walk on his own, Cardinal Ratzinger recalled Christ's words to St. Peter, recounted in the Gospel of St. John: "When you were younger, you used to fasten your own belt and to go wherever you wished. But when you grow old, you will stretch out your hands, and someone else will fasten a belt around you and take you where you do not wish to go."

"In the first years of his pontificate, still young and full of energy, the Holy Father went to the very ends of the earth, guided by Christ," Cardinal Ratzinger said.

"But afterward, he increasingly entered into the communion of Christ's sufferings; increasingly he understood the truth of the words: 'Someone else will fasten a belt around you,'" he said.

Cardinal Ratzinger pointed to a simple but key part of Pope John Paul's teaching that "the limit imposed upon evil is ultimately divine mercy." The pope saw the truth of that in the failed attempt on his life in 1981 and in his later struggles, he said.

"Impelled by this vision, the pope suffered and loved in communion with Christ, and that is why the message of his suffering and his silence proved so eloquent and so fruitful," the cardinal said.

Cardinal Ratzinger cited the late pope's Marian devotion.

"The Holy Father found the purest reflection of God's mercy in the Mother of God. He, who at an early age had lost his own mother, loved his divine mother all the more," he said.

At the end of his homily, amid applause, Cardinal Ratzinger recalled how on Easter Sunday the pope had stood at his apartment window and given his blessing to the world one last time.

"We can be sure that our beloved pope is standing today at the window of the Father's house, that he sees us and blesses us," he said.

The crowd applauded. They chanted "*santo subito*": sainthood now. The words sat well with them. This was a speaker who knew the pope and the people's heart.

BISHOP WILLIAM S. SKYLSTAD

President, United States Conference of Catholic Bishops

I ARRIVED in Rome April 2, 2005, for a routine series of meetings with the various dicasteries of the Holy See. The meetings had been on my calendar for quite some time.

This visit to the Eternal City quickly became anything but routine. The day of my arrival was the day Pope John Paul II greeted, face-to-face, his loving Lord whom he had served so faithfully for so long.

As I entered St. Peter's Square that afternoon, I was moved by the great crowd: thousands of people from around the globe, all gathered to pray, reflect and keep watch as the Holy Father slowly slipped away from earthly life. Many gazed benevolently toward the windows of the papal apartments as they awaited the inevitable news.

After his death, the crowds became even more astonishing. What struck me most deeply, however, was not the number of mourners, but their youthfulness. Thousands upon thousands came to St. Peter's Basilica to view the body. Untold millions around the globe kept their own vigil at their TV screens as the official mourning unfolded. The funeral itself was marked by attendance by leaders of nations throughout the world. Clearly, the Holy Father's impact had been felt far beyond the tiny plot of land that is Vatican City State.

One of the dominant charisms of Pope John Paul II was his ability to relate to people. He was deeply spiritual, but his faith provided the basis for his strong stance on human rights, his advocacy for the world's poor and his defense of human life everywhere. Princes and paupers and everyone in between: All lives were precious in the eyes of Pope John Paul.

Simple but profound gestures made this love of people vibrant and alive. He traveled the world. Upon arriving in a nation, his first act was to bend over and kiss the ground. In his later days, as his physical health deteriorated rapidly and his movements were curtailed, the best he could do was wave from a hospital window or from his apartment in the papal palace. Yet there is no doubt in my mind: For him, human limitation was part of the spiritual journey. As his health failed in his final days, he faced his own death with tremendous public courage. With a simple sign of the cross from his apartment window, he demonstrated his solidarity with God and the human family.

For the first time in 27 years, the church—indeed, the entire world—would witness the death of a pope and the transition to the election of the new Holy Father. The process of the conclave fascinated people everywhere. I had just finished celebrating Mass at Assumption Parish in Walla Walla, Wash., in the southern region of my own diocese, Spokane, when the grade school principal came running up to announce the news that white smoke was coming from the chimney of the Sistine Chapel.

In no time at all, the media focused its scrutiny on every word and every move of Pope Benedict XVI. His election elicited surprise and fascination from observers within the church and without. Surely the Holy Spirit had guided the church's transition into new leadership. Surely the Holy Spirit will continue to guide not only Pope Benedict, but all of us, as we continue our mutual journey of faith.

CHAPTER 3

World Reaction to Death of John Paul II

W HEN Pope John Paul II died, people responded throughout the world.

It was no surprise given his more than 26 years as a dominant figure on the world stage, using his moral leadership to promote human rights, condemn ethical failings and plead for peace.

He had the ear of presidents, prime ministers and kings, who came in a steady stream for private audiences at the Vatican. Although the pope's fading health in later years made these one-on-one meetings less substantive, his encounters with U.S. and Soviet leaders in the 1980s and '90s gave a spiritual impetus to the fall of European communism.

More than any previous pontiff, he pushed religious teachings into the center of public debate, arguing that universal moral norms—such as the sanctity of life—are not optional for contemporary society.

The pope's bold words and gestures won acclaim, but not from all quarters. As his pontificate wore on, his message increasingly went against conventional thinking on issues like abortion, gay marriage and genetic research.

Pro-life issues brought out a fighting spirit in the Polish-born pontiff. In 1994, for example, he challenged U.N. population planners on abortion and birth-control policies and steered an international development conference toward a moral debate on life and family issues.

The pope and his aides took some flak for that. But as he aged, he seemed more determined than ever to speak his mind, applying church teaching to technical questions such as economics, biology and demographics, and prodding individual consciences on what he has called a worldwide "moral crisis."

"The Gospel of Life," his 1995 encyclical on pro-life issues that he addressed to "all people of good will" and sent to government leaders around the globe, reflected the pope's sense of resolve.

"To speak out on an issue like abortion confirms this pope's leadership in a dramatic way. If a pope doesn't try to awaken ethical responsibility, what is his value?" said Vatican spokesman Joaquin Navarro-Valls.

The pope's pro-life stand also virtually excluded the death penalty, and he made frequent appeals against executions in the United States. After one dramatic plea during his visit to St. Louis in 1999, the sentence of a Missouri death-row inmate was commuted.

When it came to war, the pope gave no comfort to those pressing for the use of military force. His outspoken opposition to the U.S.-led war on Iraq in 2003 was based on the conviction that both sides should have done more to settle the dispute peacefully. He mobilized an unprecedented, though unsuccessful, diplomatic effort to help prevent hostilities and to preserve the role of the United Nations in global peacemaking. His aides successfully headed off a shooting war between Chile and Argentina in 1978.

Following the Sept. 11, 2001, terrorist attacks by extremists acting in the name of Islam, the pope led a spiritual campaign against all violence in the name of religion. He convened a meeting of Muslims, Christians, Jews and others in Assisi in early 2002; the gathering produced a joint statement against terrorism.

During jubilee celebrations in 2000, the pope continually prodded and pressured global financial powers to forgive at least part of the Third World debt—a request that added a moral dimension to the issue and helped bring about debt relief for some of the poorest nations.

The pope conferred with presidents, stood up to tyrants and preached to crowds of more than a million people. Almost immediately after his election in 1978, he began using the world as a pulpit: decrying hunger from Africa; denouncing the arms race from Hi-

GLOBAL POPE

The most traveled pope in history, John Paul II made 104 trips outside Italy covering more than 700,000 miles

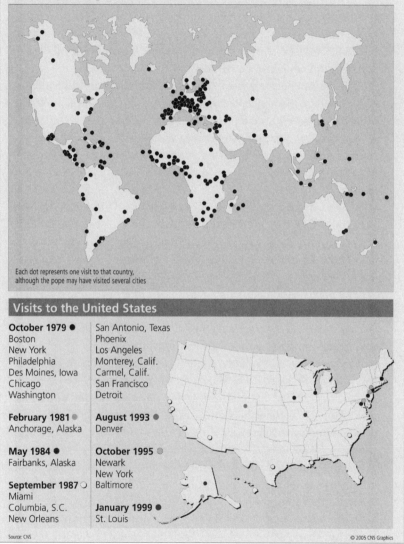

Each dot represents one visit to that country, although the pope may have visited several cities

Visits to the United States

October 1979 ●
Boston
New York
Philadelphia
Des Moines, Iowa
Chicago
Washington

San Antonio, Texas
Phoenix
Los Angeles
Monterey, Calif.
Carmel, Calif.
San Francisco
Detroit

February 1981 ●
Anchorage, Alaska

May 1984 ●
Fairbanks, Alaska

September 1987 ○
Miami
Columbia, S.C.
New Orleans

August 1993 ●
Denver

October 1995 ◐
Newark
New York
Baltimore

January 1999 ●
St. Louis

Source: CNS

© 2005 CNS Graphics

roshima, Japan; and promoting human equality from caste-conscious India.

As Poland's native son, he had a special interest and a key role in the demise of European communism. For years he criticized the moral bankruptcy of the system, to applause in the West. His visits to his homeland helped light the fire of reform, which eventually led to the first noncommunist government in the Soviet bloc.

In an astute political move, he cultivated an ally in Mikhail Gorbachev, whose *glasnost* policies set the stage for the breakup of the Soviet Union—and the return of religious freedom.

But the pope was also a sometimes-unwelcome critic of capitalism, warning that the profit motive alone would never bring justice and cautioning about the effects of "globalization" in the post-communist era.

Modern leadership is often a question of personal rapport, and Pope John Paul met with world figures across the spectrum. During his pontificate, every U.S. president made a pilgrimage to the Vatican, including President George W. Bush in 2001, 2002 and 2004.

The pope's door almost always was open to the world's powerful, a policy that brought controversial figures to his private library— among them Palestinian leader Yasser Arafat, Cuban President Fidel Castro and former Austrian President Kurt Waldheim.

Many observers, including former U.S. ambassadors to the Vatican, said Pope John Paul's influence on world events was tremendous. They praised his political savvy, reflected less in the public realm than in behind-the-scenes efforts by Vatican diplomats. The pope's tenure saw a near-doubling of the number of countries with which the Vatican holds diplomatic relations.

At the same time, his flair for the dramatic gesture helped make him the most-televised pontiff in history. That was a form of global influence that this pope never underestimated. Millions watched him walk through crowds of African poor or visit a shantytown family in Latin America. As the pope once said, one reason he kept returning to these places was that he knew the cameras would follow, spotlighting human problems around the globe.

The pope was a consistent critic of war and a booster of peace, and during his pontificate the Vatican issued major statements calling for disarmament.

But sometimes the pope's peace efforts went unheeded, to his bitter disappointment. That was true not only in Iraq; his warnings about conflagration in the Balkans and his horror at ethnic fighting in Africa illustrated the limits of papal influence.

When Pope John Paul first addressed the United Nations in 1979, he emphasized that harmonious international relations were deeply tied to a proper understanding of freedom and respect for moral precepts. That was a message he honed over the years in face-to-face meetings with world leaders and in public speeches.

Returning to the United Nations in 1995, frailer but just as forceful, he again insisted that the "family of nations" must be founded on strong moral principles and warned of "unspeakable offenses against human life and freedom" in today's world.

The pope never stopped prodding the world's conscience, nor did he shy away from appealing directly to heads of state.

Visiting Cuba in 1998, he challenged Castro's government to allow freedom of expression and a wider church role in society.

In these and other interventions, the pope felt certain that he acted in the name of civilians who had little or no voice in world events.

At his death, the words of world leaders showed that although they might not always have been convinced by him, they always respected him.

President George W. Bush praised the pope as "a champion of human freedom" and a "witness to the dignity of human life."

The president and first lady Laura Bush also attended a Mass for the pope at St. Matthew's Cathedral in Washington, just hours after the death of the 84-year-old pontiff.

In a brief televised statement from the White House, Bush called Pope John Paul "an inspiration to millions of Americans and to so many more throughout the world." In June 2004, Bush had awarded him the Presidential Medal of Freedom and called him a "hero of our time."

"The Catholic Church has lost its shepherd, the world has lost a champion of human freedom, and a good and faithful servant of God has been called home," the president said. "Throughout the West, John Paul's witness reminded us of our obligation to build a culture of life in which the strong protect the weak," Bush said. "And during the pope's final years, his witness was made even more powerful by his daily courage in the face of illness and great suffering."

Speaking earlier in the day during his weekly radio address, Bush called Pope John Paul "a faithful servant of God and a champion of human dignity and freedom."

From Poland to the Philippines to Cuba, the world's political leaders voiced appreciation for the late pope.

"He looked after Poland as a mother looks after her family," said Lech Walesa, who led Poland's Solidarity movement, which helped bring about the downfall of communist rule. Walesa became Poland's first democratically elected president in 1990.

In Cuba, President Fidel Castro published a letter to the Vatican on the front page of the newspaper *Juventud Rebelde*, April 3, saying the pope's death was "sad news" and offering "the most heartfelt condolences of the Cuban people and the government."

After Castro came to power in 1959, Cuba became an officially atheistic country, but thawing relations in recent years led to an official visit by the pope in January 1998.

Castro ordered three days of mourning, to include flying flags at half-staff and suspension of events, including anniversary celebrations for communist organizations and baseball games. He also had a book of condolences opened for the public to sign.

In China, where there had been no such warming of relations with that nation's communist government, Liu Jianchao, spokesman for China's Ministry of Foreign Affairs, issued a statement expressing his country's condolences. China prohibits religious activity by any group not specifically permitted by the government and does not recognize the Vatican's authority over Catholics in that country.

Liu's statement said in part, "We hope the Vatican, under the new pope, will create conditions conducive to the improvement of relations with China."

U.N. Secretary-General Kofi Annan praised the pope as a "tireless advocate of peace, a true pioneer in interfaith dialogue and a strong force for critical self-evaluation by the church itself."

Leaders of heavily Catholic countries joined in expressing the grief of their people.

Spanish Prime Minister Jose Luis Rodriguez Zapatero said the pope's death "represents the loss of one of the most towering world figures in recent history."

Philippine President Gloria Macapagal-Arroyo said the people of her country received the news of John Paul's death "with a deep sense of grief and loss."

Italian President Carlo Azeglio Ciampi said Italians mourned "the loss of a father" who would be remembered as a man of freedom and justice.

In East Timor, President Xanana Gusmao said the pope's 1989 visit to the island while it was still suffering under Indonesian rule "helped to break down the wall of silence and indifference of the international community."

President Jacques Chirac of France said Pope John Paul was "an enlightened and inspired priest," who "devoted himself to responding to the search for sense and the thirst for justice that is expressed today on all continents."

Even in countries with very few Catholics, the pope was recalled fondly.

Israeli Foreign Minister Silvan Shalom said, "Israel, the Jewish people and the entire world lost today a great champion of reconciliation and brotherhood between the faiths."

Palestinian leader Mahmoud Abbas said the world had lost "a very important religious figure who dedicated his life to peace and justice for all."

Pakistan's president, Gen. Pervez Musharraf, told the country's state news agency that the pope had brought people belonging to different faiths closer and had "rendered incredible services for peace."

The government of India declared a three-day mourning period, and President Abdul Kalam declared that the pope "tirelessly worked for peace on this planet and to establish an international order based on equality and justice."

Current and former leaders of nations in the former Soviet bloc credited the pope's role in peacefully changing the Soviet regime.

Former Soviet Union President Mikhail Gorbachev called the pope "the No. 1 humanist on the planet."

The death had an unprecedented impact on British public life, delaying the announcement of an impending general election and causing the postponement of the wedding of Prince Charles, heir to the British throne.

Prime Minister Tony Blair, who had been expected to announce the date of the next general election April 4, delayed the announcement by at least 24 hours. Blair said the world had lost a leader who was revered by people of all faiths. "He never waivered, never flinched, in the struggle for what he thought was right and good," he said.

Prince Charles had been due to marry his partner, Camilla Parker-Bowles, April 8. A spokesman at Clarence House, the prince's London residence, announced that the wedding would be postponed until April 9 as a mark of respect for the late pope.

The postponement of the royal wedding eased complex questions of protocol for Blair and for the archbishop of Canterbury, Archbishop Rowan Williams. The Anglican archbishop had been expected to preside at a service of blessing for the prince's wedding, to which the prime minister and other political leaders had been invited. With the delay of the wedding, the archbishop and prime minister announced they would attend the papal funeral in Rome.

The prince, prime minister and archbishop joined thousands of mourners at London's Westminster Cathedral April 4 for a vespers service for Pope John Paul. Also at the service were former British prime ministers John Major and Baroness (Margaret) Thatcher.

Prince Charles represented his mother, Queen Elizabeth II, at the papal funeral in Rome April 8. Friends of the prince said that as a man of faith he wanted to pay his respects to a great spiritual leader.

Australian Prime Minister John Howard called Pope John Paul "a pillar of strength and an apostle of peace."

Canadian Prime Minister Paul Martin remembered that Pope John Paul's visits to Canada, especially his 1987 trip to the native peoples in the North and his participation in World Youth Day in Toronto in 2002, were particularly important and unforgettable.

Church leaders from around the world hailed the late Pope John

Paul II as a force for peace who touched the lives of Christians and non-Christians alike.

Catholic bishops from the Third World or conflict-ridden areas spoke of how Pope John Paul used the power of the papacy to draw the world's attention to their plight.

In the Philippines, Cardinal Jaime Sin, retired archbishop of Manila, said the pope called the "people power" revolution that toppled the dictatorship of Ferdinand Marcos "part of the mission of the church."

The pope made two trips to the Philippines, in 1981 and 1995, and canonized the first Filipino saint.

Jesuit Father Enrique Figaredo Alvargonzales, apostolic prefect of Battambang, Cambodia, said that after the pope met with a land-mine-disabled Cambodian John Paul called for an end to the use of land mines.

"The following week His Holiness . . . spoke about the moral responsibility of the producers of land mines. He stressed the immorality of the act of using them and the need to prohibit this cruel business," said Father Figaredo.

Cardinal Nasrallah P. Sfeir, patriarch of Lebanon's Maronite Catholics, said the pope followed events in Lebanon closely, from the country's civil war through the Syrian occupation.

"He opened the eyes of the world to what is happening in Lebanon," the cardinal said.

In South Africa, Cardinal Wilfrid F. Napier of Durban said that before apartheid ended in 1994, Pope John Paul supported South Africa's bishops and strengthened their hand in opposing the country's system of forced racial segregation.

The pope "spoke out strongly against apartheid and, in calling it reprehensible, he reinforced our position," Cardinal Napier said.

Bishop John Chang-Yik of Chuncheon, South Korea, said he gave Pope John Paul more than 40 lessons in the Korean language to help the pope prepare for his first visit to Korea in 1984, reported UCA News, an Asian church news agency based in Thailand.

"Before coming to Seoul, he rehearsed the Korean-language Mass in Rome 17 times," Bishop Chang said. "The Polish pope said he himself suffered under German and Soviet control, so he couldn't speak a foreign language in Korea," which suffered under Japanese colonial rule.

In Britain, Cardinal Cormac Murphy-O'Connor of Westminster, president of the Catholic Bishops' Conference of England and Wales, said Pope John Paul was "one of the greatest popes" in church history.

Australian Cardinal George Pell of Sydney said the pope's life countered the "radical secularist view that suffering is meaningless."

In Jerusalem, Latin Patriarch Michel Sabbah received a long line of dignitaries from the Israeli government, foreign diplomats, leaders from various churches and local Christians and religious who came to his residence to pay condolences.

Cardinal Karl Lehmann of Mainz, chairman of the German bishops' conference, said the pope's support for the Polish opposition to communism helped create the conditions for the collapse of communism throughout Eastern Europe.

Throughout his pontificate, Pope John Paul II worked hard to advance Christian unity in the East and West, breaking down barriers with a combination of personal gestures and official dialogue. But in the end, the pope found that his own missionary initiatives sometimes got in the way of his ecumenical dreams. His failure to travel to Moscow and greet Russian Orthodox Patriarch Alexy II was one of the deepest disappointments of his papacy.

The tensions between ecumenism and evangelization, and between dialogue and doctrine, ran through his pontificate from beginning to end.

The pope called Christian unity a pastoral priority and said the church was committed "irrevocably to following the path of the ecumenical venture." He gave the ecumenical movement a new impetus with an encyclical in which he asked other churches how the papacy could better serve a reunited Christianity.

Yet other Vatican documents from the same period emphasized the limits of dialogue on ecumenical questions like papal primacy, apostolic succession and even use of terms like "sister churches." Dialogue also stalled over such issues as the Anglican decision in 1994 to ordain women priests.

In his final years, the pope traveled to several predominantly Orthodox countries of the East, including Romania, Bulgaria, Armenia and Georgia. A frail figure on these last journeys, he won the hearts of many Orthodox believers through his determination to witness the faith and build ecumenical bridges. In former Soviet countries, he emphasized the "ecumenism of martyrdom" and said the heroic faith of all Christians under communism was a resource for the future.

His historic 24-hour pilgrimage to Greece in 2001 overcame Orthodox opposition and public protests, largely through a dramatic papal apology for the wrongs of the past—including the sack of Constantinople by Western Christians during the Crusades.

But his visit to Ukraine the same year raised new ecumenical tensions with the Russian Orthodox Church, despite the pope's call for mutual forgiveness and a new chapter of dialogue.

The first major ecumenical act of Pope John Paul's papacy was his November 1979 visit to Greek Orthodox Ecumenical Patriarch Dimitrios of Constantinople in Istanbul, Turkey. At that meeting, they inaugurated an international Catholic-Orthodox theological dialogue.

In a joint declaration in 1987 Pope John Paul and Patriarch Dimitrios repudiated all forms of proselytism of Catholics by Orthodox or Orthodox by Catholics.

At Orthodox urging, the Catholic Church rejected "uniatism"— the uniting of a segment of an Orthodox Church with Rome—as a policy for future Catholic-Orthodox union, but at the same time it affirmed the authenticity of Eastern Catholic churches formed in the past under such a model.

Those questions all came to the fore after the collapse of Soviet communism in 1991, as Eastern Catholic communities regained legal status throughout the former Soviet empire.

In a 1992 document on post-communist Russia, the Vatican called for ecumenism in Catholic mission activity there, asking Catholic authorities to avoid competition with the Orthodox and to assist in the development of Orthodox pastoral initiatives. But despite Vatican assurances, local Orthodox communities viewed the Catholic resurgence as an attempt to proselytize among their faithful.

In 2002, when the pope created four new dioceses in Russia, the Russian Orthodox Church froze dialogue with the Vatican and accused the Vatican of expansionism into what the Orthodox regard as their "canonical territory." In the months that followed, the Russian government expelled several Catholic priests and one bishop, adding a diplomatic dispute to the ecumenical crisis.

Whenever and wherever doctrinally possible, Pope John Paul encouraged joint Christian prayer and, starting in 1994, he invited Orthodox and Protestant clergy and theologians to write the meditations for his Good Friday Way of the Cross service in Rome's Colosseum.

He used the dawning of the third millennium of Christianity to stoke the twin fires of spiritual renewal and ecumenism—convinced, in the words of his 1995 encyclical, that "the commitment to ecumenism must be based upon the conversion of hearts and upon prayer." That encyclical, titled *Ut Unum Sint* ("That All May Be One"), became a topic of ecumenical dialogues around the world in the years that followed.

In it the pope acknowledged that while Catholics view the bishop of Rome as "visible sign and guarantor of unity," the notion of that papal role for the universal church "constitutes a difficulty for most other Christians." He asked theologians and leaders of other churches to help him "find a way of exercising the primacy" that could make it a ministry of unity to all Christians.

In 1993 the church's first revised ecumenical directory in nearly a quarter-century greatly expanded the principles and applications of Catholic ecumenical relations.

Pope John Paul met with heads of the ancient churches of the East, affirming Christological agreements with all the Oriental Orthodox churches and signing landmark declarations in 1994 with Patriarch Dinkha IV, head of the Assyrian Church of the East, and in 1996 with Catholicos Karekin I of Etchmiadzin, head of the Armenian Apostolic Church.

In relations with the churches of the Reformation, it was at the pope's invitation that Catholic and Lutheran theologians developed an official joint declaration that they share the same essential belief in justification by faith—the core doctrinal dispute behind the Reformation. The declaration was signed by officials of both churches in 1999.

Pope John Paul said he was particularly moved at Masses during his 1989 visit to Scandinavian countries when Lutheran bishops approached him for a blessing at Communion time, symbolizing their desire for the day when Catholics and Lutherans could share the same Eucharist. But in an encyclical on the Eucharist in 2003, the pope said a shared Eucharist among Christian churches was not possible until communion in the bonds of faith, sacraments and church governance were "fully reestablished." These and other statements disappointed those who had hoped for faster progress on sacramental unity.

When the pope went to England in 1982, he and Anglican Archbishop Robert Runcie of Canterbury announced the formation of the Second Anglican-Roman Catholic International Commission. The final report of the first international commission—published in 1982 and covering Catholic-Anglican agreed statements on Eucharist, ministry and authority—received a cool formal response from the Vatican in 1991, but clarifications won Vatican approval three years later.

The pope affirmed the work of the World Council of Churches with his 1984 trip to its headquarters in Geneva. Almost every one of his 104 trips to other nations featured meetings with leaders of other Christian churches.

At his death, Christian leaders from around the world recalled his efforts.

The Rev. Samuel Kobia, general secretary of the World Council of Churches, said the pope "constantly affirmed as irreversible the deep involvement of the Roman Catholic Church in ecumenism. . . . He opened a dialogue with other religious traditions and addressed constantly issues of social justice and moral and ethical values."

The Rev. Robert Edgar, general secretary of the National Council of Churches, said the pope "sounded strong themes of unity among Christians."

"He advanced the cause of interfaith understanding," he said. "He engaged in a passionate quest to end hostilities . . . and to advance human rights everywhere. He spoke forthrightly on the scandal of want and need. . . . And always, he spoke to the youth, strongly connecting with them in faith and hope."

Ecumenical Patriarch Bartholomew of Constantinople noted that the pope "envisioned the restoration of the unity of the Christians and he worked for its realization."

"History will also recount his crucial contribution to the fall of atheistic communism. There are not many such brave men of vision as the departed pope," he said.

Bishop Mark S. Hanson, presiding bishop of the Evangelical Lutheran Church in America and president of the Lutheran World Federation, declared that "Lutherans will always remember John Paul II as the pope who fostered an unprecedented growth in Lutheran/Roman Catholic relations. Healing the wounds laid bare during the 16th-century Reformation took on new meaning as the Joint Declaration on the Doctrine of Justification was signed in 1999."

Bishop Frank T. Griswold, presiding bishop of the U.S. Episcopal Church declared: "The world has lost one of its great Christian leaders. . . . His voice and moral authority gave inspiration and hope to millions well beyond the Roman Catholic Church."

United Methodist Bishop Peter D. Weaver, president of the Council of Bishops, said the pope was "a courageous witness for Christ and a compassionate brother to the poor and oppressed of this world. We give thanks for his life and ministry among us and the new life he now has in Christ."

United Methodist Bishop William Boyd Grove, former ecumenical officer of the Council of Bishops, noted disagreements. "My mind was not always with the pope's mind—I disagreed with him about many things. My heart was always with him. Who could not be moved by his strength and conviction?" he asked. But, he added, "His life, like the music of Bach, has been lived *soli gloria Dei*—to the glory of God alone."

The Rev. Rob Schenck, president of the National Clergy Council, expressed fondness for the Catholic leader. "If evangelicals like me could have claimed a pope as our own, he would have been John Paul II," he said. " His Christian faith was first passionate before it was cerebral; we evangelicals like that. But John Paul did more than look like an evangelical, he acted like one, too. He traveled the world . . . preaching 'Jesus Christ' to throngs of people in settings that looked more like Billy Graham crusades than the stuffy, mystical high Masses so strange to 'outsiders' like us."

The pope's death brought an unprecedented outpouring of condolences, thanks, praise and blessing from the Jewish community.

They indicated how deeply Catholic-Jewish relations had been affected worldwide by the Catholic Church's first Polish pope—who as a youth personally experienced the tragedy of the Nazi Holocaust of the Jewish people in World War II and as pope transformed that experience into an intense Catholic theological reflection on God's eternal covenant with Jews and the sinfulness of Christian anti-Semitism.

Nobody did as much to transform Catholic-Jewish relations as John Paul II, said Rabbi David Rosen, Jerusalem-based international director of interreligious relations for the American Jewish Committee. "He will be forever remembered as a great hero of Catholic-Jewish reconciliation," he said

"The Jewish community has lost a treasured friend," said Rabbi Eric Yoffie, president of the Union for Reform Judaism.

"Pope John Paul II revolutionized Catholic-Jewish relations," said Abraham H. Foxman, national director of the Anti-Defamation League.

"He was a pope for the ages," said the Union of Orthodox Jewish Congregations of America.

"The historic and landmark contributions that he made to Catholic-Jewish relations were pioneering and invaluable," the union said.

"We will lovingly remember his historic visits to the Great Synagogue in Rome, a concentration camp in Auschwitz (Poland) and the Western Wall in Jerusalem, as he stood with us in spiritual solidarity," said the New York Board of Rabbis. "Declaring anti-Semitism a sin against God and humanity, the pope repeatedly reminded the world that we could never again remain silent while people perish because of their race or religion."

"Shalom, shalom, shalom," the board said to the late pope, repeating his final words to a delegation of 130 Jews including New York rabbis that he met at the Vatican less than three months before his death.

At that meeting, "in an extremely moving moment, three rabbis of different denominations blessed this sacred soul," the board said.

"This was a most fitting gesture for an extraordinary individual who blessed us with his voice and his vision."

In Rome, Rabbi Elio Toaff, who welcomed Pope John Paul II when he made the first visit in history by a pontiff to a Jewish temple, came to pay his last respects to the pope in the Apostolic Palace. The retired chief rabbi of Rome stood for more than a minute in silence before Pope John Paul's body, then raised his hand solemnly in blessing before walking in the long, slow line of visitors.

Rabbi Ron Kronish, director of the Interreligious Coordinating Council in Israel, said the establishment of diplomatic ties created a whole new attitude of respect for the Catholic Church among Israelis, despite the difficulties and rough points in that relationship.

In the United States, people of Polish descent felt a special loss.

Father Bogdan Milosz, pastor of Our Lady Queen of Apostles Parish in Hamtramck, Mich., a largely Polish enclave surrounded entirely by Detroit, said his city's people had been "very involved" in activities to honor Pope John Paul, beginning with an April 1 Mass at the parish church when word of the pope's declining health became known.

On April 3, Father Milosz said, 200 Catholic and other religious leaders joined with city officials for a memorial tribute at Pope John Paul II Park, which is on one of the streets of the pontiff's motorcade route when he visited Hamtramck as part of his 1987 U.S. visit.

At St. Bruno Parish in Chicago, parish administrator Father Richard Prendergast put out an empty book for people to sign, and in the initial days following the pope's death it had become a condolence book. "Different people take his death different ways," said Father Prendergast. "For some, it's very personal, very intimate. He's like a member of the family."

U.S. Catholic bishops spoke of the pope's gifts to the world.

Archbishop Charles J. Chaput of Denver said John Paul II would be remembered most of all because "he radiated hope in an age with so little of it."

Archbishop Thomas C. Kelly of Louisville, Ky., cited the pope's "advocacy for the poor and oppressed, his commitment to ecumenism, and his personal holiness. . . . His travels gave a whole new meaning to evangelization."

Archbishop Harry J. Flynn of St. Paul and Minneapolis predicted the pope would be known as "John Paul the Great" because of "his profound writings and for his unceasing focus on the dignity of each and every human being and the paramount value of human life."

Bishop Thomas G. Doran of Rockford, Ill., also noted the calls to dub the pope "John Paul the Great."

"In the history of the church, only three popes have been accorded the appellation 'the Great'—Gregory the Great, Leo the Great and Nicholas the Great," he said. He predicted John Paul would be the fourth pope accorded that honor. "When he became Roman pontiff, the Catholic Church was in disarray, as it has always been in the periods that have followed major church councils. His preternatural sense of what the church required in order to attend to the needs of the modern world and to remain faithful to its mission, coupled with his long and faithful tenure as bishop of Rome, make him worthy of the appellation John Paul the Great," he said.

Bishop Howard J. Hubbard of Albany, N.Y., said, "Pope John Paul II is a man for the ages."

"Molded in the crucible of Communist Poland he became a crusader for the world's downtrodden and oppressed. Probably more than any other individual, he brought down the Iron Curtain, and he campaigned strongly and steadily for the poor and the hungry, the elderly and the unborn, the victims of war and violence—of every religion and none," he said.

Archbishop Michael J. Sheehan of Santa Fe, N.M., said the pope's final gift was "the exemplary manner in which he taught us the significance of life, of old age, of the infirm."

In Latin America, the death of Pope John Paul II sparked an emotional outpouring. There Pope John Paul had put his personal stamp on the nations as he addressed their controversial issues of social justice, liberation theology and church political involvement.

In January 1979, fewer than 100 days after being elected, he traveled to Mexico to attend a major meeting of Latin American bishops, and, in initial news stories, his principal addresses were widely misunderstood as calls for the socially active Latin American clergy to stay out of politics.

In reality, the first pope from a communist-ruled country was warning church leaders during the Cold War to avoid entanglements in partisan politics or in partisan political ideologies. He did not tell them to sidestep political issues, nor did he avoid them.

Neither did the pope flinch from internal church controversies. He led a concerted counterattack against the use of Marxist concepts by church theologians, social thinkers, and pastoral planners. This included strong criticisms of aspects of liberation theology coupled with disciplining priests and cutting into the authority of the Confederation of Latin American Religious to name their own leaders.

His influence also reached into the region's political life, shaping church priorities in dealing with secular leaders, especially the military governments in place when the pope took office in 1978.

Papal actions included:

- Steering liberation theology away from the influence of Marxist social analysis while encouraging its thrust toward social reforms in a poverty-ridden region of the world.
- Disciplining several priests who refused to leave their high government posts in Nicaragua's Marxist-influenced Sandinista government.
- Traveling to Chile and Argentina to criticize human rights abuses under their military governments.
- Advocating religious freedom and democratic reforms in communist-ruled Cuba.
- Promoting major celebrations in 1992 for the 500th anniversary of the arrival of Christianity in Latin America while admitting that the missionary church's ties to the Spanish conquest produced "lights and shadows" for the region's indigenous inhabitants.
- Stressing the need for tighter unity of the church in the Americas by organizing a Synod of Bishops for America in 1997 and issuing a major papal document in 1999 based on the synod. The document called for new evangelization programs and greater solidarity with the poor.
- Going to Mexico in 2002 to canonize Juan Diego—the 16th-

century Indian who saw the Marian vision of Our Lady of
Guadalupe—as a sign of the church's inculturation in Latin
America.

The pope's globe-trotting included 18 trips to Latin America. The
visits gave him firsthand knowledge of the region with the world's
largest Catholic population. About 42 percent of the world's
Catholics live in Latin America.

His encounters included requiring Peruvian Father Gustavo
Gutierrez, who coined the term *liberation theology*, to revise some of
his writings and silencing Franciscan Father Leonardo Boff, a Brazilian theologian who eventually left the priesthood.

During a 1983 trip to Nicaragua, the pope wagged both his index fingers in anger at Father Ernesto Cardenal, who tried to kiss
the papal ring, because the priest had joined the Marxist-influenced
Sandinista government against papal wishes. The pope later suspended Father Cardenal from the active ministry and disciplined
several other priests who held prominent government posts.

In a 1991 show of displeasure, the pope cut into the autonomy of
the Confederation of Latin American Religious by having the Vatican choose its officers instead of allowing them to be chosen by the
membership. The decision was made after several years of controversy over the content of a confederation evangelization program
considered too Marxist by Latin American and Vatican officials.

The reaction to his death throughout Latin America was heartfelt.

In Brazil, the pope was known as "John of God," a name given
him during his first Brazilian visit in 1980. On April 3, the hymn
Bless Us, John of God, composed for him, rang out in churches and in
Rio de Janeiro's Maracana Stadium, one of the world's largest soccer
fields.

Catholics in the northeastern Peruvian Amazon city of Iquitos recalled the pope's 1985 visit to their jungle area.

At the open-air Mass, the crowd chanted a welcome from the
charapas, a nickname for Iquitos residents stemming from the local
word for a tropical turtle.

In perfect, rhyming Spanish, Pope John Paul told them, "*El papa también se siente charapa*"—the pope also feels like a *charapa*.

The incident went down in the country's Catholic lore.

"There was a special sympathy between the pope and the people of Iquitos," said Bishop Julian Garcia Centeno.

"Whenever I visited him in Rome, I would remind him that I was from Iquitos, and he would say, 'The pope is a *charapa*.'"

In Chile, tens of thousands of people flocked to church all over the country April 3 to attend special services for Pope John Paul.

In Santiago, the capital, the cathedral was packed with mourners while nearly 15,000 others spent hours in the main plaza outside, singing, weeping and holding photos of the pope.

Inside the cathedral, Santiago's Cardinal Francisco Errazuriz Ossa celebrated a Mass attended by President Ricardo Lagos and other top government officials.

Lagos decreed three days of national mourning and recalled the pope's crucial role in mediating a peace agreement between Chile and Argentina over a border dispute.

In La Paz, Bolivia, Juan Mamani recalled the papal visit of 1988, when he was 13 years old. "Seeing him has changed my life," he said. As millions of Bolivians mourned, Mamani recalled the pope as "more than the head of the Catholic Church."

"I feel I lost an older brother, an old friend," he said.

The Bolivian government declared three days of mourning.

In Mexico City, people flocked to the statue of the pope outside the Basilica of Our Lady of Guadalupe.

Throughout the weekend of the pope's death, thousands of people gathered around the statue to say goodbye, and by April 3 a sea of candles had formed. The crowd outside the basilica, which houses an image of Mexico's patron saint, Our Lady of Guadalupe, periodically broke into cheers that punctuated with "*El Papa, el Papa*, rah rah rah!"

CARDINAL THEODORE E. MCCARRICK

Archbishop of Washington

"I JUST got back from the line to pay my respects at the casket of the Holy Father," my seminarian told me. I asked him how long he had to wait on line. "Ten hours," was the young man's reply.

Two special moments will always stand out in my memory of those awesome three weeks in April 2005. One relates to the death of Pope John Paul II and the other one to the election of the brilliant and wonderfully humble man who took his place.

The first one was captured in the answer of the young seminarian who stood on line for 10 hours for just 10 seconds in prayer at the body of an outstanding and much beloved pope. Young and old, they stood there until the police closed the line when the estimated wait was more than 24 hours! They filled the city of Rome, slept in the parks and public squares, more than doubled the 3 million population of the Eternal City and made the final rites and burial of Pope John Paul II easily the largest funeral in the history of the world. For someone like me, who was privileged to have a part to play in that solemn period of prayer and grieving, it was an unforgettable time, one which spoke loud and clear of the extraordinary impact that Pope John Paul II had on our world. They came from every continent, from every religion and none, presidents and kings, scholars and artists, philosophers and pundits. Each one had been touched by his life, his teaching or his remarkable personality, and so many had been touched by his holiness. They all knew that, in different ways, they would miss him, and so they wanted to be close to him this one last time.

The second special moment was from the conclave. You know that the conclave itself is covered by the secrecy of the most solemn oath. At the same time, however, it is minutely described in a document, *Universi Dominici Gregis*, which Pope John Paul II issued to guide the Cardinals in the formalities of the election. One of the instructions which that document spells out is the precise way in which each Cardinal is to cast his vote.

We probably had all read those instructions in preparation for the balloting, but reading about it and doing it are two very different things. Each Cardinal elector was given a ballot on which the words, "I elect as supreme pontiff" were printed in Latin. Below that was a space to write in the name of the person you chose. Once you had done that, you moved in a line according to your seniority to place your ballot in a large urn on the altar of the Sistine Chapel. It was significant that as you approached the altar, the powerful painting of Michelangelo's Last Judgement was there on the wall directly before you. As you placed your ballot in the urn, you read aloud the words of an even more solemn oath: "I call as my witness Christ the Lord who will be my judge, that my vote is given to the one who before God I think should be elected."

What a profound difference this makes in your mind and in your heart. In the deepest sense, it became clear that this was not an election as we think of elections. It was really a moment of discernment to discover which of your brother cardinals was the one God wanted to be pope. In choosing Benedict XVI, I believe we got it right!

CHAPTER 4

Interregnum

WHEN John Paul died the evening of April 2, major agencies first received a cell-phone text message alert, then a two-line e-mail signed by Joaquin Navarro-Valls, director of the Vatican press office.

"The Holy Father died this evening at 9:37 in his private apartment," he said. "All the procedures foreseen in the apostolic constitution *Universi Dominici Gregis* ("The Shepherd of the Lord's Whole Flock"), promulgated by John Paul II on Feb. 22, 1996, will be followed," he added.

Following the rules outlined by the pope, those with the pope when he died informed the camerlengo, or chamberlain of the Holy Roman Church, Spanish Cardinal Eduardo Martinez Somalo, who officially verified the pope's death. He placed seals on the pope's study and bedroom. The pope's personal secretaries and the nuns who work in the papal apartments were permitted to stay until after his funeral, at which time the entire apartment was sealed.

The death set in motion a complicated period of transition, an interval marked by mourning, a slowdown in Vatican operations and the election of a new pope. It ended when the College of Cardinals, meeting in a closed-door conclave, chose a successor and announced it to the world April 19.

Regulated by ancient traditions and recent rules, the period between popes—known by the Latin term *interregnum*—began moments after the pope's death. The rules governing the interregnum are matters of church law, not dogma, and were last revised by Pope John Paul in 1996.

They confirmed that as long as the Holy See was vacant, the universal church would be governed by the College of Cardinals, which could not, however, make decisions normally reserved to the pope. Such matters had to be postponed until the new pope was elected.

The College of Cardinals was charged with dealing solely with "ordinary business and matters which cannot be postponed." There were 183 cardinals when the pope died, and all were asked to meet in Rome to help administer the transition period.

The College of Cardinals did this through two structures: a general congregation, or meeting, in which all the cardinals met daily; and a particular four-member congregation, consisting of the chamberlain, Cardinal Martinez, and a rotating team of three cardinal assistants.

As chamberlain, Cardinal Martinez Somalo was to administer the goods and temporal rights of the Holy See until the election of a new pope. His duties also included verifying the death of the pope, sealing the pope's private rooms, taking possession of papal palaces at the Vatican and elsewhere, and informing church leaders of the pope's death. The chamberlain was also authorized to grant requests to photograph the deceased pope, but only if the pope is wearing pontifical vestments.

Meanwhile, the dean of the College of Cardinals, Cardinal Joseph Ratzinger, informed the other cardinals of the pope's death and called them to the first meetings and informed the diplomatic corps and the heads of nations.

One of the first items the College of Cardinals faced when it met in daily congregations was arranging for the pope's body to be taken to St. Peter's Basilica to receive the homage of the faithful. It also set the time for a series of Masses, which were celebrated for nine consecutive days, with burial slated for April 8.

In addition, the cardinals:

- Saw that the Sistine Chapel was prepared for the conclave and the rooms of the *Domus Sanctae Marthae*, an ecclesial guesthouse, readied for the cardinal-electors to stay there once the conclave began.
- Asked two churchmen to present meditations to the cardinals on problems facing the church and the need for careful discernment in choosing the new pope.

- Read documents left by the dead pope for the College of Cardinals.
- Arranged for destruction of his fisherman's ring and personal seals.
- Set the time for the start of the conclave.

During this time, the cardinals could discuss the coming election among themselves. But they could not make pacts or agreements that would oblige them to vote for a particular candidate.

All cardinals took an oath to maintain strict secrecy regarding everything related to the conclave, even after it was over. Only cardinals under age 80—a total of 117—would be eligible to vote in the conclave. Two were ill, so only 115 cardinals entered the conclave.

The first general congregation of cardinals to discuss the pope's funeral and the mourning period and to begin planning for the conclave to elect his successor was scheduled for the morning of April 4 in the Apostolic Palace.

The cardinals in charge of major Vatican departments lost their positions with the death of the pope, although they were brought back to their jobs by the next pontiff. During the interregnum, most curial offices were overseen by the secretaries of each department, who are generally bishops.

Thus the Roman Curia kept functioning, but at a slower pace. Pope John Paul's apostolic constitution instructed the Curia to avoid action on "serious or controverted matters," so that the next pope would have a free hand in dealing with these issues. The Vatican's tribunals continued to process marriage and other cases, however, and the Vatican's diplomatic representatives remained in place. Because rules specified that during the vacancy of the Apostolic See the Vatican secretary of state (Cardinal Angelo Sodano), the president of the commission governing Vatican City State (U.S. Cardinal Edmund C. Szoka), the prefects of the Vatican congregations, and the presidents of the pontifical councils would "cease to exercise their office," the assistant secretary of state and the foreign minister handled matters in the Secretariat of State, while the secretaries of the congregations and commissions continue the work of their offices.

There were four exceptions to the job suspensions, and each reflected the pastoral concerns of the church. They included the cham-

berlain of the Holy Roman Church, who had to oversee temporal affairs of the church, and for the major penitentiary (U.S. Cardinal J.
Francis Stafford), who had to be available to provide absolution to
penitents guilty of serious sin.

The chamberlain and the major penitentiary had to then inform
the new pope of any decisions made during the interregnum.

Also continuing in their offices in order to guarantee pastoral care
for the faithful were the papal vicar for Rome (Cardinal Camillo Ruini), the archpriest of St. Peter's Basilica (Cardinal Francesco Marchi-
sano), and the vicar for Vatican City (Archbishop Angelo Comastri).

And as a sign of the church's constant love for the poor, the
pope's almoner (Archbishop Oscar Rizzato) also continued his work,
distributing charity "in accordance with the criteria employed during
the pope's lifetime. He was to be dependent upon the College of Cardinals until the election of the new pope," the 1996 document said.

During the interregnum the world's cardinals published Pope John
Paul II's spiritual testament which was written over a span of 21 years
and put the finishing touches on plans for his funeral. In his will's last
entry in 2000, examining the possibility of resigning, he wrote that
he hoped God would give him the strength needed to carry on and
help him recognize "up to what point I should continue this service."

The cardinals met daily at the Vatican to take care of the practical affairs of the interregnum and prepare for the coming conclave.
The word *conclave* comes from Latin, meaning literally "with key,"
and reflects the previous tradition of locking the cardinals in an area
where they would spend day and night until the new pope's election.

As instructed by the conclave rules, the two prelates, "known for
their sound doctrine, wisdom and moral authority," who had been selected by the group, delivered important sermons—one on problems
the church is facing, and the other on the need for careful discernment in choosing a new pope.

The first talk was given April 14 to all the cardinals at the general
congregation by Father Raniero Cantalamessa, a bearded Capuchin
friar who preached the pope's retreats at the Vatican for many years.
Father Cantalamessa has ties to the charismatic renewal movement
and often livens up his talks with references to popular culture.

The second talk was given just before the start of the conclave

April 18 by Cardinal Tomas Spidlik, an 85-year-old Czech Jesuit and an expert on Eastern Christian spirituality. Cardinal Spidlik's preaching on Vatican Radio became so famous in the 1950s that his talks were collected and published in book form.

The cardinals set April 13 as the date they would receive the official condolences of the diplomatic corps accredited to the Holy See. They also authorized U.S. Cardinal Edmund C. Szoka, who headed the Vatican City State governor's office under Pope John Paul, to mint special coins and issue special stamps during the period between popes.

Present at the cardinals' April 7 meeting were 140 cardinals, out of a total of 183 members of the College of Cardinals. They refined the schedule for the start of the conclave April 18, a Monday, to include a 10 a.m. Mass in St. Peter's Basilica and a 4:30 p.m. procession into the Sistine Chapel.

The meetings of the cardinals continued after the funeral.

Much attention during the interregnum was on the chamberlain Cardinal Martinez. The 78-year-old Spaniard had been "camerlengo" since 1993, although the job was basically just a title while Pope John Paul II was alive. In the interregnum his responsibilities ranged from ensuring that nothing was touched or tampered with in the papal apartments to selecting the technicians who swept the Sistine Chapel for electronic bugs, cameras and recording devices.

In the Vatican's employ since 1956, Cardinal Martinez had worked under five popes. In February 2004 he retired as prefect of the Congregation for Institutes of Consecrated Life and Societies of Apostolic Life.

From 1979 until his appointment to the College of Cardinals in 1988, he was one of Pope John Paul's closest aides, serving as *sostituto*, or assistant secretary of state.

Under Pope John Paul's 1996 rules, Cardinal Martinez was required to write a report on the results of each ballot, place it in a sealed envelope and give it to the new pope after he is elected. If after about 30 ballots, no papal candidate had received two-thirds of the votes, the chamberlain would have had to preside over the discussion of whether or not the cardinals wanted to move to a simple majority vote.

Although his role in the preparation and work of the conclave was key, the chamberlain's duties ended inside the Sistine Chapel with the election of a new pope.

CARDINAL EDWARD M. EGAN

Archbishop of New York

THERE are so many powerful memories and impressions of the events attendant upon the conclave of this past April that it is difficult to single out just one. Still, among those that most frequently come to mind now that some months have passed, none can compare with the countless expressions of heartfelt gratitude that I have heard or received because of the choice of the new Pontiff and the life, especially the final years, of his predecessor.

Before leaving for the conclave, I arranged for four Masses to be celebrated in St. Patrick's Cathedral in which thousands gathered with me to pray for the deceased successor of St. Peter. The first two were on the weekend of his passing, one on Saturday evening and the other on Sunday morning. For both, every pew was filled, as were the front and center aisles. The mayor of New York, the two New York senators, a multitude of other political, business, labor and cultural leaders, and literally thousands of laity of all backgrounds participated in the liturgies, which were televised across the nation and across the world as well.

After each Mass, I stood in the front aisle to be greeted by a host of Catholics and non-Catholics who wanted nothing more than to tell a representative of the church how deeply grateful they were for the courage, leadership and example of Pope John Paul II, and especially for what they had learned from him during his last years of ill-health and suffering.

Two more Masses followed. The first on Sunday afternoon was for the Polish community of Greater New York and was televised live to Poland. There were 4,000 inside the Cathedral and well over 5,000 outside. Among the dozens who spoke with me after the ceremony, virtually all—with tears in their eyes—focused on their gratitude for "Poland's greatest son," as John Paul II was described by a Polish archbishop who flew in from Rome to participate in the liturgy and address the congregation.

The fourth Mass, the next afternoon, was for the Hispanic community. St. Patrick's was once again packed to overflowing, and all with whom I had a chance to chat both before and after the Mass, centered in on one theme—gratitude. "I am not well," a rather celebrated New York Hispanic told me. "I watched our beloved Holy Father when he was hurting so badly, and he made me strong. How do I thank the church for him?"

In Rome, gratitude continued to be the dominant motif, but the focus shifted. When after the election of Pope Benedict XVI, I went to the North American College on the Janiculum Hill for a press conference, a host of seminarians descended upon me at the front door to pat me on the back and all but shout, "Thank you for Benedict!" One of the newscasters from New York whom I know quite well grabbed my arm and whispered, "I thank you too, Cardinal. A great choice." Indeed, as I was leaving the college some hours later, a writer for Catholic publications approached and kept repeating until I was out the door, "Thanks a million! Thanks a million!"

First on the streets of Rome and later back in New York, in parishes, during meetings, at dinners and even on the bustling sidewalks of Manhattan, I was stopped over and over, often by complete strangers, to be thanked for the new Pontiff. I felt almost ashamed to be accepting so many expressions of gratitude and was tempted on several occasions to remind those who were speaking to me that I was just one of 115 cardinals who had participated in the conclave. In due course, however, I settled upon simply thanking those who were thanking me for "a pope who is so 'with it' and so kind too," "a pope who has the savvy to do a 'bang-up job,'" "a pope who would surely have had my vote," and so on. (These are actual quotations. They may appear a bit overly familiar. All, however, were spoken with admiration and love.)

In the Year of the Eucharist, two bishops of Rome put gratitude, deep and sincere, on the lips and in the hearts of millions. How fitting. For as we know from the catechism, Eucharist means thanksgiving.

CHAPTER 5

A Worthy Successor

T HE DEATH of John Paul II unleashed a media frenzy unseen before in the history of the church. Even before John Paul's death, journalists and pundits had pondered the impact of his papacy and wondered who would be the next pope.

The public nature of the pope's declining health for months made preparations for a papal transition a high priority in newsrooms around the globe. News agencies prepared teams to work on the papal transition story in Rome and at home. They developed biographies of members of the College of Cardinals. They interviewed church historians, sociologists, Vatican officials and others who reflect on the needs of today's church.

When the pope appeared near death, media and pundits flew to Rome.

The cardinals around the world also prepared for this moment. Plans, personal and otherwise, were tentative, for they knew they'd be called to the Vatican as soon as the pope died and did not know how long they'd be there. They looked at the needs of the church worldwide and in their own nations and dioceses. They looked at the papacy, which had changed before their eyes with John Paul II, who had made a very visible presence on the world stage. They considered the attributes of the pope they had met on numerous occasions both in Rome and in their own homelands.

As the cardinals set off for the Vatican and began to arrive in Rome they had many questions. So did the journalists they met wherever they went—at home, in Rome's Fiumicino airport, in St. Peter's Square, at North American College where they stayed before the conclave, at Rome churches where they offered Mass, in restaurants or just on the streets. They found the media with a voracious appetite for insights and information and tried to help them within the constraints of good taste and respect for the secrecy of Vatican deliberations.

Before the funeral, several cardinals commented on what John Paul's death had meant to the world.

Ukrainian Cardinal Lubomyr Husar of Lviv, who was in a U.S. hospital recovering from eye surgery and left the hospital early to be in Rome for the pope's funeral and the meetings of cardinals, described an "emotional pain of loss."

"We lack the perspective of time to properly value his historical figure and many-sided activities," he added. However, he noted that "in his years as universal pontiff, the pope helped our Ukrainian Greek Catholic Church enormously in its transition from the state of slavery to a normal life."

Cardinal Georges Cottier, theologian of the papal household, told the French newspaper *Le Figaro*, "At the end of the 20th century and the beginning of the new millennium, John Paul II was the only moral personality able to win a universal audience, an audience that went well beyond the boundaries of the church."

He described the pontificate as "innovative and creative" and said the pope had the ability "to put anyone at ease." He never intimidated anyone, the cardinal said. "He had an exceptional ability to listen, but his tact was combined with great determination."

The internal organization of the Vatican, he said, "was not his main concern, and it is possible that this will be a problem for his successor."

Cardinal Cottier, who was over age 80 and so ineligible to vote in the conclave, expressed hope that the next pope would have learned from Pope John Paul that "the church is not an organization which considers efficiency to be a principle of governing."

"We always need popes who are saints, that is, who are great spiritual figures who preach through their example. We do not expect to have a 'successful pope.' Success would be a disaster for the church; that is not what the church seeks," he said. "The church needs witnesses of Jesus Christ."

Cardinal Miguel Obando Bravo of Managua, Nicaragua, told the

Italian news service ANSA that "the successor of Pope Wojtyla must be, like him and John XXIII and Paul VI, a pontiff able to read the signs of the times, a pontiff who loves the church and takes action to evangelize."

"He was a pope who had no fear, but who loved the truth and never hid it in an attempt to find consensus," he added. "At the same time, he was a prophet-pope who worked tirelessly to promote peace in love, in justice and in freedom."

Cardinal William H. Keeler of Baltimore, contacted by phone as he was taking a train to the airport, said the cardinals would need prayers, including those of people from the interfaith community, Muslims, Jews and representatives of all the Christian communities.

"They realize we've got a big job, and they're giving us an enormous amount of prayer support," he said.

Italian Cardinal Ennio Antonelli of Florence told reporters April 3 he had seen many newspapers' lists of top papal candidates. "Fortunately, journalists are not the ones who elect the pope," he said. "The true pastor of the church is Christ," he added. "Sometimes, it is impossible to imagine another man as pope, but then you see that the Lord knows what he is doing, that the Lord leads the church despite all our weaknesses."

French Cardinal Paul Poupard, who served as president of the Pontifical Council for Culture under Pope John Paul, said the biggest challenge still facing the church lies "in living out the Gospel."

The future pope will need to "be faithful to and build on the church's heritage and traditions while creating new ways" to merge faith and culture, "especially for young people," he said.

Scottish Cardinal Keith O'Brien of St. Andrew's and Edinburgh spoke of his trepidation at the "momentous" task of appointing a successor to Pope John Paul.

"I feel sadness at the loss of a great man who served the church to his last breath, happiness that he has gone to his eternal reward and trepidation as I join with my brother cardinals in the momentous task of selecting a new pope," he said April 5.

Discussions about who might succeed John Paul II showed the range of concerns among church leaders.

Bishop William S. Skylstad of Spokane, Wash., president of the

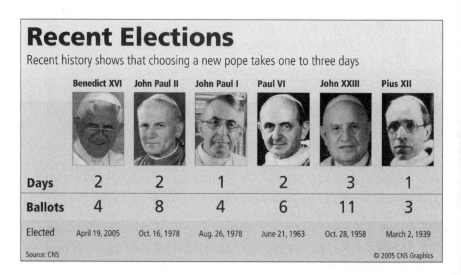

Recent Elections

Recent history shows that choosing a new pope takes one to three days

	Benedict XVI	John Paul II	John Paul I	Paul VI	John XXIII	Pius XII
Days	2	2	1	2	3	1
Ballots	4	8	4	6	11	3
Elected	April 19, 2005	Oct. 16, 1978	Aug. 26, 1978	June 21, 1963	Oct. 28, 1958	March 2, 1939

Source: CNS © 2005 CNS Graphics

U.S. Conference of Catholic Bishops, said in Rome that he was praying that the cardinals would choose a pope who is truly a pastor.

"He must be a pastor, someone who can relate to people, someone who knows the church structure and the teachings of the Second Vatican Council and someone who has a grasp of several languages," Bishop Skylstad said. "He must also be an advocate for the poor and vulnerable."

"Pope John Paul had a tremendous capacity for loving people; he really was a lover of humanity and not just of Catholics," he added.

Cardinal Francis E. George of Chicago stressed holiness and language skills when he spoke of attributes the church needed in its new leader.

The next pope, like every pope, "must be a man of deep faith, a man striving to be holy, a man faithful to Christ and his teachings, and a man who will bring them into our times," said Cardinal George.

"Pope John Paul was a genius at this," the cardinal said.

The issues the next pope will be called to deal with, he added, include "aggressive secularism" and the "scandal of the continuing gap between rich and poor."

The next pope must find new ways to dialogue with Muslims to help the world find peace and will have to face the continuing moral challenges raised by biotechnology and by changing sexual mores, he said.

Media asked Cardinal George if he thought the U.S. cardinals would look for a pope who might consider changing the church's ban against artificial birth control, especially to stem population growth as part of the battle against poverty.

"So your solution is to exterminate the poor in order to take care of poverty?" the cardinal responded.

"The doctrine of the church is not going to change," he said, although the pope and bishops try to find pastoral ways to lead people to a full acceptance of the truth.

Finding one person with all the qualities needed in a pope would be difficult, he said. But the new pope "should be able to call on people and understand . . . by talking and listening to the experience of others."

Media asked how the cardinals, coming from so many countries and backgrounds, could find consensus on one person.

"The great unifier for all of us is faith. Faith is the same everywhere," Cardinal George said, although personalities and social situations are different.

The unity of faith "creates an enormous community, with compassion and empathy. Pope John Paul II had that. He was not Asian, but when he went to Asia he was an Asian. When he went to Latin America, he became Latin American. Not because he was an actor, but because he was a man of faith, and God is everywhere," he said.

Cardinal Theodore E. McCarrick of Washington told reporters that the church had never had such a figure like the late Holy Father.

"We need a wonderful pope. We always need a wonderful pope, but maybe we need one now more than ever," he said.

The cardinal said the world today is facing "some real crises . . . of faith, of indifference and of apathy" caused in part by the way media promote wealth, power and beauty as leading to happiness.

"The church really has to be proclaiming that the beatitudes are still the way to happiness," that being kind, courageous, generous, loving of the poor and working for peace are needed, he said.

Cardinal Justin Rigali of Philadelphia said the next pope, like all popes, must be "a pastoral person who reaches out in love and truth and charity. He has to reach out in solidarity and in the proclamation of human dignity."

Although there has never been a pope from the Americas, Cardinal Roger M. Mahony of Los Angeles said he believed the next pope would not and should not be someone from the United States.

"The reason is that the United States is the last remaining superpower," he said.

Cardinal Mahony said the scenario of there being two prominent U.S. leaders on the world stage would create confusion as to who was setting the agenda or influencing global affairs.

"There would be this constant evaluation of who's leading whom: Is the pope speaking and the president following or is the president speaking and the pope following?" he said.

There would be "constant friction, people trying to second-guess."

Even though the cardinal-electors would look at each other's qualifications when choosing who would be the best person to lead the church, the election of a pope "is not a political process. It is a religious process," said Cardinal Rigali.

Each elector knows he needs "all the best of human wisdom" as well as "the assistance of the Holy Spirit" in making his choice.

The use of prayer and the intercession of the Holy Spirit are what make the election of a new pope unique and "quite different from the election of a CEO of a firm," Cardinal Rigali said.

Cardinal Adam J. Maida of Detroit said he had been praying that the Holy Spirit would show him who could best lead the church after Pope John Paul.

If the Holy Spirit "shows up as a dove, that's great; if he whispers in my ear, that's fine," he said.

Cardinal George Pell of Sydney, Australia, said the next pope should be a teacher and preacher in the spirit of Pope John Paul II, but the cardinals might not find someone with all the gifts of the late pontiff. John Paul II was, "by papal standards, very young, very energetic and very much a public performer, in a good sense of the word," he said. "You can't expect that of every pope. If an old pope is elected, for example, it could be that we won't see nearly as many papal trips." Pope John Paul was "a bit of a miracle, and I don't think anybody's expecting two miracles in a row," he added.

Cardinal Pell outlined challenges facing the church:

- The erosion of the faith, particularly in Europe. It is the basic challenge of "belief in God and the centrality of Christ," he said.
- Offering clear examples of deep faith, one of the reasons the pope was so effective among young people—"because they saw that he believed," he said.
- The inroads made by the "culture of death" on issues such as abortion, euthanasia and contraception. "There's nowhere in the Western world where we're producing enough babies to keep the population stable," he said.
- Islam, especially the church's continuing efforts to keep dialogue open in order to strengthen moderate Islamic forces. He said that John Paul refused to be "crusader-in-chief," and that spirit needs to be continued. "We're going to have to do everything we can to encourage the moderate Muslims and to sustain them in their struggle for political power," the cardinal said. A separate concern, he said, was the danger of a significant number of conversions to Islam in traditionally Christian countries of the West.
- The great missionary frontiers, especially China. Cardinal Pell predicted that with economic development, the society would open up and present opportunities for evangelization.

Cardinal Pell said he thought that questions of church governance and the balance between particular and universal churches would be "second-order" challenges for the new pope.

"There are some that suggest that a little bit of coordination, perhaps discipline in the Curia, would be advantageous. And I think there's probably something to that," he said.

Cardinal Lubomyr Husar said electing a new pope is a serious responsibility, but it is not as if the fate of the world rests on the cardinals' shoulders.

"Let's not overdramatize this," he said. "It is a serious responsibility because it is a serious job, but it is not as if the whole world depends on this. But the consequences are serious."

Cardinal Husar said an old adage applies strictly: "Work as if everything depends on you and pray as if everything depends on God."

Cardinal Husar said that when he was elected to head the Ukrainian Catholic Church people kept referring to him as the successor of Metropolitan Andrew Sheptytsky and Cardinal Josyf Slipyj, "and I am not them. I am me and the same thing will happen to the next pope."

"Someone has to fill the office," he said, but each successive pope will be different from his predecessors. "We should not create too much of a mystique about this office," he said.

He quoted a saint who once said a bishop should be a man "who is not very healthy, not very saintly and not very wise."

"He had a point," the cardinal said. "He must be a man."

"I am very much against mystifying this. The person elected must say, 'I am who I am and God will do the rest.'"

Cardinal Husar said the cardinals' task was made difficult by the fact that "there are too many of us to really know each other."

With all the challenges facing the church and the world, he said, "you cannot come up with a profile, then look around the room to see who fits."

One problem all of the cardinals see, he said, is "a lack of moral fiber all around the world."

"Addressing the problem of morality is not a matter of reciting rules, rules, rules, but of helping people to do God's will," he said.

Cardinal Husar rejected the idea that the cardinals, to guide their vote, would draw up some sort of master plan, such as choosing one of the older cardinals with a view to having a brief transitional pontificate.

"All those types of calculations are dangerous," he said.

Besides, he added, many people thought Pope John XXIII was elected to be a transitional pope, "and he called the Second Vatican Council and changed the face of the church."

Cardinal Edward M. Egan of New York said the next pope had to "be himself."

Whomever the College of Cardinals chooses to elect should not try to mimic or outdo his predecessors, he said. "Whoever is chosen—he would be very, very poorly advised to try to be Pope John Paul II, Paul VI or Pope Pius XII," the cardinal told reporters.

"None of us does very well playing roles and so whoever it is, I would hope he would come right in and be himself," he said.

"The whole idea of trying to continue what somebody else did or to do it better, I think, is a real mistake," he said.

Cardinal Egan said he would like to see renewed emphasis on the "local communities of faith which are served by dioceses and archdioceses."

Focusing on the local parishes is "what is going to gain us vocations, increased numbers—gain us unity," he said. He added that people on the local level should be allowed to make more decisions than they do now.

The next pope will have to help the church stay dedicated to addressing the spiritual needs of the world's migrants, said Japanese Cardinal Stephen Fumio Hamao.

"The successor of John Paul II, in my opinion, should continue to put emphasis on the pastoral-missionary dimension of migration as a form of new evangelization, as a contribution of the church that goes beyond mere humanitarian assistance," he said.

While the church should continue to offer important practical and material assistance to those on the move for work or study, there should be increased attention paid to "the spiritual and social well-being of those involved," said the cardinal, who served as president of the Pontifical Council for Migrants and Travelers under Pope John Paul II.

Family and marital life are often disrupted by migration, with children and women often carrying the burden that comes with families being separated, Cardinal Hamao said. The church should be on the lookout for these problems, help address them and facilitate the Catholic migrants' integration into the local Catholic community.

In a world suffering from war, hunger, environmental crises and disease, the next pope should be "an intelligent person who can provide good leadership and a critical look at issues," Cardinal Peter Turkson of Cape Coast, Ghana, said.

The cardinal noted that Pope John Paul spoke out on issues such as world hunger, ethnic warfare and the modern slave trade, and established a foundation in Burkina Faso to address problems related to drought and the expansion of deserts in Africa.

During Pope John Paul's pontificate, the Catholic population in Africa grew by 150 percent—to 137.5 million.

While membership and vocations are increasing, Cardinal Turkson said, the challenge for the church is "how we can make an impact on the political level, in terms of good government and political conflicts that degenerate into tribal conflict. It's a secular area, but we need to make an impact."

"We need to maintain an openness to the presence of God in all this," Cardinal Turkson continued. "We know what has happened in human history, but God knows it better. He knows what the church needs."

The cardinals' remarks to reporters in the days following the pope's death were quite general. They offered no names and reacted blandly to names thrown out by journalists. Many cited the Holy Spirit as the key figure in the conclave—implying they had not yet decided who would get their votes.

All that helped confirm the impression that the field was wide open, but from the cardinals' comments, some preferable traits emerged.

Many voters said holiness and an ability to offer clear, personal witness to the Gospel were the most important qualities to look for when picking the next pope.

Cardinal Philippe Barbarin of Lyon, France—one of the few who came to Rome saying he knew who he would vote for—told a French radio station that the conclave should select someone "who shows the light of Christ and the strength of the Gospel." What part of the world he comes from, or whether he is young or old, are secondary issues, he said.

Many cardinals said revitalizing the faith of Christians was at the top of the list of challenges facing the next pope. They also mentioned the erosion of traditional religious values in society, the need for continued dialogue with Islam and the renewal of missionary efforts—particularly in Asia.

Several cardinals said they would be looking for someone with pastoral experience. That did not exclude Roman Curia officials, many of whom have served as bishops.

Other cardinals suggested that the next pope would need to take Pope John Paul's strong teachings on moral and social issues and, with pastoral creativity, bring them more deeply into people's personal lives.

A Scottish cardinal said the church's priority should be "re-Christianization." "Looking around the world now, we can see moral standards have fallen—people's lives aren't as good as they used to be," said Cardinal Keith O'Brien of St. Andrews and Edinburgh, Scotland. "Re-Christianization of Scotland is one of the goals I set myself as cardinal. We now need to re-Christianize the world and the church, so Christ's followers will be as he wanted them."

Pope John Paul II's willingness to take a stand on political issues such as the war in Iraq is a model to be followed by the next pope, said Cardinal Julius Darmaatmadja of Jakarta, Indonesia. "The church should be a moral force in the world."

That ability to bridge religious, ethnic, and social divides would be important for the next pope, as would be the ability to communicate with people from different cultures, he said.

Curia officials also spoke of what would be needed in their next leader.

Pope John Paul "reached out to the entire world," said U.S. Sister Sharon Holland, one of the highest-ranking women at the Vatican as "section leader" for the Congregation for Institutes of Consecrated Life and Societies of Apostolic Life.

"His heart was for everyone," which could also be seen by the "outpouring of respect coming in from Muslims, Jews and even non-believers," said Sister Holland, a member of the Servants of the Immaculate Heart of Mary.

Pope John Paul broke numerous records in the number of encyclicals and other official documents written during a pontificate, but it was how this pope lived his life that made an impact on these Vatican officials.

The number of books, documents, and references to Mary "has been enormous," said Msgr. Arthur Calkins, a Marian expert and member of the International Pontifical Marian Academy.

But this pope also "lived with a profound Marian devotion," said Msgr. Calkins.

He paraphrased the pope's episcopal and papal motto, *Totus Tuus*, as "I am completely yours, O Mary."

"He put his love for Our Lady at center stage from the first day of his pontificate" and emphasized that a devotion to Mary "does not take away from the honor and duty to Christ, but brings us closer," said Msgr. Calkins.

Pope John Paul brought new life to Second Vatican Council teachings and church traditions, officials said.

Sister Holland said that the pope carried forward with *Gaudium et Spes*, the Second Vatican Council's Pastoral Constitution on the Church in the Modern World.

"Each pope builds on the previous pope, even if we don't see it," she said.

Sister Holland said there must be continued dialogue and respect within the church. "There has always been conflict over how to do things right in the church," she said, highlighting the "strident polarity" between so-called liberal and conservative positions. "Of course there will be differences of opinion, but we will have to dialogue, respect and represent the Gospel, and not be divisive and make a lie out of our commitment and communion" with God, she said.

CARDINAL JUSTIN RIGALI

Archdiocese of Philadelphia

FOR 26½ years Pope John Paul II reached out to the world and the world responded. One of his most insistent messages was that of divine mercy. He proclaimed God's love to humanity in the face of all its weaknesses, all its sins, all its needs. He asked people to show mercy to others. In his own pastoral love, he wanted people to understand God through the mercy revealed in Jesus Christ.

For me it was very moving to realize that John Paul II died on Saturday, April 2, at 9:37 p.m. (Rome time) after having assisted at

Mass celebrated in his room. The last Mass of his life was the Mass of the Second Sunday of Easter or Divine Mercy Sunday. The last Gospel proclaimed to him in the liturgy was the Gospel of St. John that related the institution of the Sacrament of Penance, which the Church celebrates as the sacrament of mercy.

Less than two hours after his death, at 5:15 p.m. (Philadelphia time), I was privileged to celebrate the same Mass in our Cathedral and share with the people the same Gospel that the Pope had heard for the last time. It was an exhilarating experience to celebrate the triumph of the message of divine mercy in the death of John Paul II.

It seemed to me that the days that followed his death and those that preceded and followed his funeral were also an important part of the triumph of mercy. Millions of people came to Rome. The world applauded, the world prayed and the world reflected once again on his witness to mercy. It seemed to me that the cry for his beatification, "*Santo, subito*" was the world's ratification of how well he had represented a merciful Christ.

On the morning of the election of Benedict XVI it was evident to me that there would be an unbroken continuity on the part of the new pope in bearing witness to the merciful Christ. One of the most powerful experiences of those days took place just minutes after the election itself in the Sistine Chapel.

Once the new pope had given his consent and chosen his name, he changed into his white cassock and took his place before the Last Judgement of Michelangelo. At that moment the first proclamation of the world of God to the new pope took place. It was the role of the senior Cardinal Deacon, Cardinal Jorge Medina Estévez, to approach Pope Benedict and to read from the 16th chapter of the Gospel of Saint Matthew. With the new pope, all the cardinals could experience, through the word of God, the actual transmission of the mysterious reality of the papacy. The role of Peter was being perpetuated in his newest successor, and Christ was renewing his promise to sustain him. At the same time the successor of Peter would begin his proclamation of the identity of Jesus Christ.

For me few experiences during April 2005 could equal the moment when the words of the Gospel were proclaimed: "'Who do people say that the Son of Man is?' They replied, 'Some say John the

Baptist, others Elijah, still others Jeremiah or one of the prophets.' He said to them, 'But who do you say that I am?' Simon Peter said in reply, 'You are the Christ, the Son of the living God.' Jesus said to him in reply, 'Blessed are you, Simon son of Jonah. For flesh and blood has not revealed this to you, but my heavenly Father. And so I say to you, you are Peter, and upon this rock I will build my church, and the gates of the netherworld shall not prevail against it.'"

Throughout this whole experience in the intimacy of the Sistine Chapel, another aspect that enhanced the election of the new pope was the spiritual presence of the people of God, the spiritual presence of the praying church. In no small way the prayers of the church not only sustained the cardinals but, in God's providence, helped to realize the divine choice of Benedict XVI as successor of Peter and successor of John Paul II.

CHAPTER 6

Conclave Rules

WHEN Pope John Paul II revised the conclave rules, he increased the comfort level of the cardinals' lodgings but retained the traditional seal of secrecy.

The use of the guest house was the most significant practical innovation in *Universi Dominici Gregis*. For the most part, in updating the rules for the election, the pope kept almost all the provisions set down by Pope Paul VI in 1975, including the controversial norm preventing cardinals over the age of 80 from voting.

However, he also did away with two archaic forms of election, saying the only valid method is balloting by the full College of Cardinals.

It ruled out election:

- By acclamation, when the cardinals could unanimously proclaim someone pope.
- By delegation, when a small group of cardinals was chosen to break an electoral impasse.

It confirmed that at least a two-thirds majority was needed to elect a pope.

The housing of the cardinal-electors in the *Domus Sanctae Marthae*, which is visible from street level outside Vatican City, marked a break with the centuries-old tradition of secluding the cardinals in the heart of the Vatican's Apostolic Palace for the duration of the conclave. Previously, the cardinals had to stay in makeshift rooms set up around the Sistine Chapel, quarters that were described as uncomfortable, stuffy and lacking adequate dining and bathroom facilities.

The new rules took pains to ensure that the modern lodgings away from the voting hall would not compromise secrecy. They ordered that the *domus* remain off-limits to unauthorized personnel during the conclave, and that no one was to approach the cardinals while they were being transported to the Sistine Chapel for voting.

Because the *domus* lies just inside the Vatican walls, in partial view of downtown Rome apartment buildings, some feared the "closed-door" nature of the conclave could be compromised. But Vatican officials took measures to ensure that the cardinals could not communicate with the outside world and vice versa. For example, some cardinals on the higher floors were forced to keep their window shutters closed for the duration of the election.

Although the *domus* was absolutely off-limits to "unauthorized persons" during the conclave, staff were needed to take care of the residence's normal operations. The *domus* is directed by an Italian priest and staffed by 5 nuns and 28 lay people.

While the *domus* offers relative comfort, it is not a luxury hotel. It has international cable TV, but the system was disconnected for the conclave period. There are no recreational facilities, no bar and only one small coffee vending machine for the entire building.

The rooms are simply furnished. There are 105 two-room suites and 26 singles. Cardinals drew lots for rooms. Each suite has a sitting room with a desk, three chairs, a wall cabinet and large closet; a bedroom with dresser, night table and clothes stand; and a private bathroom with a shower.

The rooms all have telephones, but the phones were turned off during the conclave. Cell phone reception also was blocked.

The most convivial place in the residence is the dining room, where the cardinals took their meals. The building's main chapel, with its ultramodern decorations, would have been crowded if all 115 voting cardinals tried to squeeze in at the same time.

The *domus* has four other tiny chapels located at the end of hallways on the third and fifth floors of each of the building's two wings. Each contains an altar and four kneelers.

Overall, the residence's atmosphere is rather austere. The marble floors are polished to mirrorlike brightness. The hallways are dimly lit; fire extinguishers stand at the far ends of each corridor.

Each floor has an open area with five or six chairs. In addition, on the ground-floor level is a modern conference room, a few smaller rooms for discussions and a large open area with tables, easy chairs and bookshelves offering an eclectic assortment of reading material.

The cardinals were warned against communicating with anyone during the conclave—by note, telephone or any other means—except in cases of proven urgency. They were banned from reading newspapers or magazines, listening to the radio or watching TV.

The cardinals and those chosen to assist inside the conclave or at the residence building had to take a solemn oath of secrecy. They also promised not to use any audio or video recording devices, and the Sistine Chapel itself was to be swept for hidden cameras or microphones—a precaution introduced by Pope Paul VI.

The section of the rules banning electronic recording or communication devices expanded on earlier precautions against the potential bugging of the conclave. Sophisticated surveillance equipment was used to scan the area in and around the Sistine Chapel and jamming equipment was installed in the Sistine Chapel under a temporary floor installed for the conclave.

Like his predecessors, Pope John Paul II prohibited cardinals from making any plans for his successor while he was still alive. In emphasizing that before or during the conclave the cardinals must not make voting pacts or promises, he invoked the threat of excommunication for those who would do so. He said it was not his intention, however, to forbid an "exchange of views" about the election while the papacy was vacant.

The effect of the rule changes meant that "the walls of the Vatican now constitute the place where the conclave is held," rather than merely the Apostolic Palace, said Archbishop Piero Marino, the Vatican's master of liturgical ceremonies, who explained the changes to media before the conclave began.

Under the rules, secret ballots were to be cast once on the first day of the conclave, then normally twice during each subsequent morning and evening session. Except for periodic pauses, the voting was to continue until a new pope was elected. For the 2005 conclave, pre-

Longtime Popes

	Years of Papacy	Months of Reign
Pius IX	1846-1878	380
John Paul II	1978-2005	318
Leo XIII	1878-1903	305
Pius VI	1775-1799	294
Hadrian I	772-795	287
Pius VII	1800-1823	281
Alexander III	1159-1181	263
Leo the Great	440-461	253
Urban VIII	1623-1644	252
Sylvester I	314-335	251

St. Peter
Considered the first pope, Peter is said to have led the church for 30+ years.

Shortest Papacy
Urban VII Sept. 15-27, 1590
He died from malaria 12 days after his election.

Source: Annuario Pontificio and New Catholic Encyclopedia   © 2005 CNS Graphics

sumably there was one vote the night the conclave opened, two the next morning and one that afternoon—when the pope was elected.

In theory, any baptized male Catholic can be elected pope, but current church law says he must become a bishop before taking office; since the 15th century, the electors always have chosen a fellow cardinal.

Each vote began with the preparation and distribution of paper ballots by two masters of ceremonies, who were among a handful of noncardinals allowed into the chapel at the start of the session.

Then the names of nine voting cardinals were chosen at random: three to serve as *scrutineers*, or voting judges; three to collect the votes of any sick cardinals who remain in their quarters at the *Domus*; and three *revisers* who check the work of the scrutineers.

The paper ballot was rectangular. On the top half was printed the Latin phrase "*Eligo in Summum Pontificem*" ("I elect as the most high pontiff"), and the lower half was blank for the writing of the name of the person chosen.

After all the noncardinals had left the chapel, the cardinals filled out their ballots secretly, legibly and folded them twice. Plans called for ballots from sick cardinals to be collected and brought back to the chapel.

Each cardinal then walked to the altar, holding up his folded ballot so it could be seen, and said aloud: "I call as my witness Christ the Lord, who will be my judge that my vote is given to the one who before God I think should be elected." He placed his ballot on a plate, or paten, and then slid it into the receptacle.

When all the ballots had been cast, the first scrutineer shook the receptacle to mix them. He then transferred the ballots to a new urn, counting them to make sure they corresponded to the number of electors.

The ballots were read out. Each of the three scrutineers examined each ballot one by one, with the last scrutineer calling out the name on the ballot, so all the cardinals could record the tally. The last scrutineer pierced each ballot with a needle through the word "*Eligo*" and placed it on a thread so they could be secured.

After the names were read out, the votes were counted to see if anyone had obtained the two-thirds majority needed for election.

The revisers then double-checked the work of the scrutineers for possible mistakes.

At this point, any handwritten notes made by the cardinals during the vote were collected for burning with the ballots. When the first vote of the morning session was inconclusive, a second vote followed immediately, and the ballots from both votes were burned together at the end.

When the pope was elected, the ballots were burned immediately. By tradition, the ballots were burned dry—or with chemical additives—to produce white smoke when the pope had been elected; they were burned with damp straw or other chemicals to produce black smoke when the voting was inconclusive. After notes from the conclave were burned with the ballots, the tally of each vote was sealed to be delivered to the new pope for safekeeping.

The most notable change introduced by Pope John Paul II into the voting process was to increase the opportunity of electing a pope by simple majority instead of two-thirds majority, after a series of ballots. Plans called for a two-thirds majority rule to hold in the first phase of the conclave: three days of voting, then a pause of up to one day, followed by seven ballots and a pause, then seven more ballots and a pause, and seven more ballots.

At that point—about 12 or 13 days into the conclave—the cardinals could have decided to move to a simple majority for papal election and limit the voting to the top two vote-getters. In earlier conclaves, switching to a simple majority required approval of two-thirds of the cardinals, but this time that decision could have been made by simple majority, too. Because Pope Benedict's election occurred on the second day of the conclave, the change was not implemented.

In the 2005 conclave, the cardinals put their ballots into newly designed urns.

For centuries, cardinals had set their ballots on a small plate and used it to tip the ballots into chalice-shaped urns. They still set the ballot on a plate, but now they also placed the ballots in silver and gilded bronze urns shaped like woks with lids.

Archbishop Piero Marini had commissioned Italian sculptor Cecco Bonanotte to make the new egg-shaped urns. The sculptor made three urns. One was for the ballots cast in the Sistine Chapel and one for ballots cast in the *domus* by cardinals too ill to go to the Sistine Chapel. Once the ballots were counted, they were placed in the third urn and carried to the stove for burning.

The urn to receive the counted ballots had a small, rough sculpture of the Good Shepherd on top; tipping the figure opened the lid to allow the ballot to be placed inside. Three sheep stand on the edge of the urn.

Archbishop Marini said the decoration, which also includes the Eucharistic symbols of grapes and wheat, stressed the spiritual significance of the balloting, which is not a political election but a religious act.

Archbishop Marini said that when one looked at the oval urns with irregular surfaces and varying shades of bronze one sensed "a space which opens up beyond the visual plane."

He described Bonanotte's design as one in which "ancient and modern harmonize in barely accented forms where the classical tradition of perfection is tempered in a vision of open lines."

There has always been great curiosity about the inside story of conclave voting. After the 1978 conclave that brought Pope John Paul II to the papacy, books were written with detailed descriptions of the shifting numbers of votes in each of the eight ballots before he was elected.

Much of the writing was speculation, but some of it was based on conversations cardinals had with close aides or friends in the excitement of the immediate post-election period. Pope John Paul apparently did not want that to happen again.

The ban on divulging information related to the papal election even extended to the meetings the cardinals had before the conclave begins. Perhaps this influenced the cardinals' decision not to talk to reporters in the week before they entered the Sistine Chapel.

St. Peter's Basilica continued to be open during the conclave. Thousands of pilgrims visited Pope John Paul's tomb in the grotto area. However, the dome of St. Peter's, which overlooks the Sistine Chapel, was closed during the conclave. Also closed were the Vatican Gardens, where the cardinals might stroll.

CARDINAL FRANCIS E. GEORGE, OMI

Archbishop of Chicago

THE death of Pope John Paul II was not unexpected. What was unexpected was the immense outpouring of love and grief that brought millions of people, especially young adults, to pay their respects in the days before his funeral Mass. Present were those who could be seen in Rome and those who could see Rome only through global television; present also were the invisible saints whose intercession was invoked in the litany we chanted as we brought the pope's body from the Apostolic Palace, through St. Peter's Square and into the basilica, where it was placed at the Altar of the Confession, above and in front of the remains of St. Peter.

The saints were invoked again as John Paul's body was taken from the basilica back to the square for the funeral Mass. Gathered in respect and sorrow were the heads of state and government for most of the countries of the world, the leaders of other churches and faith communities and the multitude that was present throughout the city.

The knowledge that the world was gathered in prayer sustained the cardinals as we felt the personal loss of John Paul II develop into a theological loss. Peter was gone; no one held the keys that Jesus had given to the head of the apostolic college. The church could not be herself, could not adequately take up the mission Christ had given her. This loss lent urgency to the discernment of the next week. Each of us had one question in mind: whose name shall I write on the ballot when we enter into conclave?

The litany of the saints was chanted once more as we went into the Sistine Chapel at the opening of the conclave. When I passed the threshold of the chapel, I looked directly at Michelangelo's fresco of the Last Judgement and felt the import of the oath each of us would swear before we voted: "In the presence of Christ who will be my judge, I swear and vow that I am voting for the one I judge to be best suited for the office of bishop of Rome." I felt intensely part of the great communion of saints, of those called by the Lord to play our roles in human history and in salvation history.

With the election of Pope Benedict XVI, the grief of the funeral and the concerns of the conclave ceded to a great sense of accomplishment. We could be fully ourselves; we could touch Peter in his successor. At the Mass inaugurating his papal ministry, the litany of the saints again accompanied us from Peter's tomb and the basilica into the square. The pope preached: "I am not alone." None of us is.

Looking at the great square filled with the world's representatives for the funeral of Pope John Paul II and then looking at it again days later from the loggia of St. Peter's as Pope Benedict XVI first greeted the people of Rome, the contrast was great. But the unity was greater. What brought people to the square in sorrow brought them also to the same square in joy: our faith. Faith sustains us in sorrow and in joy, in bad times and in good. Faith unites us to each other and to all the saints and to all those redeemed by Christ from every age and place. Faith will direct us in the years to come, during the pontificate of Pope Benedict, in communion with a holy and scholarly man who will face forthrightly the challenges to the mission of the church in our day.

CHAPTER 7

Conclave Favorites

THE CARDINALS who gathered to elect Pope John Paul II's successor represented the most international conclave ever held, with influential electors and viable papal candidates from several continents.

Pope John Paul's pontificate saw the world's Catholic population shift toward Latin America, Africa and parts of Asia, and many observers wondered if the moment had arrived for a Third World pope. Cardinals from developing countries represented nearly half of conclave voters.

Others in Rome believed that following the first non-Italian pope in 455 years, it would be time for an Italian again—one who could use the traditional skills of compromise and consensus-building to increase unity in the church.

Despite years of public speculation by the media and private reflection by the cardinals, there appeared to be no clear favorite going into the conclave to elect the 265th Roman pontiff.

"The Italian cardinals appear divided, as they were in the last conclaves (of 1978). If the Latin American cardinals were to unite behind a single candidate, that might be enough to determine the election. But it's not clear whether that will happen," said one cardinal.

Some theorized that the apparent lack of a front-runner left ample space for the action of the Holy Spirit. But it would also allow for subtle persuasion during closed-door deliberations—called "general congregations"—held by the College of Cardinals in the days before the conclave begins, and in the informal meetings that took place among small groups of cardinals in Rome.

"You can expect the cardinals to get serious about looking for a successor when they sit down in the general congregations. For the first time, they'll be discussing the future of the church without the pope being present," predicted one longtime Vatican official.

Geographically, the cardinals were more spread out than ever before, but they had come together more often than in past eras—in Rome for synods, consistories and frequent Vatican meetings, and elsewhere for regional church events. Many of the cardinals had traveled extensively, visiting church communities around the world. Most observers said that meant they knew each other far better than the cardinals who gathered at the last two conclaves.

One thing seemed certain: Having appointed more than 97 percent of the voting cardinals, the late pope would remain an influential figure in the coming conclave. None of the true *papabili*, or potential popes, had shown any indication they would alter the pastoral directions established by Pope John Paul.

The cardinals considered the strongest candidates for election included several from Italy and other European countries, at least three from Latin America and an African.

For centuries, Italians controlled the conclave and invariably elected one of their own. Some cardinals thought there were built-in reasons to elect an Italian pope: the Vatican's location as an enclave inside Italy, the fact that Italian is the common language of the Roman Curia, the role the Vatican has historically played in Italy and the pope's own position as bishop of Rome.

But in recent years no Italian cardinal appeared to have garnered the unified preconclave support of his compatriots needed to propel him to a quick election. Instead, speculation centered on two or three cardinals who represent slightly different wings of Italian Catholicism.

Cardinal Dionigi Tettamanzi of Milan, 71, was considered by many the front-runner. Short, stout, and quick to smile, he was viewed as a theological conservative with a strong social conscience. He is seasoned in church administration, having held key positions in the Italian bishops' conference. A teacher of moral theology for 20 years, he helped prepare Pope John Paul's encyclical on human life issues, *Evangelium Vitae*, and in 2000, he wrote an online "e-book" on medical ethics. He is also considered one of the Italian church's top

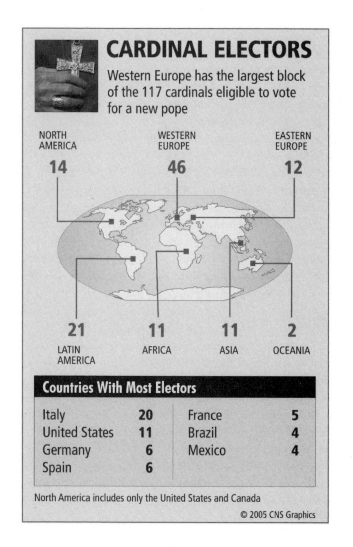

CARDINAL ELECTORS

Western Europe has the largest block of the 117 cardinals eligible to vote for a new pope

NORTH AMERICA
14

WESTERN EUROPE
46

EASTERN EUROPE
12

21
LATIN AMERICA

11
AFRICA

11
ASIA

2
OCEANIA

Countries With Most Electors

Italy	20	France	5
United States	11	Brazil	4
Germany	6	Mexico	4
Spain	6		

North America includes only the United States and Canada

© 2005 CNS Graphics

experts in marriage and family ministry, the lay apostolate and youth formation.

Increasingly, Cardinal Tettamanzi had spoken out on social issues at home and abroad, highlighting in particular the populations left behind by globalization. He drew criticism from the Right when, as archbishop of Genoa in 2001, he defended protesters at a G-8 meeting in the city and spoke movingly of the new situations of poverty in the world. In Milan, he repeatedly challenged the city's citizens to live up to Gospel values in the way they treat society's weakest members.

Cardinal Tettamanzi came to the media's attention at the 1999 European Synod of Bishops, where some leading bishops suggested a churchwide council to examine possible reforms and a less-centralized style of church governance.

Cardinal Angelo Scola, 63, is a respected academic and theologian who has headed the Patriarchate of Venice since 2002. Considered by many as a "cultural warrior," his eagerness to push church teachings in the public forum earned him plaudits from other church leaders. He travels extensively, speaks several languages and remains a prolific writer despite a heavy pastoral schedule.

Cardinal Scola, considered a friend of new church movements, spent several years with the Communion and Liberation movement as a young student and priest in Milan. He has tried to stimulate lay formation in Venice, inaugurating an important new educational complex that offers theology degrees followed by specialist studies in bioethics, business ethics, art and social sciences. He also has forged new contacts with Orthodox churches and reached out to support Christian minorities in the Middle East.

Cardinal Camillo Ruini, 73, who worked for years in the pope's shadow as papal vicar of Rome, was seen as a long-shot Italian candidate who, if elected, would press ahead with the late pope's agenda. President of the Italian bishops' conference since 1991, Cardinal Ruini got high marks for administration but low marks for charisma. After the Sept. 11, 2001, terrorist attacks, he supported the Right of the United States to respond militarily. In Italy he has pressed hard against legislative attempts to introduce euthanasia and a number of proposals that would weaken the traditional definition of the family.

Church leaders in Rome who yearned for a strong administrator as pope sometimes pointed to Italian Cardinal Giovanni Battista Re, 71, who spent years as the No. 2 man at the Vatican's Secretariat of State and has run the Congregation for Bishops since 2000.

Italian Cardinal Carlo Maria Martini, 78, a biblical scholar and retired archbishop of Milan who remains a popular pastoral figure in Italy, was expected to be influential in a conclave and had some support for the papacy despite his age.

Other Europeans frequently mentioned as potential papal candidates included Belgian Cardinal Godfried Danneels, 71, who has called for more openness and more consultation in the way the church deals with some key issues; and Austrian Cardinal Christoph Schonborn, 60, a Dominican who helped write the *Catechism of the Catholic Church*.

European cardinals represented 49 percent of conclave voters, but for the first time in history they were not an absolute majority. That fact prompted the whole church to look more closely at the wider field of cardinals.

Latin America, home to more than 40 percent of the world's Catholics and the biggest voting bloc of cardinals after Europe, had at least three cardinals frequently mentioned as strong papal candidates:

- Honduran Cardinal Oscar Rodriguez Maradiaga of Tegucigalpa, 62, whose age many thought counted against him with cardinals wary of another long pontificate. Charismatic, plain-spoken and fluent in seven languages, he served as president of the Latin American bishops' council, or CELAM, 1995–99, promoting a wide range of economic justice initiatives between North and South America.

  In the months before the conclave he made headlines when he criticized what he called a media "witch hunt" against the Catholic Church regarding clerical sexual abuse. That might have lost him points among some U.S. observers, but did not hurt his standing with some other prelates around the world.

- Brazilian Cardinal Claudio Hummes, a 70-year-old Franciscan, and head of the populous São Paolo Archdiocese. The son of German immigrants, he was named bishop of Santo Andre in 1975 and gained pastoral experience among laborers, sometimes mediating between companies and unions. He has strongly defended the church's family and pro-life teachings.

  In 2002, the late pope called him to preach his Lenten retreat—a sign of papal favor that often counts at conclave time. He is also a member of nine important Vatican agencies, more than any other Latin American cardinal.

  A constant theme of Cardinal Hummes' pastoral work has

been protecting human dignity in areas of the family, labor and economic justice. At a Christmas fund-raiser for a church-run job-training center, he said: "Jesus was born poor among the poor to call our attention to the social injustice that makes a portion of humanity increasingly poor, suffering, humiliated and excluded from sufficient access to the goods of the earth."

As a bishop in the late 1970s, he opened the doors of churches as a refuge for those hunted by the Brazilian military regime. When he headed the Archdiocese of Fortaleza in the 1990s, he strengthened his fame as a peacemaker, this time by opening the doors to new Catholic movements, such as the charismatics without generating tensions among the more progressive basic Christian communities.

■ Cardinal Jorge Mario Bergoglio, 68 and a Jesuit with a growing reputation as a very spiritual man with a talent for pastoral leadership. An author of books on spirituality and meditation, since 1998 he has been archbishop of Buenos Aires, where his style is low key and close to the people. He rides the bus, visits the poor and a few years ago made a point of washing the feet of 12 AIDS sufferers on Holy Thursday. He also has created 17 new parishes, restructured the administrative offices, led pro-life initiatives and started new pastoral programs such as a commission for the divorced. He co-presided over the 2001 Synod of Bishops and was elected to the synod council, so he is well-known to the world's bishops.

Latin Americans at the Vatican also pointed to two sometimes-overlooked church leaders in Mexico, each of whom has a reputation as a social liberal and theological conservative in the Pope John Paul tradition: Cardinal Norberto Rivera Carrera of Mexico City, 62; and Cardinal Juan Sandoval Iniguez of Guadalajara, 72.

Among the African cardinals, one stood out: Cardinal Francis Arinze, 72, a member of the Ibo tribe, who converted to Christianity as a child. He excelled as a young bishop in northern Nigeria in a period marked by strife and hunger, before being called to the Vatican in 1985 to head the Pontifical Council for Interreligious Dialogue. He firmly adhered to Pope John Paul's line on dialogue: It is essential in a shrinking world for religions to respect each other, but this can never diminish the church's duty to announce Christ.

In 2002, Cardinal Arinze was promoted to head the Congregation for Divine Worship and the Sacraments—only the second time an African cardinal has headed one of the nine top Vatican departments. In 2004, the congregation issued an important document taking aim at a wide range of liturgical abuses, and it has continued to exercise close control on liturgical translations.

During the congregation's plenary session in March 2005, Cardinal Aloysius Ambrozic of Toronto said Cardinal Arinze ran the meeting briskly, keeping order but in a "democratic and fair" way.

"He's simple, in an intelligent kind of way," Cardinal Ambrozic said. Known for his blunt talk and sense of humor, Cardinal Arinze has close ties to conservative Catholic groups in the United States.

Vatican watchers cited other potential candidates who could be found among the ranks of well-known as well as relatively unknown cardinals:

- German Cardinal Joseph Ratzinger, then prefect of the Congregation for the Doctrine of the Faith, had been the Vatican's doctrinal watchdog since 1981. In the eyes of many, he was the dominant curial figure in the last pontificate and he would be an attractive choice to those who wanted an even clearer line against dissent inside the church.

- Portuguese Cardinal Jose da Cruz Policarpo, the 69-year-old patriarch of Lisbon, was seen by some as a potential bridge candidate between Europe and Latin America. A former academic and a prolific writer, the cardinal has produced articles and books ranging from Marian spirituality—reflecting the Portuguese devotion to Our Lady of Fatima—to the moral and spiritual challenges of modern society.

  Shortly after being made a cardinal in 2001, he participated in a meeting with Pope John Paul and more than 150 other cardinals to discuss the church and the third millennium. Afterward, he said the key conclusion was that "evangelization is witness. The church must give a radical witness of holiness, charity and poverty."

  In recent years Cardinal Policarpo has made overtures to

Muslims and Jews, emphasizing the common social agenda of all believers. But, as he told the Synod of Bishops in 2001, the church cannot follow "a merely cultural and sociological notion of dialogue." For the church, he said, dialogue starts with faith in Jesus and in the Gospel. The church listens to others after listening to the word of God, responding to questions and challenges by living the faith more deeply and completely.

■ Cardinal Nicolas Lopez Rodriguez of the Dominican Republic, 68, who organized the church's celebration of the fifth centenary of the evangelization of the Americas in Santo Domingo in 1992. A past president of CELAM, he has emphasized evangelization in the region and insisted that the church's concern for the poor must not be "exclusive or excluding." A strong voice on family issues, he has been sharply critical of U.S.-supported abortion and sterilization campaigns, comparing them to the work of "death squads."

■ Indian Cardinal Ivan Dias of Mumbai, formerly Bombay, was considered an Asian long shot among papal contenders. A longtime Vatican diplomat and fluent in 17 languages, the 68-year-old prelate was named to Mumbai in 1996. Cardinal Dias has endorsed the teachings of the controversial Vatican document, *Dominus Iesus*, saying the church has no choice but to announce Christ as the only mediator between God and humanity. He is the type of pastoral leader the Vatican hopes will lead the evangelization advance in India and the rest of Asia. Insiders add that the cardinal has a sense of humor and that his jokes made the late pope laugh.

CHAPTER 8

Opening of the Conclave

A DIGNIFIED and solemn spirit permeated St. Peter's Basilica April 18 during the opening Mass of the conclave to elect the 265th pope. The basilica was packed long before the 10 a.m. liturgy, which began with a procession of the 115 cardinals who would elect the successor to Peter.

Cardinal Joseph Ratzinger presided, looking *papabili* despite his 78 years, which some thought might preclude him from consideration. Although Italian media had named him front-runner from the start, many dismissed this as just the Italian custom of floating names in the media as trial balloons. Also named by Italian media was the man they deemed Cardinal Ratzinger's political or theological opposite, Cardinal Carlo Maria Martini, 78, a Jesuit and the retired archbishop of Milan. However, Cardinal Martini suffered from Parkinson's disease, and many deemed both his age and health issues making his election unlikely. Some *Vaticanisti*, as veteran Vatican watchers are called, suggested the two names were placeholders on the right and left to help cardinals line up candidates in between.

The Mass in St. Peter's was the last public event before the 115 cardinal-electors began secret balloting in the Sistine Chapel. The cardinals, wearing red vestments, filed into the packed basilica two by two, looking somber as they kissed the altar.

During the homily, Cardinal Ratzinger, dean of the College of Cardinals, delivered a stern warning about a "dictatorship of relativism" and other modern threats to the faith.

He prayed that after Pope John Paul, God would again give the church "a pastor according to his own heart, a pastor who guides us to knowledge in Christ, to his love and true joy."

He spoke about the "ideological currents" roiling the church in recent decades. "The small boat of thought of many Christians," he said, "has often been tossed about by these waves—thrown from one extreme to the other: from Marxism to liberalism, even to libertinism; from collectivism to radical individualism; from atheism to a vague religious mysticism; from agnosticism to syncretism."

"Every day new sects are created and what St. Paul says about human trickery comes true, with cunning which tries to draw people into error," he said.

Cardinal Ratzinger, who had dealt with theological concerns all around the world as head of the Vatican's doctrinal congregation under the late pope, said having true faith today is often labeled "fundamentalism"; meanwhile, he said, "we are moving toward a dictatorship of relativism" that insists there is no certain truth.

The cardinal said all of these threats underline the need for Christians to make a journey toward Christ. "We should not remain infants in faith," he said.

Cardinal Ratzinger did not mention the papal election until the last line of his homily. The liturgical prayers and readings, however, made frequent reference to the need to choose a good pastor.

"O God, eternal Father, you who govern your people with the care of a father, give your church a pontiff pleasing to you for his holiness of life, totally consecrated to the service of your people," said the opening prayer.

The Gospel reading recalled how Christ selected his disciples for special ministry: "It was not you who chose me, but I who chose you and appointed you to go and bear fruit that will remain."

The cardinals had been meeting daily for two weeks to discuss church issues and to begin considering potential candidates for the papacy. Despite an official news blackout by the cardinals, leaks and rumors fueled speculation about a wide array of *papabili*.

As the cardinals processed from St. Peter's, the congregation gave special attention to those deemed leading candidates. Besides Cardinal Ratzinger, other frequently mentioned names were Italian Cardinals Dionigi Tettamanzi of Milan and Angelo Scola of Venice; Brazilian Cardinals Claudio Hummes of Sao Paolo and Geraldo Majella Agnelo of São Salvador da Bahia; Portuguese Cardinals Jose da

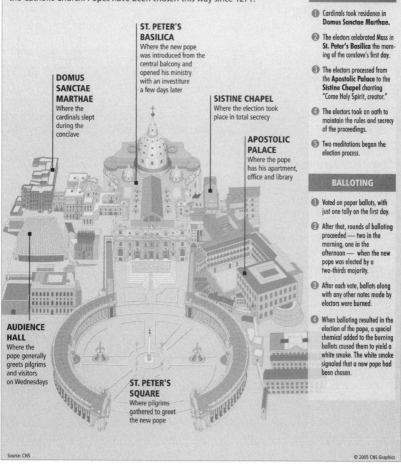

CONCLAVE OVERVIEW

Cardinals met under an oath of secrecy to elect the new leader of the Catholic Church. Popes have been chosen this way since 1271.

DOMUS SANCTAE MARTHAE
Where the cardinals slept during the conclave

ST. PETER'S BASILICA
Where the new pope was introduced from the central balcony and opened his ministry with an investiture a few days later

SISTINE CHAPEL
Where the election took place in total secrecy

APOSTOLIC PALACE
Where the pope has his apartment, office and library

AUDIENCE HALL
Where the pope generally greets pilgrims and visitors on Wednesdays

ST. PETER'S SQUARE
Where pilgrims gathered to greet the new pope

PREPARATIONS

1. Cardinals took residence in **Domus Sanctae Marthae.**

2. The electors celebrated Mass in **St. Peter's Basilica** the morning of the conclave's first day.

3. The electors processed from the **Apostolic Palace** to the **Sistine Chapel** chanting "Come Holy Spirit, creator."

4. The electors took an oath to maintain the rules and secrecy of the proceedings.

5. Two meditations began the election process.

BALLOTING

1. Voted on paper ballots, with just one tally on the first day.

2. After that, rounds of balloting proceeded — two in the morning, one in the afternoon — when the new pope was elected by a two-thirds majority.

3. After each vote, ballots along with any other notes made by electors were burned.

4. When balloting resulted in the election of the pope, a special chemical added to the burning ballots caused them to yield a white smoke. The white smoke signaled that a new pope had been chosen.

Source: CNS

© 2005 CNS Graphics

Cruz Policarpo of Lisbon and Jose Saraiva Martins, head of the Vatican's sainthood congregation under Pope John Paul; Nigerian Cardinal Francis Arinze, head of the Vatican's congregation for worship and sacraments under Pope John Paul; and Argentine Cardinal Jorge Bergoglio of Buenos Aires.

The conclave was the largest in history. It was also the most geographically representative, with cardinals from 52 countries. Cardinal Ratzinger and Cardinal William Wakefield Baum, an American and retired curia official, were the only two electors who had taken part in the last election in 1978.

U.S. Catholics at the Mass had their own ideas about the papal election.

"I'd like to see a Latin American. The church has so many followers there," said Ivonne Fleitas, a Cuban-American Catholic from Miami.

Another American, Gennaro Cibelli, a Catholic from Clarksville, Md., said it was important to choose someone with a "sturdy character."

"He doesn't have to be a carbon copy of John Paul, but someone with the same moral fortitude," he said.

As in past conclaves, Italians comprised the largest delegation, with 20 of the 117 eligible voters. In comparison, the conclave that elected Pope John Paul II had 27 voting Italians, or 24 percent of the 111 participants. There were 11 U.S. cardinals eligible to vote in the conclave, the second-largest group from one nation.

Of the 11 cardinals, Cardinal Baum, the retired head of two Curia offices, was the most senior and had voted twice before. He was named to the College of Cardinals in 1976 when he was archbishop of Washington, and voted in the two conclaves in 1978 at which Popes John Paul I and II were elected.

The U.S. cardinals also included Cardinals Edward M. Egan of New York; Francis E. George of Chicago; William H. Keeler of Baltimore; Bernard F. Law, retired archbishop of Boston; Roger M. Mahony of Los Angeles; Adam J. Maida of Detroit; Theodore E. McCarrick of Washington; Justin Rigali of Philadelphia; J. Francis Stafford, head of the Apostolic Penitentiary, a Vatican court, and former archbishop of Denver; and Edmund C. Szoka, president of the commission that governs Vatican City State and former archbishop of Detroit. Another American, Cardinal Lubomyr Husar, a Ukrainian-born U.S. citizen, is counted among Ukrainian cardinals. He is the major archbishop of Kiev and Aalyeh, Ukraine, and head of the Ukrainian Catholic Church.

Two cardinal-electors did not participate in the conclave for health reasons. Filipino Cardinal Jaime Sin, retired archbishop of Manila, and Mexican Cardinal Adolfo Suarez Rivera, retired archbishop of Monterrey, were too ill to make the trip to Rome, leaving 115 cardinals under age 80, the largest number to vote in a papal election to date. Cardinal Sin's absence meant that Cardinal Baum was the senior cardinal priest in the conclave.

Cardinals are divided into a three-tier internal hierarchy: cardinal bishops, cardinal priests and cardinal deacons. The cardinal bishops include only six Latin-rite cardinals, one of whom, Cardinal Joseph Ratzinger, was then dean of the College of Cardinals. Cardinals who head archdioceses make up the bulk of the rank of cardinal priests, while cardinal deacons are mostly members of the Roman Curia.

According to Pope John Paul II's conclave rules, one of the senior cardinal priest's duties is to deliver a spiritual "exhortation" should voters not be able to agree on a candidate with a two-thirds majority after about six days.

To ensure the right atmosphere for the election of a new pope, the Vatican published a book of rites and prayers to accompany the cardinals as they entered the conclave, voted, elected a new pope and introduced him to the world.

The *Ordo Rituum Conclavis* (Rites of the Conclave) prepared by Italian Archbishop Piero Marini, the papal master of liturgical ceremonies, was approved by Pope John Paul II in 1998, but not released until after the pope's death. The 343-page book with prayers in Latin and an Italian translation begins by noting that the election of a pope "is prepared for and takes place within liturgical actions and constant prayer." The election of a pope, it said, "is of supreme importance in the life of the people of God in pilgrimage on earth."

The Ordo called for the Mass to begin with the antiphon from the Book of Samuel, "I will choose a faithful priest who shall do what I have in heart and mind."

The prayers of the faithful, written in 1998, include pleas that God safeguard and protect his church; that the Holy Spirit enlighten the cardinals; that all humanity form one family; and that God grant eternal rest to the soul of the deceased pontiff.

The Mass for the election of the pope is the only rite in the book to be celebrated publicly before the new pope is presented to the

world. Other rites pertain to the entrance into the conclave and related activities.

After the Mass was celebrated in the morning, the book called for
the cardinals to gather in the late afternoon in the Pauline Chapel of
the Apostolic Palace. The dean of the college, Cardinal Ratzinger,
addressed the cardinals: "After having celebrated the divine mysteries, we now enter into conclave to elect the Roman pontiff. The
whole church, united with us in prayer, invokes the grace of the Holy
Spirit so that we elect a worthy pastor of the entire flock of Christ,"
he said.

In a procession behind the cross, the cardinals walked into the
Sistine Chapel singing a litany of saints of the East and West and a
series of invocations to Christ with the refrain, "Save us, Lord." It
was the final act in a drama marked by liturgical pageantry, private
contemplation and consensus-building among the cardinals entrusted with choosing the next pope.

Cardinal Roger M. Mahony, writing afterward, said that experience "was the most moving" of conclave rites for him personally.
"We processed into a special sacred space where the presence of God
was so evident and the long history of God's plan of salvation was
further revealed. It was simply stunning and poignant."

Cardinal Francis E. George was struck by the litany. "I felt intensely part of the communion of saints, of those called by the Lord
to play our roles in human history and in salvation history," he said.

The faces of the cardinal-electors betrayed little emotion as they
filed from the Hall of the Blessings, through the *Sala Regia* and into
the historic chapel, dominated at one end by Michelangelo's fresco of
the Last Judgement.

In a corner at the opposite end stood the small stove where ballots would be burned, signaling to the waiting world whether a new
pope had been elected.

Once the cardinals had taken their places in the chapel, the Book
of the Gospels was enthroned in a position visible throughout the
celebrations and deliberations of the cardinals. When everyone was
in place, the cardinals chant the ancient invocation of the Holy
Spirit, *Veni, Creator Spiritus*.

Then the dean prayed: "O Father, you who guide and protect your church, give your servants the spirit of intelligence, truth and peace, so that they strive to know your will and serve you with total dedication."

Following the new rite, the cardinals took an oath to "faithfully and scrupulously observe" the rules for electing a pope; each swearing that if he were elected he would "faithfully fulfill the Petrine ministry as pastor of the universal church and will strenuously affirm and defend the spiritual and temporal rights as well as the freedom of the Holy See." They also promised to keep secret everything having to do with the election.

When the last cardinal had placed his hand on the open Book of the Gospels and sworn the oath, Archbishop Marini said: "*Extra omnes,*" ordering all those not directly involved in the conclave out of the Sistine Chapel.

Czech Cardinal Tomas Spidlik, who at 85 was not an eligible voter, remained inside to lead the cardinals' reflection on their responsibilities in electing a new pope. After the meditation, he and Archbishop Marini left the chapel.

Finally, only the voting cardinals were left inside and the first vote was taken. Each cardinal marked his ballot in secret, folding it twice and depositing it in a silver and bronze urn. After the ballots were counted, they were burned with special chemicals to produce the black smoke signifying an inconclusive vote.

Each day, the cardinals were to recite morning and evening prayer together and concelebrate Mass. They were to listen to Scripture and have time for prayer before each ballot was cast and before the ballots were counted.

As each cardinal placed his vote in the urn, he promised that his vote was cast for the candidate he believed deserved to be elected.

Cardinal Theodore E. McCarrick recalled how momentous it felt to be part of the election.

"Reading about it and doing it are two very different things," Cardinal McCarrick said. "It was significant that as you approached the altar, the powerful painting of Michelangelo's Last Judgement was there on the wall directly before you," he added.

Each conclave session ended with a brief prayer of thanksgiving and an invocation to the Blessed Virgin Mary.

On the conclave's opening evening, black smoke poured from the Sistine Chapel chimney, signaling that the cardinals had failed to elect a pope on their first ballot.

Thousands of people who had gathered in St. Peter's Square April 18 went away disappointed, but hardly surprised. Few expected a candidate to immediately obtain the two-thirds majority needed for election.

A first wisp of light-colored smoke raised expectations in the crowd, but it was soon followed by thick clouds of dark smoke.

The cardinals returned the next day for three more ballots—with occasional pauses for reflection—when they chose the 265th pope.

During the conclave, tourists and locals poured into St. Peter's Square, expectantly watching the chimney sticking out between the basilica and the Apostolic Palace for a sign of the smoke many had only read about in history books. Thousands of people waited patiently for hours in sometimes chilly temperatures, resting weary feet by leaning against barricades or stretching out on the cobblestones.

In the front row of plastic chairs set up in front of the basilica, surrounded by study-abroad students from Christendom College in Front Royal, Va., sat three young women from Harding University in Searcy, Ark. In Rome for two weeks after the end of their program in Athens, the Harding students—members of the United Church of Christ—learned to pray the rosary from their newfound Catholic friends.

"We had to cover our heads when we went into mosques, so why not pray the rosary when we're at the Vatican?" said Lindsey Blackburn, 20. "We didn't think we'd be this excited because we're not Catholic, but everybody else's excitement kind of pours out onto us," said Blackburn, who jumped to her feet at the first sign of smoke.

Few people seemed to have any favorites among the cardinals. Most, in fact, said they trusted the conclave to elect the right person.

One Italian woman, however, waiting for the smoke signal April 18, showed her support for the Italian cardinal from Genoa with a sign that read "Tarcisio Bertone for pope."

But by then, the cardinals were locked inside the Sistine Chapel.

"The Holy Spirit will see it," she said.

As in elections past, confusion over the smoke's color led some to believe prematurely that a new pope was at hand. The evening of

April 18, the first day of voting, black smoke wafted up, then turned gray for 30 seconds, causing hundreds to rush in a stampede toward the basilica, cameras raised above their heads, until the color darkened once more and the square emptied out.

On April 19, the crowd let out a collective sigh of disappointment when black smoke appeared at about 11:50 a.m., only to turn to applause 10 minutes later when the color lightened and the basilica's bells rang out to mark the noonday hour, leading people to think that the bells were sounding to announce a successful ballot. The white smoke people were waiting for, however, did not appear until hours later with the election of Pope Benedict XVI.

Once chosen, the newly elected pope was asked by Italian Cardinal Angelo Sodano, "Do you accept your canonical election as supreme pontiff?" The book gave no formula for the assent, nor did it recognize the possibility that the person elected might refuse. The second question asked was: "With what name do you wish to be called?"

Since he was already a bishop, once he accepted the office Cardinal Ratzinger immediately became the bishop of the church of Rome, the true pope and head of the college of bishops and acquired full and supreme power over the universal church.

Immediately after the election, the cardinals were called to pray inside the Sistine Chapel. The liturgy included a choice of two readings, either from the Gospel of Matthew—"You are Peter and upon this rock I will build my church"—or from the Gospel of John where Jesus says to Peter, "Feed my sheep." The former reading was chosen, and marked a powerful moment for Cardinal Justin Rigali.

"With the new pope, all the cardinals could experience, through the Word of God, the actual transmission of the mysterious reality of the papacy," Cardinal Rigali said. The role of Peter was being perpetuated in his newest successor and Christ was renewing his promise to sustain him. At the same time the successor of Peter would begin his proclamation of the identity of Jesus Christ."

The cardinals approached the new pope and paid homage to him, then sang the Te Deum hymn of thanksgiving to God. Then the senior cardinal deacon, Chilean Cardinal Jorge Medina Estevez, went to the central balcony of St. Peter's Basilica and declared to the public, "Habemus papam" (We have a pope).

When the conclave began, 66 cardinals above the age limit of 80 were not allowed into the Sistine Chapel to take part in the voting process. But just because the octo- and nonagenarians of the College of Cardinals were not permitted to vote, it did not mean they were not part of the deliberations. The over-80 cardinals took part in pre-conclave meetings, where all cardinals had the chance to speak up about the different issues under discussion.

"Even though (the over-80s) aren't directly influencing the conclave, they do represent the church at large, and they can give others their insights based on their long experience," said Cardinal Cahal Daly, 87, retired archbishop of Armagh, Northern Ireland.

Msgr. Charles Burns, a Scottish historian and retired official of the Vatican Archives, said setting an age limit on who can attend a conclave "was not meant to punish" older members. Pope Paul instituted the age restrictions "out of regard for the older" cardinals, so they would not feel the burden of having to make the long trip to Rome, said Msgr. Burns.

Retired Australian Cardinal Edward Cassidy flew from Australia to Rome and said it was "fair to the older men to let them be free to come and take part or not; they are not obliged," as the cardinal-electors are, to get to Rome. He said that even though at 80 he was "in good health and could go (into a conclave) if I had to," he would not favor changing the age restrictions for voting members.

He said too many old or infirm electors "could give a very unpleasant view with cameras showing people being carried up steps" to get into a conclave. "It might make people wonder, 'Are these the people who will choose the next pope?'" he said.

But just because someone turns 80 "doesn't mean their 'sell-by' date has expired," observed a Vatican expert. Msgr. Burns also noted that "The cardinal-electors could choose an octogenarian to be pope; he wouldn't last 26 years, but it does show (the over-80s) can't just be cast aside."

Ambrogio Piazzoni, vice prefect of the Vatican Library, said having a ceiling on the voting age actually serves a more practical purpose because it keeps conclave numbers steady and predictable and voters relatively young.

CARDINAL ROGER M. MAHONY

Archbishop of Los Angeles

THE month of April 2005 will remain fresh and vivid in my memory the rest of my life. Those incredible days between the death of Pope John Paul II and the election of Pope Benedict XVI were ones of extraordinary faith, grace and a deep sense of God's presence.

The assurance of Jesus Christ which came to mind most often was: "And behold, I am with you always, until the end of the age" (Matthew 28:20). Between April 2 and April 19 the church did not have a visible successor of Peter; but we still had the powerful presence and guidance of Jesus, and the reminders of his presence were everywhere.

The great numbers of pilgrims who came to Rome to bid farewell to a beloved Holy Father were such an inspiration, especially with the vast majority being young people. The faith, prayer, and devotion of the people—often waiting for many hours in lines—gave witness to the presence of Jesus among us during those days of loss. Those pilgrims came to say thank you and goodbye to a beloved grandfather in faith, someone who inspired us with his own personal life of prayer, and one who challenged us to live out to the full our Gospel commitments.

The depth and spiritual richness of the church's liturgy captivated the world and helped all peoples, regardless of their own personal faith, to enter into the ritual prayer of the church. The unfolding of the various liturgies reflected the simple but powerful nature of the church's prayer and worship. It was a special spiritual moment for millions around the world. For example, the chanting of the litany of the saints on the occasion of the funeral for Pope John Paul II, as the cardinals processed into the Sistine Chapel, and at the beginning of the Mass of Inauguration of Pope Benedict XVI brought alive our understanding of the communion of the saints and the pilgrim nature of the church.

While it is difficult to isolate any particular moment as more moving than another, our procession into the Sistine Chapel to begin the conclave was the most moving for me personally. In previous years I had visited the Sistine Chapel for its artistic wonder and beauty. This time, we processed into a special sacred space where the presence of God was so evident and the long history of God's plan of salvation was further revealed. It was simply stunning and poignant.

The feeling which stirred in my heart most frequently was that of inadequacy. I kept asking myself: "What am I doing here?" This role in our church's history belongs to men who are deeply spiritual and great pastoral leaders in the church; and I never felt that description fit me. But my consolation came in discovering that so many other Cardinals were feeling the same thing.

I returned to Los Angeles with a renewed commitment to the church of Jesus Christ and with a new zeal to bring the good news of Christ to all. With so many personally touched by the graced events of April 2005, I am confident that the church will enthusiastically follow Jesus' command: "Put out into deep water and lower your nets for a catch" (Luke 5:4).

CHAPTER 9

"Habemus Papam"

WHITE SMOKE from the Sistine Chapel chimney
wafted aloft a gray sky at 5:49 p.m. on April 19. Fifteen
minutes later, the bells of St. Peter's Basilica began peal-
ing continuously to confirm the election.

The speed of the election caught people by surprise. Few felt the
College of Cardinals, which had entered the conclave barely 24
hours before with many candidates and no clear favorite, could have
reached a decision so quickly.

But the spiritual leader of the world, the head of more than 1 billion Catholics worldwide, had been chosen. And with some 100,000
people in the square, at 6:40 p.m., Chilean Cardinal Jorge Medina
Estevez, the senior cardinal in the order of deacons, appeared at the
basilica balcony and intoned to the crowd in Latin: "Dear brothers
and sisters, I announce to you a great joy. We have a pope. His pro-
nouncement—"We have a pope"—brought the loudest cheers of the
evening.

Then the crowd waited in high anticipation to hear who had
been elected, and Cardinal Medina Estevez continued: "The most
eminent and reverend lordship, Lord Joseph Cardinal of the Holy
Roman Church Ratzinger."

People burst into applause. Some jumped for joy, some knelt to
pray and some simply stood and watched.

They listened for the name chosen by the 78-year-old German,
who had been guardian of the Church's doctrine for the last 24 years
as head of the Congregation for the Doctrine of the Faith.

"Benedict XVI," announced Cardinal Medina Estevez. Moments
later the crowd began to chant the name in Italian, and like a clas-

White smoke from the chimney of the Sistine Chapel signals to the world that the cardinals have chosen a new pope. CREDIT: KNA-BILD.

sic soccer cheer, "Be-ne-det-to," reverberated across the square.

Benedict XVI emerged from a red velvet curtain at the central window of St. Peter's Basilica to the cheering crowd. Flags from Poland, the United States, Brazil, Argentina, Mexico and other countries waved furiously above the heads of people.

He spoke his first words as pope: "After the great John Paul II, the cardinals elected me, a simple, humble worker in the vineyard of the Lord," he said, in a brief talk broadcast around the world.

"I am consoled by the fact that the Lord can work and act even through insufficient instruments, and I especially entrust myself to your prayers.

"In the joy of the risen Lord, and trusting in his permanent help, we go forward. The Lord will help us, and Mary his most holy mother is on our side. Thank you," he said.

Then Pope Benedict gave his blessing to the city of Rome and to the world. He stood and listened to the endless applause that followed, smiling and raising his hands above his head.

The election marked the first German pope since Victor II, who reigned from 1055–1057, and the second non-Italian in a row to be elected after Italians had held the papacy for more than 450 years.

The new pope was chosen by at least a two-thirds majority of 115 cardinals from 52 countries, who cast their ballots in secret in the Sistine Chapel.

In St. Peter's Square, cell phones and cameras came out of pockets and purses; telephone lines jammed almost immediately, leaving those eager to announce their presence at a historic moment unable to communicate with friends and family. Every few minutes, rhythmic clapping rippled through the square.

Many people had heard the news on Vatican Radio or on television before the bells began ringing, and had run to St. Peter's Square. One Norwegian journalist ran nearly two miles and arrived, soaked in sweat, before the new pope's entrance onto the balcony.

As they saw people running toward the basilica, Andrew and Shanna Linbeck of St. Michael's Parish in Houston hurried from the Vatican Museums. The Linbecks, who traveled to Rome specifically for the conclave, said they appreciated the festive atmosphere as the crowd waited to see who the next pope would be.

"It's almost like a football game, with a band and everything," said Andrew Linbeck as the sounds of drums and horns floated out from under the colonnade.

Linbeck said he was pleased with the cardinals' vote.

"This is a great tribute to John Paul II. When we were at the Mass that Cardinal Ratzinger celebrated Monday before the conclave, you could tell he had the presence," Linbeck said.

Despite the excitement, it seemed the faithful might take a while to get used to a new face.

A 22-year-old from Como, a town in northern Italy, mused, "It's strange—it's so strange. It's not Wojtyla."

An elderly Italian woman, wiping away tears, expressed her

doubts while talking to someone on her cell phone, but her daughter reassured her, patting her on the back and saying, "You'll like him, you'll see."

As the crowd dispersed, flooding the streets around the Vatican, the mood calmed somewhat, and people took time to reflect on the events they had just witnessed.

The thought of being elected the leader of the universal church made him lightheaded and doubtful, said Pope Benedict afterward. During the "slow unfolding of the voting process" at the conclave, it eventually became evident that "the guillotine was coming closer and was meant for me," he told pilgrims from his native Germany at an April 25 audience. The thought of becoming the next pope "made my head spin," he said. "I had thought that up until now my life's work was done and that the years ahead of me would be more restful." But a fellow cardinal-elector had given the future pope a letter reminding him of a phrase he had used during his homily at the funeral Mass of Pope John Paul II: "If the Lord calls you, you must obey," said Pope Benedict. Pope Benedict said that during the voting when he began to emerge as the clear favorite he prayed to God "to spare me." He said he told God, "You have candidates who are younger, better, stronger and have more élan than me."

"Evidently God did not listen to me," he said wryly.

The pope said he gathered strength for accepting the cardinals' decision from the letter. He said the "touching" letter reminded the pope of the theme he chose for the mid-April funeral Mass homily that when one is called by God that call "cannot be rejected."

"So I had no other choice than to say yes," he said. Pope Benedict asked his audience to continue to pray for him and have trust in him. "If I ever make an error or when the pope says something that is not easy to understand, because the pope has to say these things, I ask for your trust from now on," he said.

Pope Benedict said because Pope John Paul was seen as an open and fatherly figure, it created a church that "was not closed up inside itself" and was "open to all."

"The church is not old and immobile but young," he said.

Pope Benedict said it was "not true that today's young people were only drawn" to a consumerist and materialist lifestyle.

PAPAL COUNT

Pope Benedict XVI is the 54th non-Italian and the eighth German pope to lead the church. The vast majority of popes have been Italian.

ITALIANS

211

NON-ITALIAN EUROPEANS

42

NON-EUROPEANS

10

UNCERTAIN

2

Pope Victor II

Pope Benedict XVI is the first German pope since Pope Victor II, who reigned from 1055-1057.

Source: CNS/2005 ANNUARIO PONTIFICIO   © 2005 CNS Graphics

"Young people want what is great and good," he said.

When the pope spotted some blue and white Bavarian flags being waved by pilgrims in the Vatican audience hall, he said, "Now I have something to say to the Bavarians."

Even though "I have spent the past 23 and a half years in Rome, I am still Bavarian, even if now I am bishop of Rome," he said.

Despite his long career in the Roman Curia, there was significant curiosity about Benedict XVI. The first question centered on what he would do first. His predecessor had kept the cardinals in conclave in 1978 until Mass the next morning. Benedict ended the conclave that elected him shortly after his election but invited the electors to join him at dinner that night and at Mass the next morning.

Dinner was simple because staff at the *Domus Sanctae Marthae* hadn't expected the conclave to end so soon. The only sign of celebration had been a special dessert and the singing of a few hymns by the electors.

The next morning at Mass in the Sistine Chapel where the cardinals had elected him, Benedict XVI delivered a heartfelt homily. After Mass, he pledged that he would lead the church on the path of unity, dialogue and evangelization.

The white-haired pope faced 114 cardinals seated at the same long tables used in the papal election and spoke from a chair beneath Michelangelo's fresco of the Last Judgement.

Dressed in light gold vestments, he read his four-page Latin message in a clear and forceful voice. He paid tribute to Pope John Paul II and outlined the priorities of his own pontificate.

"I address everyone with simplicity and affection to assure them that the church wants to continue to build an open and sincere dialogue with them in the search of the true good of man and society," he said.

Pope Benedict said that, like his predecessor, he considered the Second Vatican Council the compass for the modern church. In particular, he stressed his commitment to ecumenism and dialogue and said he was aware that "concrete gestures" were sometimes needed to promote breaking through old antagonisms.

At the same time, he said the chief priority for the modern church is to announce Christ to the world. "The church must revive within herself an awareness of the task to present to the world again with the voice of the one who said: 'I am the light of the world. He who follows me will not walk in darkness, but will have the light of life,'" he said.

"As he begins his ministry, the new pope knows that his task is to make the light of Christ shine before the men and women of today: not his own light, but that of Christ," he said.

The 9 a.m. liturgy was broadcast live on giant TV screens in a virtually empty St. Peter's Square where some 100,000 people had gathered the evening before for the dramatic announcement of Pope Benedict's election and cheered him at his first public appearance.

The pope said he had been completely surprised at his election. He said he began his papacy with two emotions: a sense of "inadequacy" and the confidence that God would help him.

As head of the Vatican's doctrinal congregation since 1981, then-Cardinal Joseph Ratzinger was a controversial figure for many in the church because of his strong line against dissent, his disciplining of theologians and his criticism of some of the ways the Second Vatican Council has been implemented.

Pope Benedict XVI also stressed the need for close unity between the pope and the world's bishops. This collegial communion, he said, favors "unity in the faith, on which depends in large measure the effectiveness of the church's evangelizing efforts in the modern world." He asked bishops to accompany him "with prayers and with advice, so that I may truly be the 'servant of the servants of God.'"

Pope Benedict pledged to make the search for Christian unity a special priority. He called ecumenism a "compelling duty" and said he would "spare no energy" in trying to bring Christian churches together. He said ecumenism must go beyond theological dialogue and probe the historical motives for the divisions among Christians. "What is most needed is that 'purification of memory' so often mentioned by John Paul II, which is the only thing that can lead souls to welcome the full truth of Christ," he said.

In his promise to keep dialogue open, the new pope also mentioned the followers of other religions and people who are "simply searching for an answer to the fundamental questions of existence and have not found it yet." He said he made this overture with the awareness that the church's mission is to bring the light of Christ to all peoples.

Acknowledging his predecessor's special relationship with young people, the new pope pledged that the church would continue to dialogue with them. He said he intended to travel that August to Cologne, Germany, for World Youth Day celebrations—a tradition begun by Pope John Paul.

Pope Benedict underlined the importance of the current Eucharistic year, also an initiative of the late pope, saying the Eucharist would be at the center of the Cologne festivities and of the Synod of Bishops the following October. He asked all the faithful to reflect on the centrality of the Eucharist. Many other things—including church unity, evangelization and charity toward all, especially the poor—depend on it, he said.

The new pope recalled Pope John Paul with great affection and said he felt encouraged by the late pontiff as he began his own papacy. "I seem to feel his strong hand squeezing mine; I seem to see his smiling eyes and listen to his words, addressed particularly to me in this moment: 'Do not be afraid!'" he said.

Pope Benedict said the death and funeral of Pope John Paul represented "an extraordinary time of grace for the whole world." He said it was a moment in which one could feel "the power of God who, through his church, wants to form a great family of all peoples."

The pope spoke briefly about the church's continued commitment to peace and justice issues. He said he would continue the dialogue of his predecessors with "the various civilizations," convinced that the conditions for a better future in the world depend on mutual understanding.

Pope Benedict told the cardinals he felt an "enormous weight of responsibility" as the new pontiff but was certain of divine assistance. "By choosing me as the bishop of Rome, the Lord wanted me as his vicar, he wanted me to be the rock on which everyone can lean with assurance," he said. "I ask him to supplement my scarce resources, so that I may be a courageous and faithful pastor of his flock, always obedient to the inspirations of his Spirit," he added.

Within 16 hours of the pope's election, the Vatican created a series of new e-mail addresses so people around the world could send a message to the new pope. Well-wishers could send Pope Benedict XVI an e-mail in English, Spanish, German, Italian, French and Portuguese. "In just two days after the accounts were set up, we received over 56,000 e-mails," said Legionaries of Christ Father Fernando Vergez, an official in the Vatican's Internet office. "We didn't publicize anything," he said. "People just know that when there is a special event we usually highlight it on our Web site," he said.

Most people chose the English e-mail address, which received more than 30,000 e-mails in 48 hours. One long e-mail from "Kurt" in the Philippines said, "It's my first time to write the pope a letter." He asked Pope Benedict "to continue the works of your predecessors and continue to touch lives as Pope John Paul II did."

"Debbie" wrote that she was not Catholic, but that she was seeking prayers "for my three sons," one of whom was "trying to make some life decisions" and another who was "signing with a college tomorrow to play soccer for them at Missouri Valley."

"Helen" in the United States wrote the pope that it was "a great honor to be able to e-mail you and express my feelings."

"We know that there are a lot of pressures on you right now, but I will always be in prayer that you will be guided by Our Lord," she wrote.

The Vatican Web site, www.vatican.va, featured a brand-new home-page design with the words *Habemus papam* (We have a pope) and *Benedictum* XVI emblazoned under the new pope's chosen coat of arms. Internet users could click on one of the six languages listed on the home page to get to the page featuring the pope.

Father Vergez said the Internet office would put up links to see the video footage of the April 19 *sfumata* or the moment white smoke billowed out of the Sistine Chapel chimney signaling the election of a new pope. He said other events such as the introduction of the new pope and his appearance on the balcony of St. Peter's Basilica to give his apostolic blessing to the city and the world would have video links also.

"Our hope is to be able to offer video links" via streaming video or archived material of "all the main events" of Pope Benedict's pontificate, said Father Vergez. He said the Vatican Internet office wanted its Web site to offer the extra video links after the enormous popularity of its live broadcast of Pope John Paul's April 8 funeral Mass. "There were over 1 million visitors to our site that day, with 54,000 people connected (to the live video feed) simultaneously," said Father Vergez. He said the Vatican Web site only used to offer video coverage of the Wednesday general audiences and rare events. But after seeing the huge demand for video links to major Vatican events, "we cannot go back; we want to try to offer (video links to) all the main events in the future," said the priest.

Two days before his inauguration, Benedict XVI met with the cardinals present in Rome. He thanked the world's cardinals for placing their trust in him and asked them for their continued prayers and counsel. "Dear brothers, to you go my most personal thanks for the trust you have placed in me by electing me bishop of Rome and pastor of the universal church," he told them.

Rather than outline any projects or directions for the church, Pope Benedict said he convoked the meeting to share "in a simple and fraternal way" what he was feeling.

The pope said he felt "an intimate need for silence and two complementary feelings: a heartfelt desire to give thanks and a sense of human impotence in the face of the serious task that awaits me." Pope Benedict said the cardinals' "act of trust" also was "an encouragement to undertake this new mission with more serenity because, in addition to the indispensable help of God, I know I can count on your generous collaboration."

"I ask you, never let me lack your support," he said. "If, on the one hand, I know the limits of my person and of my abilities, on the other hand I know well what is the nature of the mission entrusted to me and which I undertake with an attitude of interior dedication," Pope Benedict said. The new pope said his position is not about honor but about service, and he, together with the cardinals, must do their personal best to fulfill God's will.

Speaking on behalf of the group, Cardinal Angelo Sodano, Vatican secretary of state, promised that the cardinals would support and assist Pope Benedict with his ministry. In Pope John Paul II's death and funeral and in the conclave and the election of Pope Benedict, he said, "we all have been witnesses of the assistance that the Lord always grants his holy church."

The church, he said, is "a tree that receives new life each day and thrives."

"We cardinals are happy that the one giving vigor today to the tree of the church is Pope Benedict XVI. To him go all of our devotion, our total collaboration and our fraternal affection in Christ Jesus," Cardinal Sodano said. At the end of the audience, each of the cardinals went up to greet Pope Benedict and kiss his hand. When the more elderly cardinals or those who use a cane or a wheelchair approached, the pope stood and went to greet them.

The pope and the cardinals sang the *Regina Coeli* prayer together. Then after Pope Benedict said, "Thank you and see you Sunday" for the installation Mass, the cardinals broke into the chanted *Oremus Pro Pontifice* ("Let us pray for the pontiff").

"Let us pray for our Holy Father, Pope Benedict. May the Lord preserve him, and give him life, and make him to be blessed upon the earth, and deliver him not up to the will of his enemies," they sang.

Los Angeles Cardinal Roger M. Mahony, right, joins other cardinals at a memorial Mass in honor of Pope John Paul II in St. Peter's Basilica April 13. Catholic Church tradition calls for a nine-day period of memorial Masses for a deceased pontiff. PHOTO BY NANCY WIECHEC © 2005 CATHOLIC NEWS SERVICE.

A deacon reverences the congregation at one of nine memorial Masses held in honor of Pope John Paul II in St. Peter's Basilica. PHOTO BY NANCY WIECHEC © 2005 CATHOLIC NEWS SERVICE.

Cardinals and bishops celebrated the last of nine memorial Mass for Pope John Paul II in St. Peter's Basilica April 16. The service marked the end of the official nine days of mourning for the deceased pontiff. PHOTO BY NANCY WIECHEC © 2005 CATHOLIC NEWS SERVICE.

St. Peter's statue is silhouetted as the sun sets behind the Vatican April 16, three days before the world's cardinals chose the 264th successor of Peter. PHOTO BY NANCY WIECHEC © 2005 CATHOLIC NEWS SERVICE.

Seven U.S. cardinals pose for a group photo at the North American College in Rome April 17 before going heading to the Vatican for the start of the conclave. From left are Cardinals Justin Rigali of Philadelphia, Adam J. Maida of Detroit, Edward M. Egan of New York, Roger M. Mahony of Los Angeles, Francis E. George of Chicago, William H. Keeler of Baltimore and Theodore E. McCarrick of Washington. Three other U.S. cardinals holding Vatican appointments participated in the election. PHOTO BY NANCY WIECHEC © 2005 CATHOLIC NEWS SERVICE.

Anticipation ran high in St. Peter's Square as a crowd watched for the first smoke signal to come from the Sistine Chapel chimney. PHOTO BY NANCY WIECHEC © 2005 CATHOLIC NEWS SERVICE.

A U.S. *pilgrim prays in St. Peter's Square the morning of the conclave's second and last day.* PHOTO BY NANCY WIECHEC © 2005 CATHOLIC NEWS SERVICE.

Students from the North American College shout in joy as bells ring in St. Peter's Square hailing the election of the new pope. PHOTO BY NANCY WIECHEC © 2005 CATHOLIC NEWS SERVICE.

The new pope greets the world from the central balcony of St. Peter's Basilica. PHOTO BY NANCY WIECHEC © 2005 CATHOLIC NEWS SERVICE.

U.S. Cardinal Francis George, far right, stands with other cardinals on a side balcony of St. Peter's Basilica as the new pope addresses the world. PHOTO BY NANCY WIECHEC © 2005 CATHOLIC NEWS SERVICE.

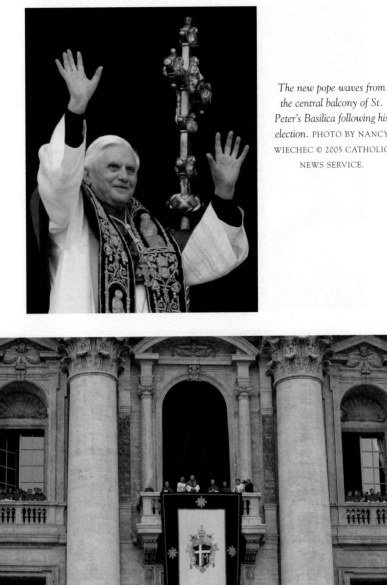

The new pope waves from the central balcony of St. Peter's Basilica following his election. PHOTO BY NANCY WIECHEC © 2005 CATHOLIC NEWS SERVICE.

The new pope gives a blessing from the central balcony of St. Peter's Basilica. To both sides, cardinals stand in support of the church's new leader. PHOTO BY NANCY WIECHEC © 2005 CATHOLIC NEWS SERVICE.

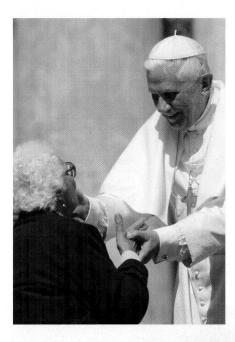

Pope Benedict XVI greets an elderly woman during his second general audience in St. Peter's Square. PHOTO BY NANCY WIECHEC © 2005 CATHOLIC NEWS SERVICE.

The new pope points upward as he talks about his predecessor, John Paul II, during his first Sunday noon blessing. PHOTO BY NANCY WIECHEC © 2005 CATHOLIC NEWS SERVICE.

The pope waves to the crowd
gathering for his second general
audience in St. Peter's Square.
PHOTO BY NANCY WIECHEC
© 2005 CATHOLIC NEWS
SERVICE.

Cardinals seated
along the walls of the
Sistine Chapel
celebrate Mass with
newly elected Pope
Benedict XVI
April 20. CREDIT:
POOL PHOTO.

Conclave Memorabilia

CONCLAVE memorabilia is always of interest to students of church history, and a seminary in Chicago has managed to accumulate memorabilia from past conclaves. When Pius XII became pope on March 2, 1939, Chicago's Cardinal George Mundelein was among the cardinal-electors in the Sistine Chapel. Though the cardinals are sworn to secrecy about details of the voting, Cardinal Mundelein stuffed his pockets with cards, trinkets and other souvenirs from the papal election

SANTA MESSA
PER L'ELEZIONE DEL ROMANO PONTEFICE
E INGRESSO IN CONCLAVE
LUNEDÌ, 18 APRILE 2005

before returning to Chicago. They are now preserved in a small museum in the library of the seminary and town that bear his name, the University of St. Mary of the Lake-Mundelein Seminary in Mundelein.

"Cardinal Mundelein had a propensity for collecting memorabilia," Father Thomas Baima, university provost, told the *Catholic New World*, newspaper of the Chicago Archdiocese. "He brought back several interesting pieces that afford us a glimpse of the 1939 conclave." The museum also has a similar collection of souvenirs that Cardinal John Cody brought back from the 1978 conclave in which Pope John Paul I was elected. After the pope's death 34 days later, Cardinal Cody returned to Rome for the conclave that elected Pope John Paul II. Among the items are several blank ballots, printed with the Latin words *"Eligo in Summum Pontificem . . ."* ("I elect as Supreme Pontiff . . ."), which the cardinals used to cast their votes.

Other memorabilia in the seminary's collection include coins, a wax stamp used by Cardinal Mundelein to seal his ballots and lists of the cardinals with their Vatican room numbers. At that time, they were sequestered in the rooms surrounding the Sistine Chapel. When not voting in the Sistine Chapel, the cardinals often used the lists of cardinals to pay informal visits to each other, discussing the worthiness of this or that candidate. Cardinal Cody brought back the list from the 1978 conclave, which

Memorabilia from the 2005 conclave, photographed in the archives of the Archdiocese of Baltimore.

contains the names and room numbers of well-known prelates including German Cardinal Joseph Ratzinger, now Pope Benedict XVI; U.S. Cardinal Terence Cooke; and of course Polish Cardinal Karol Wojtyla, who became Pope John Paul II. Also on display in the museum is a "tally sheet" which the cardinals used to keep score of who was getting how many votes. The tally sheet that Cardinal Mundelein brought back does not contain any voting tallies, however, since the cardinals vow to keep that information secret.

One curious item in the museum is a lead filament used to wire the window shut in Cardinal Mundelein's room—a primitive but effective way of keeping the window closed since the cardinals were forbidden to communicate with the outside world during the conclave.

CHAPTER 10

"What's in a Name?"

"WHAT'S in a name?" That famous query from Shakespeare's *Romeo and Juliet* was on the minds of many in St. Peter's Square when the world learned the 264th successor to St. Peter would be called Benedict XVI.

The newly elected pope reportedly told the cardinals that he had chosen Benedict for several reasons. In part, it harks back to the last Benedict, pope from 1914 to 1922, who sent a seven-point letter to the countries involved in World War I in an effort to halt the hostilities.

His pontificate was relatively short, just under eight years. Benedict XVI, elected at age 78, probably is not expecting a long pontificate, some theorized. Then there is the new pope's affinity for the spirituality of St. Benedict, whose rule for living, working and praying in community still guides the lives of Benedictine abbeys around the world. "The Benedictine spirituality is a very balanced, human one," Abbot Notker Wolf, abbot primate of the Order of St. Benedict, said. The heart of monastic life, he said, "is just living out the Gospel."

Pope Benedict XVI was born in Bavaria, where Benedictine roots run deep. With 17 abbeys in the region, "Bavaria is called *terra benedictina*—Benedictine land," Abbot Wolf said. "Benedictine wisdom has permeated society there." For years the new pontiff has made an annual spiritual retreat at the Benedictine abbey in Scheyern, Germany, the abbot said.

He also has visited other Benedictine abbeys. Father Cassian Folsom, prior of St. Benedict Monastery in Nursia, Italy, the saint's birthplace, recalled a visit from then-Cardinal Ratzinger in 2003.

"He gave a wonderful homily, blessed our new library and was delighted to be here. And of course, we were even more delighted," Father Folsom said.

Some suggested that the new pontiff's choice of the name Benedict could be a symbol of his desire to revitalize Catholicism in an increasingly secular Europe, as he indicated in his homily at the Mass before the conclave. St. Benedict is credited with having spread the faith throughout Europe in the early sixth century. "The faith in Europe is extremely fragile. It's a terrible crisis," Father Folsom said. "St. Benedict was a master of the faith in a time of similar crisis. He went about witnessing to the faith not by special programs or strategies or long-range planning, but by being faithful in the little things of every day in the monastic vocation."

Those who live by the Rule of St. Benedict find it as relevant today as it was when the saint established his first monasteries. Monasticism emphasizes "the primacy of God, the importance of prayer, putting things in their right order," said Father Folsom, who went to Nursia from the Benedictine abbey in St. Meinrad, Ind. "God first, and other things come from that. It's also a way of life that emphasizes prayer and communion with God."

The structure of Benedictine life also provides guidelines for the exercise of authority, Abbot Wolf said. "It's a very human rule" that maintains respect for the individual within the communal life. While the members of the community are under the authority of an abbot, "the abbot has to convoke the entire community for serious questions," he said. "There's a sharing of responsibility." Most of all, the abbot said, Benedictine spirituality, with its hours for prayer, work and rest, is a model to the world of "a balanced way of living."

At his first Wednesday audience, April 27, the pope himself shared reasons for choosing *Benedict*. "I wanted to call myself Benedict XVI to bind myself to the venerated Pope Benedict XV, who guided the church in a troubled period because of the First World War. He was a courageous and authentic prophet of peace and worked with valiant courage first to prevent the drama of war and then to limit its nefarious consequences," he said. "In his footsteps, I want to place my ministry at the service of reconciliation and harmony among individuals and peoples, deeply convinced that the great good of peace is, first of all, a gift of God, a fragile and precious gift to invoke, safeguard and build day after day with the help of everyone," Pope Benedict said.

The second reason for choosing the name, he said, was to evoke the spirit of St. Benedict, founder of Western monasticism. In his prepared text, the pope had noted that St. Benedict is a copatron of Europe along with Sts. Cyril and Methodius. In his Italian-language talk, he went off script to pay homage to Sts. Bridget of Sweden, Catherine of Siena and Edith Stein, who also are invoked as patrons of Europe and Italy.

Pope Benedict said the expansion of Benedictine monasticism had "an enormous influence on the spread of Christianity over the whole continent."

"St. Benedict is very venerated in Germany, particularly in Bavaria, my homeland; he is a basic point of reference for the unity of Europe and a strong reminder of the undeniable Christian roots of its culture and civilization," he said. Pope Benedict asked the saint "to help us keep Christ firmly at the center of our existence. May he always have first place in our thoughts and in all our activities."

The last Pope Benedict served 1914–22, a period that included World War I during which he made unsuccessful efforts to negotiate peace. Pope Benedict XV, born Giacomo della Chiesa in 1854, was the son of Italian nobility whose mother was related to Pope Innocent VII (1404–06). According to an entry in the New Catholic Encyclopedia, "he was small, stoop-shouldered and very thin (dubbed 'the midget' by some, even after he became pope) with the left side of his body higher than the right and he limped."

After serving in the Vatican diplomatic corps, he was named archbishop of Bologna, Italy, and was consecrated in the Sistine Chapel in 1907 by Pope Pius X. He was made a cardinal in 1914, three months before the death of Pius X. According to the encyclopedia article, "He probably took the name Benedict in memory of the last pope elected from the see of Bologna, Benedict XIV (1740–58). The coronation was held in the Sistine Chapel, because of the crisis of World War I." Usually papal coronations were held outside in St. Peter's Square.

On Aug. 1, 1917, Pope Benedict XV made a formal peace proposal that included "substitution of the 'moral force of right' for military force; reciprocal decrease in armaments; arbitration of international disputes; freedom of the seas; renunciation of war indemnities; restoration of all occupied territories (and) examination 'in a conciliatory spirit' of rival territorial claims," according to the encyclopedia article.

"That for which the whole world has long sighed, which Christianity has implored with such fervent prayer, and for which we, too, interpreter of the common sorrow, have never ceased to pray . . . has come in a moment: At last, the clash of arms has ceased," the pope said in his 1918 encyclical *Quod Iam Diu* on the future peace conference.

"True, peace has not yet in solemn fashion brought to an end the great war, but to peace the road has been opened happily with the armistice which has, meanwhile, suspended slaughter and devastation by land, sea and air," he added.

His peace proposal was rebuffed, but he made efforts to relieve people's suffering from the war. Among other things, he established an international missing-persons bureau, established relief agencies and assigned priests to visit the wounded and prisoners of war. "So generous was he in such activities that at his death the Holy See was virtually bankrupt," the encyclopedia article reported.

After the war, "the pope deplored some aspects of the settlement, considering the reparations imposed on Germany too harsh and believing that the treaty contained the seeds of future wars," the article said.

Benedict XV wrote a dozen encyclicals, including *Spiritus Paraclitus* (1920) on modern biblical criticism. His apostolic letter *Maximum Illud* (1919) is credited with calling for the development of local clergy by missionaries.

He established the Sacred Congregation for the Oriental Church, now known as the Congregation for Eastern Churches, in 1917, and he saw the number of countries with diplomatic ties to the Holy See rise from 14 to 26.

He canonized three saints in 1920—Joan of Arc, Margaret Mary Alacoque, and Gabriel of the Sorrowful Mother.

In 1922, at age 67, Pope Benedict fell ill and died. He was sick for only a few days with influenza, which turned into pneumonia. "The Holy See had to borrow money to pay for the funeral, the conclave and the coronation of Pius XI," the New Catholic Encyclopedia said.

The pope's choice of the name Benedict held special significance for a group of black-robed monks in the throng celebrating the event in St. Peter's Square. Abbot Notker Wolf, abbot primate of the Order of St. Benedict, said that when he heard that Cardinal Joseph Ratzinger had chosen the name Benedict, "I was very happy."

"I felt recognized," he added. In further recognition, U.S. Benedictine Brother Gregory Gresko of Mary, Mother of the Church Abbey in Richmond, Va., sang the Gospel in Latin during the Mass. The 34-year-old monk, a songwriter who sings in a Christian rock band called Mary's Men in Black, is studying at St. Anselm University in Rome.

The new pope's name evokes both the legacy of the early 20th-century Pope Benedict XV and a spiritual tradition dating back to the sixth-century saint credited with spreading Christianity throughout Europe as the Roman Empire collapsed. "Before the conclave, Cardinal Ratzinger made a critique" of modern society, urging the cardinal-electors to take a stand against relativism, Abbot Wolf said. Upon hearing the new pope's name, "I said this is the answer to his critique," the abbot said. "The Rule of St. Benedict is just the opposite (of relativism). It is a moderate rule based on living out the good news."

CHAPTER 11

Inauguration

THE MORNING of April 24, Pope Benedict XVI with some 150 cardinals processed into a sun-bathed St. Peter's Square to begin the Mass and receive the main symbols of his office: the fisherman's ring and the pallium.

In a liturgy rich with symbols and promises, Pope Benedict formally began his ministry as head of the universal church, and Catholics from around the world pledged their love and obedience to him.

"At this moment, weak servant of God that I am, I must assume this enormous task, which truly exceeds all human capacity," Pope Benedict said in his homily. The 78-year-old pope said he would rely on the prayers of all Catholics and the grace of God. "I do not have to carry alone what in truth I could never carry alone," he said. The new pope said his inaugural Mass was not the moment to present "a program of governance," but rather a time to promise to try be a good shepherd to Christ's flock, to rescue those who are lost, to help the poor and to build unity among all believers in Christ.

More than 350,000 people turned out for the inaugural Mass, some making their way to the Vatican well before the 10 a.m. start time. Michael, a junior at Villanova University and a member of the Syro-Malankara Church, asked a passerby where to find the start of the line—12 hours before the Mass was to begin.

His experience at the March 26 Easter Vigil, when he came within three feet of then-Cardinal Joseph Ratzinger, spurred him to return. "I prayed to the Holy Spirit the last time I was here that I could kiss the pope's ring or somehow meet him," he said. "And then after Cardinal Ratzinger's election, I realized he's the pope now, and I had prayed to see the pope. So I had to come." About 200 people milled about the square the night before the new pope's first Mass in public; a few lit candles and prayed. A small group of Polish pilgrims unfurled a flag that read "Always Faithful." Bedsheets with painted slogans hung from the windows of a school on the street leading to the square, declaring in Italian and German the students' love for Pope Benedict.

Italian officials set up a labyrinth of barricades from St. Peter's Basilica down to the Tiber River, blocking roads around the Vatican to the frustration of pilgrims. Authorities called in police and medical reinforcements—including units from Italy's northern Alto Adige region who could communicate with German-speaking pilgrims—to handle the large numbers expected in Rome for the inauguration.

By 8 a.m. thousands had staked out their viewing posts, others taking a more leisurely approach by fortifying themselves with cappuccinos at cafes, reflecting the calm but expectant mood of the crowd.

Among the people at the Mass were delegations from more than 130 countries and from dozens of Orthodox, Anglican and Protestant churches. Florida Gov. Jeb Bush, brother of U.S. President George W. Bush, led the five-member U.S. national delegation. Canada's governor general, Adrienne Clarkson, led the five-member Canadian delegation.

The German-born pope's 81-year old brother, Father Georg Ratzinger, was seated in the front row by the altar, not far from German Chancellor Gerhard Schroeder and President Horst Koehler. The crowd was dotted by faithful waving flags, especially German flags. Italian President Carlo Azeglio Ciampi, King Juan Carlos of Spain and Britain's Prince Philip were seated alongside the altar.

Religious calendars created complications for some delegations. Israel was represented by its ambassador to the Vatican, although the inauguration took place on the first full day of the weeklong Passover observance. Sixteen Orthodox churches sent representatives even though April 24 was Palm Sunday on the Julian calendar most of them follow.

Chilean Cardinal Jorge Medina Estevez placed the pallium, a long woolen stole, around the neck of Pope Benedict, reminding him that Jesus has entrusted him with taking up the ministry of St. Peter to shepherd Christ's flock.

Italian Cardinal Angelo Sodano, Vatican secretary of state, handed Pope Benedict the fisherman's ring, which the new pope placed on the ring finger of his right hand. Cardinal Sodano prayed that "the Spirit of love" would fill the new pope with the strength and meekness needed to minister to Christians "in the unity of communion."

In his homily, Pope Benedict said, "One of the basic characteristics of a shepherd must be to love the people entrusted to him, even as he loves Christ, whom he serves."

"Loving means giving the sheep what is truly good, the nourishment of God's truth, of God's word, the nourishment of his presence which he gives us in the Blessed Sacrament," he said. The new pope asked for the prayers of the entire church that he would grow in his love for the Lord and for the members of the church and prayers that he would be strong in the face of those who threaten the church. "Let us pray for one another, that the Lord will carry us and that we will learn to carry one another," he said.

His homily was interrupted repeatedly by applause, and Pope Benedict received a long ovation when he finished. After he received the symbols of his office, Pope Benedict received the act of obedience of his new flock, symbolized by 12 people from eight countries.

Bishop Andrea Erba of Velletri-Segni, Italy, who represented diocesan bishops, leads the diocese of which the former Cardinal Joseph Ratzinger was titular head while serving as dean of the College of Cardinals.

Father Enrico Pomili, representing all priests, is pastor of the Rome parish of Santa Maria Consolatrice, Cardinal Ratzinger's titular church until he became dean of the college in 2002.

The others included a transitional deacon from Africa; a Discalced Carmelite priest who serves as a consultant to the Congregation for the Doctrine of the Faith; a Benedictine abbess; a Korean married couple; a young woman from Sri Lanka; and a young man from Congo. Italian Cardinal Angelo Sodano, South Korean Cardinal Stephen Kim Sou-hwan and Cardinal Medina represented the College of Cardinals.

Among the thousands of people who gathered in St. Peter's Square and filled the surrounding streets for the Mass were many who felt represented by the 12.

Francisco Navarro, 36, of Los Angeles said he was not disappointed that the world's cardinals had chosen a German instead of a Spanish or Latin American pope. "The pope is the pope," he said. "I'm happy with it. I hope God will guide him. We feel blessed to be here, to be as one: no racism, no nothing."

Petra Keller, 36, who is German but lives in Rome, said: "We are proud, yes, but Germans generally are never proud of their country because of their history. They are more proud where he is from, in Bavaria." Keller said that in general "Germans are very critical. They are waiting to see what he is like because he seems to be very conservative."

Barbara Schwartzenberg, 49, of Baton Rouge, La., said, "It is nice we have another non-Italian pope to show the universality of the church."

While the Gospel was chanted in Latin and Greek, the other Bible readings were in English and Spanish. The prayers of the faithful were recited in German, French, Arabic, Chinese and Portuguese. In French, the people prayed: "For our Holy Father Benedict XVI, who today begins his ministry as the Roman pontiff, may he serve the church and be a courageous witness of the Gospel."

The bread and wine consecrated by Pope Benedict during the Mass were brought up to him by Catholics from Hungary, Croatia, Kenya, Burkina Faso, Italy, China and Peru; many in the procession wore their national costumes. During the offertory procession and the act of obedience, Pope Benedict smiled broadly, listened attentively, stroked the cheeks of the young and offered his blessing.

At the end of the Mass, Pope Benedict took his first ride in the popemobile, standing in the back of the open vehicle, waving to the crowd and blessing them with his right hand, newly weighted by the fisherman's ring. Standing on tiptoe on the bases of columns, sitting atop parents' shoulders, binoculars in hand, and packed cheek to jowl into St. Peter's Square, people craned their necks to catch their first glimpse of Pope Benedict XVI at his inauguration Mass.

While pilgrims found the experience of attending Pope Benedict's Mass exciting, most took a "wait and see" approach to the new pontiff.

Claudio, 25, from the northern Italian Piedmont region, said he thought Pope Benedict's background in theology would serve him well in his new office. "This is a man who must tell society what he thinks," he said.

Teresa Vandre, 32, of San Francisco, said she was concerned about Pope Benedict's "conservative bent."

"I'd like to see the Catholic Church do many things, like include women and allow priests to marry, but those are pipe dreams with this pope," she said.

Many in attendance said the media attention since Pope John Paul II died April 2 would benefit the church, possibly increasing the unity of the faithful. "A lot of non-Catholics have been asking me lots of questions. They want to know more, and that can only be a good thing, I think," said Jason Coeur-de-Leone of Mauritius.

Tara Termine of Killingworth, Conn., said the press coverage "has put the church back in the world's eye. In recent history people have lost interest in religion, and it's important that this pope unite everyone again."

A Beijing woman studying economics in British Columbia took photos from the outskirts of the square as the pope appeared in front of the basilica, but from that distance he appeared as just a tiny dot on the screen of her digital camera. "I feel so moved to see so many people. I'm not Christian, so I can't understand them coming to see one man, but I can understand their love and loyalty for their religion," she said.

Benedict then went into St. Peter's Basilica where a chair was set on an oriental rug before the main altar. Members of the government delegations were led into the basilica to greet him and pose for photographs.

The next day Pope Benedict met with the delegations from the other Christian churches and from other religions. A separate audience was held for Catholic pilgrims from Germany.

With Pope Benedict XVI's first public Mass, the Vatican inaugurated new rites, rituals and vestments. Developed during the pontificate of Pope John Paul II, the changes were kept as drafts until Pope Benedict approved them the day after his April 19 election, said Msgr. Crispino Valenziano, a consultant to the office of papal liturgical ceremonies. When asked if Pope Benedict had requested any changes to the liturgies, the monsignor said, "No comment." However, he said, Pope Benedict's reaction to the rites as a whole was that they express "all of ecclesiology," providing a tangible expression of what the Catholic Church believes about itself.

Msgr. Valenziano said the revised Rites for the Beginning of a Pontificate represent the first systematic and formal reworking of the rites since the Second Vatican Council.

Pope Paul VI began his pontificate with the traditional coronation, although later he dispensed with the tiara. The inaugurations of Popes John Paul I and John Paul II were simplifications of the old coronation ceremony, Msgr. Valenziano said.

The biggest visual changes in the new rites, he said, are the fisherman's ring and the pallium, the woolen stole symbolizing a bishop's authority. Both, he said, are based on ancient designs. The fisherman's gold ring, incised with a scene of St. Peter casting out his net, is similar to the old rings that popes used also as seals. Designed by the Rome Association of Goldsmiths, it does not have a gem in it, Msgr. Valenziano said.

Pope Benedict's pallium is similar to that worn by popes in the first millennium, he said. Pope John Paul's pallium was a circular band worn over the shoulder with a 12-inch long strip hanging down the front and the back. The new pallium wraps around the pope's shoulders and hangs down his left side just below his knees. The end piece is made of black silk, a symbol of "the black sheep which the shepherd rescues and carries over his shoulder back to the flock," Msgr. Valenziano said.

Two major changes were made to the inauguration Mass. The service began inside St. Peter's Basilica with all the concelebrating cardinals forming a circle around the main altar. Pope Benedict and the patriarchs of the Eastern Catholic churches went down to St. Peter's tomb under the altar, paying their tribute to the apostle. "Places are especially important," Msgr. Valenziano said. "Although the Basilica of St. John Lateran is his cathedral, the ministry of the pope begins at St. Peter's because he is the successor of St. Peter." By walking into the square from the apostle's tomb, the monsignor said, the new pope tells the world, "I begin my ministry from the place where the apostle's ended."

The second change involved the act of obedience, which in the past was made by every cardinal present at a papal inauguration.

The new rite was designed to demonstrate that the entire church recognizes the newly elected pope, Msgr. Valenziano said.

Msgr. Valenziano said the new rites also called for the pope to go almost immediately to the Basilica of St. Paul Outside-the-Walls to pay homage to the other martyr considered cofounder of the church of Rome. Pope Benedict visited that basilica April 25.

The next major liturgies were focused on the Diocese of Rome, which the pope heads.

He took possession of his cathedral, St. John Lateran, but also was reminded of what the early fathers of the church said about the role of bishop. Cardinal Camillo Ruini, papal vicar of Rome, reminded Pope Benedict that "you are elevated to watch over us, not because you are superior to us," that "your honor is true only if you do not obscure the honor of your brothers and sisters" and that his role is to be "the servant of the servants of God."

After leaving St. John Lateran, the new pope stopped at the Basilica of St. Mary Major and offered his prayers to the Blessed Virgin Mary, particularly for the Diocese of Rome.

Priest's Chalice Used by Cardinal Ratzinger, Pope John Paul II

OF THE first two priests to use Father Brian Klingele's personal chalice, one was a pope and one would become one. In fact, it was in the space of only two days in June 2002 that the chalice bought for Father Klingele as an ordination gift was used first by the cardinal who would become Pope Benedict XVI, and then used a day later by Pope John Paul II.

Father Klingele, associate pastor at St. Peter Cathedral in Kansas City, Kan., was a seminarian at the North American College in Rome at the time. His parents, with assistance from Holy Trinity Parish in Lenexa, Kan., where he had worked summers as a seminarian, bought him the chalice. The Gothic-style, gold-colored metal chalice features 12 silver medallions on its base, each depicting one of the Twelve Apostles.

There is a custom among some priests and seminarians who are serving or studying in Rome to request that the pope use their chalice for one of his private Masses. "That's what I wanted," said Father Klingele. "I thought it would be great to have (Pope John Paul II) be the first one to use it." But first it needed to be blessed and consecrated. Father Klingele reasoned that the pope would not have time to do this, so he decided to ask a cardinal for help. He chose then-Cardinal Joseph Ratzinger.

"I knew he had a simple little Mass every Thursday morning in a chapel at a residence for German student priests within the Vatican," he said. Father Klingele—still a seminarian at the time—met him in the sacristy before the Mass, and Cardinal Ratzinger consecrated it. "I was almost ready to put it back into the box," said Father Klingele. "I thought he'll consecrate it and then I'd have the pope be the first to use it. "But (the cardinal) picked it up and said, 'Ah, this is very, very worthy. May I use this for the holy Mass?'" recalled Father Klingele. "When a cardinal says, 'May I use your chalice?' you don't say no."

It wasn't exactly what he had been hoping for, but after the Mass Father Klingele put the chalice back into the box, placed a note to Pope John Paul, and gave it to a Swiss Guard. Later it was returned with a card of thanks and a couple of rosaries inside. Pope John Paul II had used it to celebrate Mass on the feast of the Sacred Heart. "I wonder if (Pope John Paul) thought about the priest who owned the chalice, and prayed for him," said Father Klingele. "I'm sure he did. He was that kind of person."

And every time Father Klingele uses the chalice, he thinks about the two popes who used it as well. But the story doesn't end there. Despite the chalice's papal pedigree, however, Father Klingele does not keep it hidden away. Rather, it is on hand in the cathedral sacristy for use at daily Mass. "I like to point out that whether it's a simple chalice or an elegant chalice, whether it was blessed by a bishop or the pope, whether it's a Mass celebrated by the Holy Father or a newly ordained priest, it's the same Jesus," he said. "That's what is special about it to me," the priest added. "The fact that the pope used it is special, but the fact that it contains the precious blood of Jesus is much more significant."

CHAPTER 12

Who Is Benedict?

WITH the election of Benedict XVI friends from Germany and Rome wanted the world to know the man they knew. From the town of Pentling, Germany, where the pope owns a house, emerged a picture of a man who enjoyed books, flowers and cats.

From his birthplace in Germany's Marktl am Inn, where the pope has been an honorary citizen since 1997, came reminders that he is always welcome there.

From Vatican colleagues who worked with him through his years as the fierce defender of orthodoxy, came a warning: Do not believe everything reporters have told you.

Rupert Hofbauer, a Pentling neighbor who cares for the home that then-Father Ratzinger built decades ago, said his relationship with the pope goes back to 1969, when Father Ratzinger was a professor of theology at nearby Regensburg University.

"This house is his own," he said, pointing next door. "I was there when he bought the plot, hired an architect and built it." He said the professor needed somewhere quiet but within walking distance of the university because he did not drive. "It became his permanent home, and he returned as often as he could. He usually celebrated New Year's together with his brother, Georg, just the two of them. In summer they would often sit on his balcony, reading, or walk around the garden. Then they would retire indoors and make themselves a simple supper." When the pope's sister, Maria Ratzinger, was alive, the three siblings often took long walks in the woods, he added.

Hofbauer's family benefited from the relationship. "Whenever we had family problems, I could go and talk to him. He also positively influenced my children, both of whom are successful. He was their role model and took an active interest in their growing up." Once, when his sons were little and playing, they crashed through the garden fence. The neighbor "just smiled and said that fences can be fixed," Hofbauer recalled. "He always reminded me to be kind to the children, even when they were unruly, saying they would eventually grow out of it."

The house is simple. The ground floor contains a bathroom and a small bedroom, with a single bed, a desk and glass doors leading into the garden. The ground floor also has a chapel with glass doors leading into the garden. The chapel has a wooden floor, a simple cross on the wall, and no chairs or benches.

The pope "was really a man of God, all along. I know that he prayed in this chapel many times a day," Hofbauer said. The upstairs has a bedroom, living room, kitchen and another bathroom. The bedroom was used by the pope's late sister, Maria. "He kept it just like it was when she died" in 1991, Hofbauer said. Beside the bedroom is the living room, where the cardinal would often sit with his brother, reading and writing. The room opens onto a balcony overlooking the garden.

Hofbauer said his neighbor liked Hofbauer's cat, Chico, who "often wandered over into the garden of the cardinal, who loved him," he said. "I also have a dog, Igor, who frequented the garden," he added, but the cardinal preferred Chico. "There are dog and cat people in the world, and he is definitely a cat person," he said.

Hofbauer was especially proud of the garden. "The pope's favorites are roses, but he likes all flowers," he said. "He told me that he wants flowers in bloom in the garden through to autumn. So I plant them, in all colors, and I send him photographs all the time, because I know that he misses his home a lot."

With his election as pope, Benedict XVI's favorite son status only increased in his birthplace, Marktl am Inn. The house where Pope Benedict was born, at Marktplatz 11, has become the focus of international attention in the town of 2,700 residents. The local bakery now offers Vatican bread and Ratzinger cake, and one of the stores sells pope honey and Benedict XVI tea. Residents eagerly share their connection to the new pope, whose family moved away when he was 2.

"Joseph and I had the same midwife and were baptized in the

same font," said Gunter Volker, a federal police officer. Pope Benedict was born to Joseph and Maria Ratzinger, April 16, 1927, which was Holy Saturday that year. He was baptized later that morning, which was so cold that his siblings, Georg, who is three years older, and Maria, who was 5 at the time, were not allowed to attend. Georg, who became a priest, studied music and became director of the world-famous Regensburg boys' choir. Maria looked after the household of her brother Joseph for many years and followed him to Rome.

The font is now in the heritage museum, next to a display about the pope, who visited the predominantly Catholic town and its museum and said Mass for the townspeople when he became an honorary citizen in 1997.

He was happy about his Bavarian roots, recalled museum director Josef Gassner. "When I guided him through the exhibit, he would pick up everyday items with obvious joy and say he remembered them from his childhood."

People of Marktl boast of the town's Bavarian heritage and its beautiful surroundings and life that moves at a slower pace. Located along the Inn River, some 10 miles from the Austrian border, the town is surrounded by two nature parks and boasts some of the most spectacular scenery of the upper Bavarian region.

The Cafe am Rathaus, at Marktplatz 2, just steps away from the pope's birthplace, keeps a special table reserved permanently for Pope Benedict, with his picture and a candle that is lit for him daily. "We want him to know that Marktl is his home, always," said owner Gisela Rompf. "This is his table, we are his people and he is always welcome here."

Away from that pastoral setting, at the Vatican, the cardinals who elected Pope Benedict and the priests who worked with him in the doctrinal congregation recognize that Cardinal Ratzinger, who spent 24 years defending Catholic doctrine and moral teaching, got mixed reviews in the media after many of his pronouncements. They stressed, however there was always a deeply spiritual, quiet, kind pastor behind them.

His conclusions about specific theologians and their teaching, about trends in theology and about moral questions have been described either as clear or as sharp. Some have questioned whether he

HABEMUS PAPAM!

Highlights in the life of Pope Benedict XVI

April 16, 1927
Born Joseph Ratzinger in Marktl am Inn, Germany

1945
Deserted from German army and held
briefly as U.S. prisoner of war

Berlin ★

GERMANY

Regensburg
Freising
Munich
Marktl

June 29, 1951
Ordained a priest, along with
his brother Georg

1957
Earned doctorate in theology from University of Munich

1958-77
Taught dogma and theology at five German universities

1962-65
Served as expert at Second Vatican Council

1969-77
Vice president, University of Regensburg

March 24, 1977
Ordained archbishop of Munich and Freising, Germany

June 27, 1977
Elevated to College of Cardinals

1981-2005
Prefect, Vatican Congregation for the Doctrine of the Faith

April 19, 2005
Elected 265th pope of the Catholic Church.

Languages
German, English, Italian, French, Spanish,
some Portuguese

Hobbies
Plays piano
Author of more than two dozen books
translated into English

Source: CNS   © 2005 CNS Graphics

always had to act when he did or if advancement in theology required time and room for debate and correction by colleagues; but when Cardinal Ratzinger put on his scholar's hat and engaged in public debates with other scholars, there was no denying the twinkle in his eyes and the smile on his lips.

He enjoyed the sparring.

The October before his election he and an Italian historian discussed history, politics and religion in a Rome debate. The cardinal told the scholar and Italian government officials, members of Parliament and Vatican officials in the audience, "We find ourselves in a situation in which it would be opportune to dialogue.

"Our moral capacity has not grown at the same rate as our potential power," especially when it comes to the ability to manipulate, prolong or terminate human life, he said. His somber assessment of the world's moral confusion did not outweigh the obvious delight he took in the opportunity to engage in a public debate, where theological and philosophical terms and names could be tossed into the conversation with no need for explanation.

Even while serving as the Vatican's moral and doctrinal "watchdog," a task often covered in silence, the future Pope Benedict continued to be a prolific public speaker, author and subject of interviews. He has published more than 60 books: scholarly theological tomes; responses to questions; collections of speeches and essays; and memoirs of his first 50 years of life, published in English in 1998 as *Milestones: Memoirs 1927–1997.*

In *Milestones*, he wrote about being born on Holy Saturday and baptized the same day in the newly blessed waters. "Personally, I always have been grateful for the fact that in this way my life from the beginning was immersed in the paschal mystery, which could not be anything other than a blessing," he wrote.

The future pope's father was a policeman, and the family moved frequently during his youth. According to his memoirs, he was only vaguely aware of the poverty and political strife building up in Germany before the outbreak of World War II. He joined his brother, Georg, at the minor seminary in 1939 and said he found it difficult to study in a room with 60 other boys but got used to that. "What weighed more heavily on me was that every day included—in homage to a modern idea of education—two hours of sports," he wrote. He was the smallest boy in the class, and the games were "a true torture."

Ordained in 1951, he received a doctorate and a licentiate in theology from the University of Munich, where he studied until 1957. He taught dogma and fundamental theology at the University of Freising in 1958–59, then lectured at the University of Bonn, 1959–1969, at Munster, 1963–66, and at Tubingen from 1966 to 1969. In 1969 he was appointed professor of dogma and of the history of dogmas at the University of Regensburg, where he also served as vice president until 1977.

A theological consultant to West German Cardinal Joseph Frings, he attended the Second Vatican Council as an expert or *peritus*. At the council, he played an influential role in discussions among the German-speaking participants and gained a reputation as a progressive theologian. After the council, he published several major books, including *Introduction to Christianity, Dogma and Revelation and Eschatology*. He was named a member of the International Theological Commission in 1969. Pope Paul VI appointed him archbishop of Munich and Freising in 1977 and named him a cardinal later that year.

Book-length interviews with then-Cardinal Ratzinger—the 1985 *Ratzinger Report*, the 1996 *Salt of the Earth* and the 2002 *God and the World*—showed a prelate with clear ideas, worried about the state of the church and not the least bit hesitant to respond to questions.

The interviews cover many of the same topics the doctrinal congregation had issued statements on: the Second Vatican Council; theological dissent; liberation theology; ecumenism and interreligious dialogue; the special place of the Jews in salvation history; liturgy; the role of women in the church; and collegiality and papal primacy. But they also attempted to delve into his spirituality, prayer style and the events that shaped his life.

He told Peter Seewald, author of the 1996 and 2002 books, that he believes God "has a great sense of humor."

"Sometimes he gives you something like a nudge and says, 'Don't take yourself so seriously!' Humor is in fact an essential element in the mirth of creation. We can see how, in many matters in our lives,

God wants to prod us into taking things a bit more lightly; to see the funny side of it; to get down off our pedestal and not to forget our sense of fun," he said.

In a 2000 interview, Seewald asked the future pope if he had ever been tempted to leave the Catholic Church. The cardinal said it would "never have entered my head," because his whole life has been bound up with the church. However, he said, "there are things about her (the church), big and little, that are annoying. From the local church right up to the church's overall leadership, within which I now have to work," he told Seewald in an interview conducted in 2000.

When Cardinal Ratzinger wrote the meditations for the Good Friday Way of the Cross service at Rome's Colosseum in 2005, he spoke much more soberly about members of the church who no longer believe in Christ as the true savior, who abuse others, who do not believe in the real presence of Jesus in the Eucharist or who have abandoned the sacrament of reconciliation. His words on sexual abuse and other clerical scandals were much stronger than any public comment he had made since 2001, when the doctrinal congregation began requiring bishops to report abuse cases to the congregation. In the 2005 meditation, he wrote: "How much filth there is in the church, and even among those who, in the priesthood, ought to belong entirely to him."

In a November 2002 speech in Spain, Cardinal Ratzinger said, "In the church, priests are also sinners." However, he said, "I am personally convinced that the constant presence in the press of the sins of Catholic priests, especially in the United States, is a distortion of the reality because the percentage of these offenses among priests is not higher than in other categories, and perhaps it is even lower."

Serving as dean of the College of Cardinals, the future pope opened the April 18–19 conclave with a homily many people saw as negative or pessimistic. It was not a new accusation. Cardinal Ratzinger had spoken on more than one occasion about his belief that the Catholic Church would get smaller and smaller, but that eventually the world would discover the hope and joy present in the small community of true believers and be attracted again to the Christian faith.

"When I said that," he told Seewald, "I was reproached from all sides for pessimism. And nowadays nothing seems less tolerated than what people call pessimism—and which is often in fact just realism."

The challenges the church faces continue to change, he said, but God continues to be with it. As the chief defender of Catholic doctrine and morality, Cardinal Ratzinger had a major role in drafting the 1992 Catechism of the Catholic Church and, especially, its 1997 revised passages on the death penalty—judged unacceptable in most cases—and on homosexual orientation, which it said was "objectively disordered."

While he has said all people must be treated with love and respect, he said no one can change Christian moral teaching that homosexual acts are sinful, and no one can equate a gay union to marriage between a man and woman without denigrating the human, moral, social and religious significance of marriage.

One question on many minds since Pope Benedict's election was what would happen to the teachings of the Second Vatican Council and to its liturgical reforms.

In *The Ratzinger Report*, he was quoted as saying the postconciliar church "seems to have passed over from self-criticism to self-destruction" with a growth of dissent and more people abandoning church practice. The cardinal said it was not the fault of the council, but of Catholics who thought that renewal of the church and dialogue with the modern world meant embracing the world's agenda without any sense of responsibility or limit.

Nevertheless, Pope Benedict told the world's cardinals April 20 "I want to forcefully affirm the strong desire to continue in the task of implementing the Second Vatican Council." He said Vatican II's documents were especially relevant to the modern church and today's globalized society and that the council's "authoritative" rereading of the Gospel would guide the church in the third millennium. Pope Benedict did not mention the council's liturgical reforms.

In the early 1980s, then-Cardinal Ratzinger repeatedly mentioned his belief that the council's liturgical reforms did not include the mandate that the priest face the congregation while celebrating Mass. He said he felt the church should have preserved the ancient practice of the congregation and priest facing East during the Eucharistic prayer.

By the time he published *The Spirit of the Liturgy* in 2000, he acknowledged that issuing new rules to have the priest celebrate with his back to the people was no longer pastorally practical. "Nothing is more harmful to the liturgy than a constant activism, even if it seems to be for the sake of genuine renewal," he said. He gave a similarly pastoral reply when Seewald asked him if the Mass should be celebrated in Latin. "That is no longer going to be possible as a general practice, and perhaps it is not desirable as such," he said.

But he did call for "a new liturgical consciousness, to be rid of this spirit of arbitrary fabrication" that might be clever or entertaining but not "the Holy One being offered to me."

The other question in people's minds concerned what would be Pope Benedict's approach to ecumenical and interreligious dialogue. It was prompted by the doctrinal congregation's questions over the years about joint ecumenical agreements, but mostly because of the congregation's 2000 document *Dominus Iesus* on salvation in Christ alone, its 2000 document on sister churches and its 2001 criticisms of Jesuit Father Jacques Dupuis, author of a book on religious pluralism.

Speaking to seminary rectors two months after *Dominus Iesus* was released, the cardinal said it "expresses with great clarity the central point of our faith, that is, that the Son of God was made man and that a bridge exists between God and man." The document was the focal point of ecumenical and interreligious controversy because of its firm statement that Christ and the church are necessary for salvation, leaving those who do not believe in Christ or are not part of the church feeling as if the congregation were denying that their faith offered the possibility of salvation.

The cardinal said at the time he was most disappointed in the negative reaction of Jewish leaders and groups to the document. "I did not expect it at all because for me it is evident that we come from the roots of Israel and that their Bible is our Bible and that Judaism is not just one of many religions, but is the foundation, the root of our faith. We share the faith of Abraham," he told Vatican Radio.

The other 2000 document insisted the term *sister churches*, frequently used among Christians, was to be used by Catholics only in reference to the Orthodox and other churches that "have preserved a valid episcopate and Eucharist." The document was criticized by many Anglicans and Protestants as well as by Catholic ecumenists.

Catholics involved in interreligious dialogue also expressed concern after the congregation's 1998–2000 investigation of Father Dupuis' 1997 book, *Toward a Christian Theology of Religious Pluralism,* an investigation focused on the issues raised in *Dominus Iesus.*

In early 2001, the congregation praised Father Dupuis' desire to explain the theological significance of the presence of so many religions in the world, but it said the book contained ambiguous statements and insufficient explanations that could lead readers to "erroneous or harmful conclusions" about Christ's role as the one and universal savior.

Under Cardinal Ratzinger, the doctrinal congregation was increasingly sensitive to criticism about the methods it used when investigating theologians and their work. In 1997 Cardinal Ratzinger said his new Regulations for Doctrinal Examination would safeguard the rights of theologians under review. The biggest change was the possibility that the theologian could name an advocate and an adviser to assist in his examination.

The commentary issued with the notification on Father Dupuis went out of its way to say the "tone" of the Vatican statements was not meant to sound authoritarian, but it had to be assertive and definitive so that the faithful would know that "these are not matters of opinion or questions for dispute but central truths of the Christian faith that certain theological interpretations deny or place in serious danger."

Addressing the cardinals who elected him the day before in the Sistine Chapel, Pope Benedict said that the new pope would assume as "his primary commitment that of working tirelessly toward the reconstitution of the full and visible unity of all Christ's followers. This is his ambition, this is his compelling duty." He said that the new pope also "is aware that to do so, expressions of good feelings are not enough. Concrete gestures are required to penetrate souls and move consciences, encouraging everyone to that interior conversion which is the basis for all progress on the road of ecumenism."

He also told the cardinals, "I address myself to everyone, even to those who follow other religions or who are simply seeking an answer to the fundamental questions of life and have not yet found it."

"The church," he said, "wants to continue to build an open and sincere dialogue with them in a search for the true good of mankind and of society." And while not shy about talking tough, as a cardinal Pope Benedict avoided "fire and brimstone" phrases and cautioned others about attributing apocalyptical threats to God or to the Blessed Virgin Mary.

In 1996, four years before Pope John Paul II released the so-called third secret of Fatima, Cardinal Ratzinger told a Portuguese Catholic radio station that the pope had shown him the message. "I am certain," he said, "that the Virgin does not engage in sensationalism; she does not create fear. She does not present apocalyptic visions but guides people to her Son. And this is what is essential."

The Vatican published the complete text of the Fatima message in 2000, interpreting it as a vision of a long war waged by atheistic regimes against the church. It included a figure of a "bishop in white" who falls in a hail of gunfire, which was presumed to be a reference to the assassination attempt against Pope John Paul in 1981. At a press conference marking the publication of the text, Cardinal Ratzinger said, "There does not exist an official definition or official interpretation of this vision on the part of the church." Like any private revelation approved by the church, he said, the Fatima message "is a help which is offered" to Catholics for living their faith, "but which one is not obliged to use."

In a commentary on the message, he said the vision described the path of the church through the 20th century as "a journey through a time of violence, destruction and persecution." Cardinal Ratzinger said he believed the particular period of struggle described by the vision had ended, making it appropriate to reveal the secret's contents.

The reality of evil and of threats against the church are issues Pope Benedict had experienced. When the future pope was a child in Adolf Hitler's Germany, school officials enrolled him in the Hitler Youth movement. He said he soon stopped going to the meetings. But when he was 16, he and his classmates were conscripted into an anti-aircraft unit that tracked Allied bombardments; although in uniform and staying in barracks with other soldiers, the seminarians also continued their studies. Later, young Ratzinger was drafted into a worker battalion, then into the army. In the spring of 1945, when Hitler had died and it appeared the war was almost over, he deserted his unit and returned home. When the U.S. military arrived, he was arrested with other members and former members of the German army and placed in a prisoner-of-war camp for several months.

In *God and the World*, Seewald asked the then-Cardinal Ratzinger about Hitler, the devil and evil. "One certainly cannot say that Hitler was the devil; he was a man," the cardinal said. However, he added, "I believe one can see that he was taken into the demonic realm in some profound way, by the way in which he was able to wield power and by the terror, the harm, that his power inflicted."

Benedict XVI, who came to the papacy from the Vatican bureaucracy, is the first German pope in 948 years, but he was a major figure on the Vatican stage for nearly a quarter of a century. As the guiding light on doctrinal issues during Pope John Paul II's pontificate, Pope Benedict was one of the most respected, influential and controversial members of the College of Cardinals.

Over the years, he met quietly once a week with Pope John Paul to discuss doctrinal and other major issues facing the church. Insiders said his influence was second to none when it came to setting church priorities and directions and responding to moral and doctrinal challenges.

White-haired and soft-spoken, Cardinal Ratzinger came across in person as a thoughtful and precise intellectual with a dry sense of humor. A frequent participant at Vatican press conferences, he was a familiar figure to the international group of reporters who cover the church. He was also well-known by the church hierarchy around the world, and his speeches at cardinal consistories, synods of bishops and other assemblies often had the weight of a keynote address. When Cardinal Ratzinger spoke, people listened.

Sometimes his remarks were bluntly critical on such diverse topics as dissident theologians, liberation theology, "abuses" in lay ministry, homosexuality, women as priests, feminism among nuns, premarital sex, abortion, liturgical reform and rock music. As Pope John Paul's pontificate developed, some Vatican observers said Cardinal Ratzinger's influence grew. He was to become "the last check on everything," the final word on orthodoxy. "Everything is passed through his congregation," one Vatican official said.

"I'm not the Grand Inquisitor," Cardinal Ratzinger once said in an interview, referring to the head of a medieval church tribunal focused on heresy. But to the outside world, he was known as the Vatican's enforcer. He made the biggest headlines when his congregation silenced or excommunicated theologians, withdrew church approval of certain books, helped rewrite liturgical translations, set boundaries on ecumenical dialogues, took over the handling of cases of clergy sex abuse against minors, curbed the role of bishops' conferences and pressured religious orders to suspend wayward members.

In 2003, the doctrinal congregation issued a document that said Catholic politicians must not ignore essential church teachings, particularly on human life. That set the stage for a long debate during the 2004 U.S. election campaign on whether Democratic Sen. John F. Kerry, a Catholic who supports legalized abortion, should be given Communion.

Cardinal Ratzinger's congregation also published a document asking Catholic lawmakers to fight a growing movement to legalize same-sex marriage.

In his first decade at the helm of the doctrinal congregation, Cardinal Ratzinger zeroed in on liberation theology as the most urgent challenge to the faith. He silenced Latin American theologians like Franciscan Father Leonardo Boff and guided the preparation of two Vatican documents that condemned the use of Marxist political concepts in Catholic theology.

But after the collapse of Marxism as a global ideology, Cardinal Ratzinger identified a new, central threat to the faith: relativism. He said relativism is an especially difficult problem for the church because its main ideas—compromise and a rejection of absolute positions—are so deeply imbedded in a democratic society.

More and more, he has warned, anything religious is considered "subjective." As a result, he said, in places like his native Germany the issue of abortion is being confronted with "political correctness" instead of moral judgment.

He said modern theologians are among those who have mistakenly applied relativistic concepts to religion and ethics. He said Jesus is widely seen today as "one religious leader among others," concepts like dogma are viewed as too inflexible and the church is accused of intransigence.

Cardinal Ratzinger was particularly sensitive to wayward trends in

Asian theology, especially as they find popular expression. He banned the best-selling books of a late Jesuit theologian from India and declared a Sri Lankan theologian excommunicated for his writings on Mary and the faith. The Sri Lankan theologian later reconciled with the church.

After review by Cardinal Ratzinger's congregation, U.S. Father Charles Curran, who questioned church teaching against artificial birth control, was removed from his teaching position at The Catholic University of America in Washington in 1987. Early in 2005, Cardinal Ratzinger made a similar judgment about Jesuit Father Roger Haight, who was banned from teaching Catholic theology over his book touching on the divinity and salvific mediation of Jesus.

That same year, he issued a document on papal primacy—a topic of intense ecumenical discussion—saying that, as a matter of faith, only the pope has the authority to make changes in his universal ministry.

Despite his reputation as a hardliner, however, the man who emerged in the days immediately after the death of Pope John Paul II was a figure more pastoral than pugnacious, more comforting than condemning. His simplicity was reflected in the fact that before his election, Pope Benedict lived in an apartment just outside the Vatican's St. Anne's Gate, walking to work daily across St. Peter's Square, rarely attracting people's notice.

Until just days before his election, most people in Rome had discounted the idea that he could ever be elected pope. They argued that he was simply too controversial and might divide the church. So when the 78-year-old German emerged from the conclave April 19 as Pope Benedict XVI after just four ballots, it represented a turnaround of sorts.

From the comments of several cardinals afterward, it became clear that a significant change in perception had occurred among some of the voters, and that this helped propel Cardinal Ratzinger past the two-thirds majority needed for election. The man known for years as a tough disciplinarian was almost uniformly described in post-conclave interviews as a mild, meek and caring person, someone open to ideas and suggestions.

"He's a very loving, lovely person, very unassuming, and shortly you will see this," Cardinal Edward M. Egan of New York said after the election. Cardinal Roger M. Mahony of Los Angeles cautioned people against judging the new pope on his reputation and said people "will have to get to know this man as we know him."

What happened to soften Cardinal Ratzinger's image and make him more appealing to the wide spectrum of cardinals from 52 countries? Many pointed to the cardinal's spiritual and organizational leadership during the interregnum. In particular, they were impressed by his sermon during Pope John Paul's funeral—not just his words, but also his rapport with the huge crowd of mourners.

South African Cardinal Wilfrid F. Napier of Durban said that while Cardinal Ratzinger may have built a reputation for severity as head of the doctrinal congregation "that is certainly not the Cardinal Ratzinger we've come to know in the last two weeks."

"He was very caring, gentle, humble and approachable," Cardinal Napier said. "You could see this in the way he interacted with the crowd at Pope John Paul's funeral—for example, when he patiently allowed the crowd to keep chanting during the Mass instead of cutting it off. We could see that this was the kind of person who was able to read situations and respond to them."

Clearly, Cardinal Ratzinger's position as dean of the College of Cardinals gave him wider recognition and more exposure, making him a point of reference for all the cardinals. Chairing the daily meetings before the conclave he was able on several occasions to articulate his views on the challenges the church faces.

When Pope John Paul died, Cardinal Ratzinger already had a core of firm supporters among curial cardinals and others. Despite a news blackout, the level of that support—some 40 electors—leaked out to Italian newspapers. So did some revealing anecdotes, as when Italian Cardinal Giacomo Biffi, retired archbishop of Bologna and a backer of Cardinal Ratzinger, spoke to the assembled cardinals and ended his strong speech on the need to protect Christian identity with the words: "You already know who I'm voting for!"

Another factor was continuity. In the wake of the global outpouring of respect and affection for Pope John Paul after his death, many cardinals seemed to be looking for someone of recognized stature to pick up the mantle of church leadership. That may have made them less inclined to vote for some of the newer, less-known candidates.

Cardinal Ratzinger was seen as Pope John Paul's right-hand man throughout most of his papacy. During the interregnum, the cardinal reinforced his prominence in sermons and talks and began looking more and more like the heir apparent. "We all felt like he was a brother with superior qualities," said Cardinal Christoph Schonborn of Vienna, Austria.

To the outside world, Joseph Ratzinger seemed to undergo somewhat of a transformation during the papal election. He went into the conclave sounding like an angry prophet and came out sounding like a humble shepherd. A few weeks before the conclave, in exceptionally strong language, he denounced the "filth" inside the church. At the conclave's opening Mass, he warned of an ominous "dictatorship of relativism" in today's world and compared the church to a small boat being tossed by the waves of ideologies, surrounded by human trickery and cunning.

When he emerged after the election as Pope Benedict, smiling shyly at a cheering crowd in St. Peter's Square, he described himself as "a simple, humble worker in the vineyard of the Lord." The next day he told the cardinals who elected him that he wanted their prayers and their advice and pledged to lead the church along the path of dialogue and unity traced out by his predecessor. His speech contained several passages that calmed those who feared a sharp departure from the reforms of the Second Vatican Council. It also contained a hallmark statement of the old Cardinal Ratzinger: that the church's dialogue and its work in the world are framed by its most basic duty, announcing the Gospel of Christ to all people.

His neighbors in Borgo Pio, the tiny Rome neighborhood just east of the Vatican where he had lived before moving to the Apostolic Palace, painted a different picture of the theologian. They saw a different side of the man. "I like him more than Wojtyla (Pope John Paul II)—maybe that's because I knew him," said Carla, who preferred not to give her last name. As co-owner of a fruit and vegetable shop in Borgo Pio, she saw the future pope pass by nearly every day on his afternoon walk. "This pope is more intelligent, where the other was more instinctive; he drew forth passion. This one is more rational—but he is delightful. The fact that he's timid endeared him to all of us."

Angelo Mosca, who runs an electrical supply shop in the "Borgo," said that "Cardinal Ratzinger used to come to buy light bulbs and batteries or ask for a minor repair, and I went to his house many times to fix something or other," said Mosca. "He is an exceptional person, with an indescribable humility." About five years ago Mosca, on one of his repair visits to the then-cardinal's fourth-floor apartment, brought along some documentation regarding miracles by a monk who worked with Padre Pio da Pietralcina. "He listened to me with the greatest kindness. The professor was listening to his student as if the student was the professor," said Mosca.

Walter Colantoni, an optician a block away from Pope Benedict's old apartment, filled then-Cardinal Ratzinger's first eyeglass prescription in 1988. "He has two pairs, one small and one larger, both for reading," said Colantoni, who greeted the cardinal with a wave every afternoon as he strolled down the street. "He's a simple, cordial person—as is being revealed now. Before, people only knew him through his writings and thought he was severe, but he's not. He's humble, without any pretext. We will miss him because he was a constant presence in the neighborhood."

After the election, as people sought to uncover the man behind the doctrine, the new pope's relationship with cats seemed to become almost as important as his relationship with cardinals.

Story after story recounted his love of felines, some implying he had a veritable menagerie at home. On Vatican Radio, Italian Cardinal Tarcisio Bertone of Genoa, who worked under Cardinal Ratzinger at the doctrinal congregation, portrayed the new pontiff as something of a Dr. Doolittle. "I tried to understand the language he used with cats, who were always enchanted when they met him. I thought maybe it was a Bavarian dialect, but I don't know." Ingrid Stampa, the pope's housekeeper for 14 years, finally spoke out to deny that he owned a cat. Instead, the cardinal apparently fed strays that lurked around his building, and according to his brother Georg's housekeeper in Germany, the two possess a collection of cat plates there.

With his election as pope, even details about Cardinal Ratzinger's daily sustenance emerged, focusing on his preference for Austrian and German food like strudel and sausages. Roberto Proscio, who used to work at a Rome restaurant specializing in Tyrolean cuisine, said the future pope always ordered a Viennese soup and drank orange soda when he came for dinner. When Cardinal Ratzinger visited Proscio in his new restaurant outside the city, he tried pasta and beef Wellington, though the restaurateur sent out a Bavarian cream for dessert in deference to the German prelate's culinary leanings.

The new pope is not a sportsman like John Paul, who played soccer, skied and hiked. But he rooted for Bayern-Munich, the hometown soccer team during his 1977–1982 tenure as head of the Archdiocese of Munich and Freising. In his Vatican Radio interview, Cardinal Bertone said Pope Benedict later befriended the team's Italian coach and gave him signed copies of some of his books.

A Virginia priest who worked for two years at the Vatican with the future Pope Benedict XVI saw then-Cardinal Joseph Ratzinger as the epitome of someone with a brilliant mind. "The breadth of his understanding and knowledge of the church is equal to none," said Dominican Father Brian Mulcahy, of Charlottesville, Va. Father Mulcahy said the new pope is very much like Pope John Paul in his ability to understand all sides of an issue. "He's not an ideologue, in any sense of the word." He noted that both men participated in the Second Vatican Council. "Both men were framed by the theology of the Second Vatican Council," and "both saw the last 26 years as the time to properly implement the ideas of Vatican II."

Though he thinks the two popes were like-minded philosophically, having been shaped by similar forces during their formative young adult years in Europe during World War II, Father Mulcahy said they could not have been less alike in temperament. He described Pope Benedict as a quiet man who plays the piano for relaxation and who would be unlikely to imitate his predecessor's outgoing approach of picking up babies in the crowd and feeding off the energy of children and teens. "Perhaps the cardinals were looking for someone who in no way would feel like he had to try to be like John Paul," Father Mulcahy said. He added that he was completely astounded that his former boss was elected pope and that he agreed to accept his election. Cardinal Ratzinger had actually been trying to retire for years, but remained in his position at the pope's request, the priest said.

"He would have loved to retire and to take the time to study and write some of the books that have been rattling around in his head for years," Father Mulcahy said, adding that Pope Benedict also might work to rebuild the church's fading numbers in Western Europe, a subject on which he wrote a book, A *Turning Point for Europe*.

Pope Benedict XVI delighted pilgrims and passers-by two days after he was elected and went outside the Vatican walls to visit his old apartment. A crowd of several hundred people thronged the apartment entrance after the new pope arrived in a car and went inside, apparently to rearrange his belongings for the move into the Apostolic Palace. The evening before, the pope had kissed two French children on his way out of the apartment. "I'm really very touched," Pope Benedict said, smiling as he waved to the crowd. The pope also took time to drop in on some of his neighbors in the building, which stands just across the street from Vatican City and houses several cardinals. "It was like a good neighbor saying goodbye," said Cardinal Dario Castrillon Hoyos, who lives in the building. "The pope was in his old apartment, perhaps looking over papers. . . . Then he had the courtesy to go and visit the apartments of the other residents. I never imagined that. He used the stairs," Cardinal Castrillon told Vatican Radio. In another of the first acts of his papacy, the new pope returned to the Congregation for the Doctrine of the Faith and greeted officials and staff there.

After the papal election, U.S. bishops, most of whom had met the future pope during their *ad limina* visits to the Vatican, which always included visits to many different congregations and councils, recalled warm personal encounters with then-Cardinal Joseph Ratzinger.

Archbishop Wilton D. Gregory of Atlanta had gone to the Vatican frequently during his six-year stint as vice president and then-president of the U.S. Conference of Catholic Bishops. "Every time I went to Rome . . . we had a meeting with Cardinal Ratzinger," he said. "It was always the easiest of the meetings that we had, insofar as he was always well-prepared." The new pope is "very, very professional, very organized and very cordial—a man you can talk to and raise the most sensitive issues with," he added. "He is very, very forthright and straightforward and well-informed and not threatened by questions."

Archbishop Gregory emphasized that the images presented by the media of Pope Benedict XVI or any public figure "are never the whole story." He spoke about a close friend, Msgr. Thomas Herron of the Archdiocese of Philadelphia, who died of pancreatic cancer last May. The two met in Rome in 1976, and Msgr. Herron later went on to work in the doctrinal congregation. Last year when Archbishop Gregory visited the dying priest, Msgr. Herron shared with him a letter he had received from Cardinal Ratzinger. "Cardinal Ratzinger wrote Tom a personal letter that was one of the warmest, most comforting letters that I've ever read," the archbishop said. "That's the kind of man that is now Benedict XVI."

Archbishop William J. Levada of San Francisco, who has worked closely with the new pope in several posts since 1981, said: "I have come to know him as unfailingly gracious and fair by personal temperament as well as keenly interested in and knowledgeable about pastoral concerns throughout the universal church." One of Benedict's first major appointments was to name Archbishop Levada his successor as head of the doctrinal congregation.

Auxiliary Bishop Joseph N. Perry of Chicago said he first came to know the new Pope Benedict through the "paper trail" of his theological work. He's one of the few popes who comes to us with a plethora of writings and literature," Bishop Perry said.

Auxiliary Bishop Francis J. Kane of Chicago recalled meeting Cardinal Ratzinger while attending "bishop school"—a Vatican seminar for new bishops—shortly after his episcopal ordination. "I think he's considered rather rigid and conservative (but) I found him very willing to listen to us," he said. "I think he will be somebody who will listen to what people are saying. But he is also someone who is very clear in what he thinks and believes."

Archbishop Daniel M. Buechlein of Indianapolis, who worked with the cardinal as head of the U.S. bishops' committee on the implementation of the catechism, agreed, saying that those who have criticized him as too harsh do not really know him. "He's a humble man—very gentle, very patient," he said. "He'll talk with anyone who stops him in the street." Pope Benedict's former job put him in the role of chief defender of Catholic beliefs, Archbishop Buechlein said. "He did that with strength, but never with a mean spirit," he added.

Cardinal Ratzinger visited the United States on several occasions.

On those visits and in other dealings with U.S. church leaders, he expressed his views on a wide range of issues, from theological dissent to seminary formation, from Scripture study to the cultural challenges to faith. On one such visit he said the only power the papacy has "is power of conscience."

Cardinal Ratzinger visited Dallas and St. Paul-Minneapolis in 1984, New York in 1988, Philadelphia and Washington in 1990, Dallas in 1991 and San Francisco in 1999. He also participated in a summit of U.S. archbishops at the Vatican in 1989 and was the Vatican point man in consultations with the U.S. bishops as they developed pastoral letters on nuclear deterrence and on women. He dealt directly with the U.S. hierarchy on specific issues of moral teaching, including such matters as the use of condoms by people with AIDS, pastoral ministry to those who are homosexually oriented and the responsibilities of Catholic politicians on legislation and public policy issues with a moral dimension.

The new pope's February 1984 visit was to give a keynote address on bishops, theologians and moral issues at an annual four-day symposium in Dallas on medical and moral questions, attended by 240 Western Hemisphere bishops. "Today we seem to know more about how to build bombs than to judge whether it is moral to use them," he told the group. His audience was composed mainly of U.S. bishops, who the year before had adopted a landmark pastoral letter on war, peace and nuclear deterrence—a letter he had publicly defended in the face of criticisms from some European bishops. He called the inadequate attention to morality "the key question of our day" and added, "The renewal of morality is not just some rear-guard action of a zealot opposed to progress, but the critical question upon which any real progress will depend." At the Dallas meeting he said bishops should consult with theologians in preparing statements on moral or doctrinal issues, but he also outlined "rules and limits" theologians must follow when they criticize church teachings.

On his subsequent stop in St. Paul-Minneapolis, he addressed the different challenges the church faces in different parts of the world. Christian faith has moral consequences, he said, and "if we do not have spiritual and moral reasons on how to answer the challenges of our time, if we only have technical power, then we are really poor and the problems are unresolvable."

"In a vital organ some tensions are normal," he said as he spoke of the different concerns the Vatican had in different parts of the world—issues such as feminism and marriage and sexuality in the United States, liberation theology in Latin America, inculturation in Africa and Asia, and intellectual critiques of church tradition in Europe. On the whole, he said, the U.S. church and the Vatican were in harmony.

Pope Benedict's 1988 visit to New York was organized by the Rev. Richard John Neuhaus, a prominent Lutheran thinker who later joined the church and is now a priest of the New York Archdiocese. In a public lecture on biblical interpretation, Cardinal Ratzinger said most Bible scholars use "a good deal of prudence" in their efforts to understand Scripture, but he sharply criticized "materialist and radical feminist" analyses of sacred texts. He said those methods "do not even claim to be an understanding of the text itself" and "are no longer interested in ascertaining the truth, but only in whatever will serve their own particular agenda." Several gay rights activists were arrested when they interrupted the lecture, shouting insults at him in protest against church teaching on homosexuality.

After the lecture he engaged in two days of dialogue on biblical interpretation with a group of Catholic, Protestant and Orthodox scholars, including Sulpician Father Raymond E. Brown, long regarded as one of the leading Catholic biblical scholars in the country and a frequent target of criticism from some conservative Catholic quarters. Afterward the cardinal publicly commended Father Brown, and Father Brown said the cardinal's views presented "no threat to honest and responsible biblical scholarship." The cardinal also met privately with a small group of Jewish leaders at the residence of Cardinal John J. O'Connor, then archbishop of New York.

In 1990 the future pope flew to Philadelphia to give the keynote address for a symposium on the priesthood at the archdiocesan seminary. He stressed a commitment to truth, scriptural formation and a deep Eucharistic spirituality as central elements of priestly formation. He said a priest "has to lead people to reconciliation" and "must be ready before all else to stand by people in their tribulations." He said spiritual development has to be an ongoing process, building "over and over again." He spoke bluntly about the difficulty of celibacy, saying it "stands in starkest contradiction to the normal fulfillment of life. When a man accepts it interiorly . . . he must somehow assent to the renunciation of his own life's aspirations."

Three days later, speaking at the John Paul II Institute for Studies on Marriage and Family in Washington, he decried the culture of death arising from people's failure to attend to their spiritual needs and the moral demands of life. "The unshackling of sexual desire, drugs and the sale of armaments have formed an unholy trio whose lethal net stretches ever more oppressively over the world's peoples. . . . Only in a relationship with God can human life become true living," he said.

Back in Dallas for the 1991 medical-moral symposium for bishops, he said a legitimate conception of the supremacy of conscience cannot reduce the idea of conscience to "firm subjective conviction" without reference to objective norms of good and evil. If that were the case, he said, "Hitler and his accomplices" would be in heaven "since they carried out all their atrocities with fanatic conviction and complete certainty of conscience." He said a strictly subjective conception of conscience sets up "morality of conscience and morality of authority as two opposing models," viewing authority as an external restraint that compromises personal freedom and autonomy, rather than as a bridge between the person and truth. "Such a modern, voluntaristic concept of authority can only distort the true theological meaning of the papacy," he said. "The true nature of the Petrine office has become so incomprehensible in the modern age no doubt because we only think of authority in terms which do not allow for bridges between subject and object."

"The pope does not impose from without," he added. "Rather he elucidates the Christian memory and defends it. . . . All power that the papacy has is power of conscience."

In an interview with the *Texas Catholic*, the Dallas diocesan newspaper, he acknowledged that the doctrinal congregation has a bad media image in the West. "How we can introduce into the media our message is a very important issue," he said. "The media are the mediator of our message," he added. "True . . . the media are media of our time, of our liberal time and our secular time, which in many aspects is opposed to the Christian faith. And so it is quite difficult to translate our message." During the interview he described Pope John

Paul's 1988 letter, "The Dignity of Women," as a "first step" in giving definition to a Catholic Christian feminism. "It is an important challenge to find the Christian articulation of the special dignity of women," he said.

In 1999 the future pope made his last visit as a cardinal to the United States, going to San Francisco to consult for four days with members of the doctrinal committees or commissions of bishops' conferences in the United States, Canada, Australia, New Zealand, and islands of the Pacific. Following the consultation, in an interview with Catholic San Francisco, the local archdiocesan newspaper, he called subjectivism a pervasive "problem in our culture, not only American culture but Western society."

If moral absolutes are denied, he said, society is left rudderless because "all opinions are equivalent."

"If we cannot have common values, common truths, sufficient communication on the essentials of human life—how to live, how to respond to the great challenges of human life—then true society becomes impossible," he said.

He gave a public lecture on Pope John Paul's 1998 encyclical "Faith and Reason." Speaking of Christianity's claim to universality in the lecture, he said, "Revelation is not something extraneous to cultures, but rather it responds to an inner expectation within cultures themselves." An authentic proclamation of the Gospel "allows people to preserve their own cultural identity" and forms a believing community "marked by a universality which can embrace every culture," he said. At a press conference he acknowledged tensions between the Vatican and some segments of the theological community but added that "tensions can be a good thing," and the doctrinal congregation was working "to have good relations between the theological community and the magisterium," the church's teaching authority.

A Catholic News Service report on that press conference said the cardinal also "indicated that judging a Catholic politician's vote on abortion legislation as sinful must take into account circumstances, freedom, intention and informed conscience, and that ultimately the question lies between the person and his or her confessor." In the midst of the 2004 U.S. presidential campaign, a private memo from

Cardinal Ratzinger to Cardinal Theodore E. McCarrick of Washington, then heading a task force of bishops on the political responsibilities of Catholics when dealing with public policy on fundamental moral issues such as abortion, was leaked to the media. It made no mention of the factors of individual circumstances, freedom and intention, and it was seized upon by some U.S. Catholics to support the idea that bishops should deny Communion to legislators who consistently vote in favor of legal abortion. Cardinal Ratzinger's office issued a public statement that his memo was in harmony with the task force's position that such decisions should be left to the local bishop in light of the circumstances in each case.

Coat of Arms

POPE BENEDICT revealed who he is in designing his papal coat of arms. He dispensed with the image of the three-tiered tiara that traditionally appeared at the top of each pope's coat of arms and replaced it with the pointed miter. He also added the pallium, the woolen stole symbolizing a bishop's authority, to the elements surrounding the shield. "Benedict XVI has chosen a coat of arms that is rich in symbolism and meaning, so as to put his personality and his papacy in the hands of history," said Italian Archbishop Andrea Cordero Lanza di Montezemolo, an expert on heraldry and creator of Benedict XVI's new insignia.

"For at least the past eight centuries, popes have had their own personal coats of arms in addition to the symbols of the Apostolic See," the archbishop said in the Vatican newspaper. While each papal shield is unique, the elements surrounding it had more or less remained the same for centuries—until now. Gone is the beehive-shaped crown whose actual use in important ceremonies was abandoned during the papacy of Paul VI. For Pope Benedict's ensign, the more modest and recognizable miter has taken its place. But the silver miter has three gold stripes to mirror the symbolism of the papal tiara's three tiers: "order, jurisdiction and magisterium," said Archbishop Cordero Lanza di Montezemolo. A vertical gold band connects the three stripes in the middle "to indicate their unity in the same person," he said. The white pallium with black crosses draped below the shield "indicates the (bishop's) role of being pastor of the flock entrusted to him by Christ," wrote Archbishop Cordero Lanza di Montezemolo.

What has not changed and has been part of papal emblems for centuries is the Holy See's insignia of two crossed keys, which symbolize the

powers Christ gave to the apostle Peter and his successors. The gold key on the right represents the power in heaven and the silver key on the left indicates the spiritual authority of the papacy on earth. The cord that unites the two keys alludes to the bond between the two powers. Nestled on top of the keys lies the unique shield of Pope Benedict, which is based on his coat of arms as archbishop of Munich and Freising, Germany, and is particularly rich in personal and spiritual symbolism, wrote Archbishop Cordero Lanza di Montezemolo. The shield is divided into three sections—each of which has its own symbol. The central element on a red background is a large gold shell that has theological and spiritual significance for the pope, the archbishop said. The shell recalls a legend in which St. Augustine came across a boy on the seashore who was scooping water from the sea and pouring it into a small hole he had dug in the sand. When the saint pondered this seemingly futile activity, it struck him as analogous to limited human minds trying to understand the infinite mystery of the divine.

"The shell reminds me of my great master Augustine, of my theological work and of the vastness of the mystery which surpasses all our learning," wrote then-Cardinal Joseph Ratzinger in his 1997 memoirs *Milestones*. Archbishop Cordero Lanza di Montezemolo wrote that the shell has long symbolized the pilgrim, "a symbolism Benedict XVI wants to keep alive" after Pope John Paul II, "the great pilgrim." The shell is also present in the coat of arms of the Schotten monastery in Regensburg, Germany, to which the pope "feels very spiritually close," the archbishop said. The upper left-hand section of the shield depicts a brown-faced Moor with red lips, crown and collar; it is a symbol of the former Diocese of Freising dating back to the eighth century. Though it is not known why the Moor came to represent Freising, in *Milestones*, the pope said for him "it is an expression of the universality of the church, which knows no distinctions of race or class since all are one in Christ."

Finally, a brown bear loaded with a pack on his back lumbers up the upper right-hand section of the shield. The bear is tied to an old Bavarian legend about the first bishop and patron saint of the Diocese of Freising, St. Corbinian. According to the legend, when the saint was on his way to Rome, a bear attacked and killed his horse. St. Corbinian punished the bear by making him carry the saint's belongings the rest of the way to Rome. Archbishop Cordero Lanza di Montezemolo said the bear symbolizes the beast "tamed by the grace of God," and the pack he is carrying symbolizes "the weight of the episcopate."

The pope said in his memoir, "I have carried my pack to Rome and wander for some time now through the streets of the Eternal City. When release will come I cannot know. What I do know is that I am God's pack animal, and, as such, close to him."

CARDINAL WILLIAM H. KEELER

Archbishop of Baltimore

THE person and the office of Pope John Paul II, his trips around the world, with his emphasis on the liturgical renewal fostered by the Second Vatican Council and his repeated commitment to the implementation of the council, together with his outreach to youth, to other Christians and to other faith families helped to set the scene. Beyond question, the example he gave us in his final weeks with us made a deep impression on people everywhere.

Pope John Paul II clearly looked ahead to a new phase in the life of the church, one which would follow on his death.

He convened the cardinals a number of times for consistories. The result was that the cardinals knew each other better than had been the case in the past. Our synods of bishops also helped: we were together for a month in each case. Also, through travel, the cardinals came to know each other better.

When we arrived in Rome, we found and made many opportunities to get to know each other better.

In the general congregations, we began our more intense mutual conversations. In these sessions, we had an opportunity to speak from our own perspective. We spoke initially in Italian, with Cardinal Ratzinger, dean of the College of Cardinals, very ably recognizing speakers and moving the discussions along. Soon enough, English was used and then simultaneous translation. Through these discussions we gained an impressive overview of the major challenges facing the church today and of her strengths as well.

To the election: the experience in the Sistine Chapel was one of great peace and amazing beauty; the greatest Christian art is in this one hall. I could look up and opposite me see the frescos by Botticelli, Ghirlandaio, Perugino and Rosselli. Overhead was the Creation by Michelangelo and to my left, the Last Judgement, by the same artist. Pope John Paul II, in his last published poem, visualized the Cardinals assembling in the Sistine Chapel to elect his successor and mused how between creation and judgment they shall meet, to be guided by Him to him whom they are to choose.

After the election, before he went out on the balcony, the new Holy Father met each of us in the Sistine Chapel. I brought the love of the Archdiocese of Baltimore, and he said, "We must keep praying for each other."

At his inaugural Mass, attended by hundreds of thousands and watched by millions around the world, he confirmed his intention to follow in the path of Pope John Paul II and continue the implementation of the Second Vatican Council, and also his outreach to the youth, to other Christians, especially the Orthodox, to all religious bodies and to the world. Justice and peace are clearly priorities with him. The name he took honors the memory of Pope Benedict XV, of World War I days, as well as the patron saint of Europe.

I have known him for 22 years, and especially from 1989 on, when the archbishops of the United States and the officers of our bishops' conference went to Rome for a weeklong meeting with the Pope and the officials in Rome who were responsible for making and carrying out policy for the universal church. Like my mother, a school teacher, he is sweet and clear. I worked with him when I was vice-president and then president of our bishops' conference, from 1989 to 1995, and found him very perceptive and helpful, especially on the issue of inclusive language, which is a problem peculiar to our English.

When Pope Benedict met with the cardinals in Rome, he said to me, "Cardinal Keeler, yours is the first diocese in the United States." I responded, "And, Holy Father, we have the first cathedral, which we are restoring now. The bishops of the United States are coming next year in November for the rededication. It would be wonderful if you could come to rededicate this cathedral." He replied: "I will see. . . ."

CHAPTER 13

The World Reacts to Benedict's Election

THE ELECTION of the head of the more than 1 billion Catholics drew responses from around the world. Religious and political leaders and the German community hailed the pontiff from Bavaria, the first German pope in centuries. Church leaders praised Pope Benedict XVI as a standard-bearer of Catholic values and a worthy successor to Pope John Paul II.

Cardinal Aloysius Ambrozic of Toronto said that in electing Pope Benedict the cardinals were motivated by a desire to continue the work of Pope John Paul. "He is unquestionably one of the best theologians we have. He is an extraordinarily clever man," Cardinal Ambrozic said.

The cardinal said that because of the nature of Cardinal Ratzinger's position as head of the Congregation for the Doctrine of the Faith he was not able to demonstrate other facets of his personality. "There's a real difference between the image and the reality. The media doesn't really know the man," he said.

Archbishop Mario Conti of Glasgow, Scotland, called Pope Benedict "a very humble, personable man." He is a man of great theological ability, linguistically talented, kindly of manner and of enormous pastoral and administrative experience. He was, of course, very close to Pope John Paul, knew his mind and collaborated very closely with him. But he is his own man and will bring his own gifts to the papacy, to the church and the world," he said. The archbishop said Pope Benedict showed the world a different side of his personality when he celebrated Pope John Paul's April 8 funeral Mass. "He spoke simply, directly and movingly. Many who had only known him as the great enforcer were surprised at his kindly, gentle, affectionate words that day."

Maronite Bishop Bechara Rai of Jbail, Lebanon, said Pope Benedict's approval of an Arab catechism allowed the local church to "avoid some words and expressions" to show "respect (to) the Arab sensibility." He also said the new pope is "someone who is esteemed by theologians."

"He is of the same thinking of John Paul II, especially for the traditional vision of the church and theology. I think his appointment is providential, because the church needs to be in a period of calm," Bishop Rai said.

In Mexico, home to the world's second-largest Catholic population, bells rang out in churches throughout the capital soon after the white smoke emerged from St. Peter's Basilica. President Vicente Fox, the country's most openly Catholic leader in decades, said the new pope can count on Mexico "to stand by his side," and that he would have "a permanent, open invitation to visit our country as soon as might be possible."

In London, worshippers at Westminster Cathedral clapped during the daily Mass when the new pope's name was announced. The cathedral bells rang, and Auxiliary Bishop George Stack of Westminster said, "I am sure you will join the church throughout the world in praying that he is given the strength to be a true servant." Archbishop Patrick Kelly of Liverpool, England, described Pope Benedict as "wise, profound and humble."

"I expect him to be a very different pope; it is very difficult to follow in someone's footsteps, but I am sure he will find his own path," he said.

Archbishop Rowan Williams of Canterbury, spiritual head of the worldwide Anglican Communion, said the appointment was of "great significance to Christians everywhere."

"I look forward to meeting him and working together to build on the legacy of his predecessor," Archbishop Williams said. He was encouraged by Pope Benedict XVI's commitment to Christian unity and believed his papacy would give special energy to a "united Christian witness" in an increasingly secularized Europe. The only head of a church present for Pope Benedict's installation and his April 25 meeting with ecumenical representatives, Archbishop Williams spoke with reporters afterward. Because of the large number of representatives at the audience, he said, "it was not possible to speak in any great depth, but the pope and myself were able to exchange a few words and promised to pray for each other." The archbishop was encouraged by the fact that in the first days following his election "Pope Benedict has gone out of his way to underline the sense of priority of ecumenical work. He has spoken of the service of unity, and we have taken that very much to heart." The Anglican leader said the pope has expressed his commitment to ecumenism since his election, "so we look forward in hope and sympathetic interest to how this very fruitful dialogue . . . is to be pursued." Archbishop Williams said he also was pleased about the new pope's emphasis on "the theme of united Christian witness."

"I sensed a real willingness to draw others into that common encounter—not aggressive or triumphalistic—with secularism as a philosophy," he said. Especially in Europe, the archbishop said, there is a need to find the proper balance between the separation of church and state, on one hand, and the freedom of Christians to make their beliefs known publicly, on the other. The archbishop said he had been assured that current Anglican-Roman Catholic projects will continue. Archbishop Williams also said the illness and death of Pope John Paul II, his funeral, the conclave, the election of Pope Benedict and his installation had given "a foretaste of a worldwide fellowship gathered for worship, glorifying God together," in a way that overcame denominational and doctrinal divisions. "It is as if we have been given a glimpse of other levels of unity," he said. Too often, the archbishop said, the faith of ordinary Europeans has been ignored, but the massive media coverage of Pope John Paul's death and Pope Benedict's election gave many Christians an opportunity "to talk 'to camera' about their faith."

According to Archbishop Williams, Pope Benedict's election comes at a time when the Anglican Communion is "struggling to find a robust, sustainable doctrine of the church" that will help the communion remain united even in the face of sharp differences over such issues as the ordination of openly gay men as bishops and the blessing of gay unions. The agreements reached with the Catholic Church over basic doctrines and teachings are a resource for the internal unity of the Anglican Communion as well as for the movement toward unity with the Roman Catholic Church, he said.

Britain's Chief Rabbi Jonathan Sacks said that he hoped the new pope would continue to work at improving relations between Christianity and Judaism. "As a global leader in a global age, his voice will be important in framing some of the great challenges of the 21st century," he said.

Cardinal Cormac Murphy-O'Connor of Westminster, England, said Pope Benedict has made it very clear since his election that "there is no going back" on the Catholic Church's commitment to Christian unity, and he has given "his own imprimatur" on ecumenism. "Someone said our God is a God of surprises, and who knows, Pope Benedict, too, may be a pope of surprises," the cardinal said.

He said Benedict XVI was the right choice. "He's aware, as few others are, of the challenges facing the church in today's society. If there was one candidate who particularly impressed us," it was then-Cardinal Ratzinger.

He said the pope's election had brought "a sense of continuity, solidarity and affirmation of faith," as well as of a "job well done" among the 115 participating cardinals. He was a "very, very strong candidate," and it was not a surprise when he won on the fourth ballot. Asked about the final ballot, he said there had been a "gasp all-round" when Pope Benedict reached a majority of "over 77 or 78 votes." He said the new pope sat with his head down when Cardinal Jorge Medina Estevez approached to ask if he accepted. "We knew it was ended then—although he couldn't have been unaware that this was quite likely to happen, the moment it actually does is always a special one," he said.

"Benedict XVI now has a platform and place—and wider responsibilities for the whole church—which he didn't have before, and I think he's aware of this," Cardinal Murphy-O'Connor said. "At his age, he must feel he isn't a young man and be very conscious, not of unworthiness, but of the huge task that awaits him. What's important in a pope—and he would appreciate this—isn't just that he's doctrinally very secure, but also the kind of image of the church we're going to have with him," he said. "When he was head of his congregation, he had a particular task to do in making sure the church's traditions were upheld, doctrinally and morally. Now that he's pope, it's an entirely different concept altogether. He has to be Peter for the whole church—not only a very intelligent man, but also pastoral and spiritual."

Writing in the *Sunday Telegraph*, a London-based national newspaper, April 24, the cardinal wrote that Pope Benedict was "courteous, highly intelligent and invariably kind," rather than the hard-line conservative often depicted in the world media. "Returning home, I am surprised at the picture painted of Pope Benedict in some of the British press reports," the cardinal wrote. "Pope Benedict has, I know, a particular knowledge and concern for the church in this country and a deep desire to further the cause of Christian unity with fellow Christians here." On April 20, the *Daily Telegraph* bore the headline "God's Rottweiler is the new pope." On the same morning—the day after the election—a headline in the *Daily Mail* said, "Cardinals Pick the Rottweiler," while the *Sun* carried a headline that read, "From Hitler Youth to Papa Ratzi."

The Islamic Society of North America, a U.S. organization, lauded Pope Benedict's election, and voiced hopes he will "reinforce the direction of the church taken during the last few decades."

"We will continue to cooperate, build alliances, promote dialogues and strengthen conversations with the Roman Catholic Church because the Quran commands us to seek common grounds with 'people of the book,'" said a statement released April 21 by the society's secretary-general, Sayyid M. Syeed. The center is one of the major Muslim organizations in the United States and Canada and provides religious training and educational and administrative support to some 300 affiliated mosques and organizations. It is the Islamic cosponsor of a Midwest Catholic-Muslim dialogue, one of three such regional dialogues in the United States cosponsored on the Catholic side by the U.S. Conference of Catholic Bishops. "The Muslim community in America has been celebrating a close relationship of understanding and cooperation with the Catholic community for decades," the statement said. "Our common concerns about moral decadence, religious bigotry and issues of peace and justice have enhanced personal friendships and support at different levels." The society said it hoped Pope Benedict "will build upon John Paul II's legacy of interfaith outreach and reconciliation based on mutual respect and religious tolerance."

During his papacy Pope John Paul visited a number of Muslim countries and met with Muslim leaders. On a trip to Syria he became the first pope to enter a mosque. There is an official dialogue between the Vatican and the Islamic clerics of al-Azhar University in Cairo, Egypt, the oldest and most prestigious university in the Muslim world.

German Catholics said Pope Benedict could help reconciliation among some European countries. About 100,000 German pilgrims, many waving flags and banners, were among the 350,000 people who attended the installation; the largest number of Germans came from the southern state of Bavaria, where Pope Benedict was born.

Michael Ilyander, a 40-year-old university professor who came with fellow Bavarians, said he believed Pope Benedict had a "fantastic opportunity" to heal the World War II wounds still existing between Germany and neighboring countries. "As a universal theologian and philosopher, our new pope's horizons go far beyond Germany," Ilyander said. "Although his manner and attitude seem conservative, he also embodies a Bavarian tradition of liberalism with very positive aspects, which he can rediscover as pope."

Sacred Heart Father Heinrich Wilmer, a principal from the state of Lower Saxony, Germany, said he and 1,800 students and parents had planned to come for the scheduled April 24 beatification of the founder of the Sacred Heart Fathers. When the beatification was postponed after the death of Pope John Paul II, the group decided to come anyway. "Everyone was surprised and stunned" when German Cardinal Joseph Ratzinger was elected pope, Father Wilmer said. "I myself will go back full of strength, energy and hope," he said after the installation Mass. "I think this will give everyone a new, fresh attitude toward our Catholic Church."

"I'm proud of my country—it's the first time in my life I haven't been ashamed to hold up our flag," said Theresa Konopka, a lay Catholic from the former capital, Bonn. "Some people have said they expect a new evangelization to come out of Germany, something that has been hard to imagine. Perhaps we can now see how (Pope Benedict's) election could really give new force to our church."

Michael Holzer, a student from Nuremberg who came for the weekend with members of a Catholic youth group, said he was "not surprised" so many young Germans made the journey for the installation. "Although he's been in Rome a long time, he's still a Bavarian German inside," said Holzer. "I think he's a good, strong person for the job—this is a great chance for the German church." Angela Stefan, a student from the pope's hometown of Marktl am Inn who slept in St. Peter's Square with a group of 100 Catholics and Protestants, said she came to Rome to "feel the atmosphere" after joining street celebrations at home.

After the inauguration Mass, German President Horst Koehler and Chancellor Gerhard Schroeder became the first heads of state and government to greet the new pontiff.

"It's a cause of great joy that a German has been elected," said Peter Antes, president of Germany's Association of Church Historians. "But he is also viewed as a more Roman than German figure now—a truly catholic theologian who thinks in universal church categories rather than in a necessarily German way."

Christian Weisner, the chairman of Germany's We Are Church movement, which has campaigned for voluntary priestly celibacy and the ordination of women, said he hoped Pope Benedict would favor "a church of dialogue and collegiality" in line with reforms at the 1962–65 Second Vatican Council. "I don't expect him to accept our demands. But he is an intellectual person, and I hope he has the wisdom to see what's needed in the church," Weisner said shortly after the pope's election. Pope Benedict "must realize he's now in a different position. He has to be pope for the whole church, and I think this will be an enormous task for him," he said.

News of the election in Rome was celebrated by more than 500 people in the main square of Pope Benedict's birthplace of Marktl am Inn, as well as in nearby Traunstein, where he spent part of his childhood. In a congratulatory message, Chancellor Schroeder described the election as a "great honor for the whole country," adding that the pontiff knows "the world church like no one else" and is a "worthy successor" to Pope John Paul II.

Father Paul Zulehner, dean of Vienna University's theology department, said that Pope Benedict's election had "placed the church in a new position," but also predicted he would be a "pope of transition."

"Those who hoped for a new departure on celibacy and women's ordination will resign their hopes—the new pope has worked to stop these things, and they'll now be beyond discussion," he said. "But this election could also provide the basis for a religious revival in German-speaking countries. There's a feeling that he's one of us, and that we're now the center of the church," he said. Germany's Catholic Church makes up approximately a third of the country's population of 82 million and has faced divisions during the past decade over moral and social issues.

In a statement posted on the German bishops' Web site, Cardinal Karl Lehmann of Mainz, chairman of the German bishops' conference, described the new pope as a "living symbol of the continuing witness of the church."

Cardinal Lehmann, who often disagreed with positions taken by then-Cardinal Ratzinger, said that as head of the doctrinal congregation the cardinal had one of the most sensitive tasks in the church: the maintenance of the substance of Catholic faith. "It is almost obvious that, with the variety of current opinion, not least in the church itself, not every (person) could or would follow him. But, even from those who disagreed with him, he won respect for his theological achievement and the recognition of his nonconformist courage in dialogue and the confrontation with contemporary forces," the cardinal said.

Cardinal Joachim Meisner of Cologne said, "We will experience through the new Holy Father a good and consistent continuation of the pontificate of his great predecessor John Paul II. If some people accuse him of being too conservative, the answer is: Every Christian must always be a conservative, and not a producer. A Christian should not produce the Gospel, he must take it on and keep it." Cardinal Meisner, a close friend of Pope Benedict, called him "the Mozart of theology," adding that he and other cardinal-electors were "happy with the work done."

Archbishop Robert Zollitsch of Freiburg told German television: "(As a conservative,) he'll have it harder than others, especially in

Germany. He once told me: I have a certain image in Germany. I'll have to live with that."

Among other reactions, Pope Benedict's 81-year-old brother, Father Georg Ratzinger, said he believed his brother would "make a good pope" but was also "a very different type than John Paul II."

"They had good relations, but he doesn't have the capacity for such direct, immediate contact with people," the priest said. "My brother has achieved a great deal in life, but this pontificate could be too heavy a burden for him."

When it was announced that German Cardinal Joseph Ratzinger had been elected as the new pope, Benedict XVI, hundreds of people gathered at the cathedral in Cologne, expressing a mixture of joy and dismay that one of their own had succeeded the popular Pope John Paul II.

Johannes Schumann, 21, said he was very happy a German had been chosen. "I thought there would never be a German pope after the Nazis," he said. "Here in Germany the level of faith is going down, and maybe a German pope can strengthen faith in Germany."

Reactions from German-Americans in Brooklyn, N.Y., suggested that Pope Benedict XVI's German nationality would most likely take a back seat to his performance and philosophy. Msgr. Edward Scharfenberger, pastor at St. Matthias in Ridgewood, home of one of the few German-language Masses in the Brooklyn Diocese, said he was sure there'd be "a great deal of pride" in the pope's German ancestry, but he also thought the expressions of pride would be subdued.

Germans made up one of the largest immigrant communities, "but they're also probably the most assimilated," agreed Msgr. Anthony Danna of Our Lady of the Miraculous Medal in Ridgewood, another former German enclave that is now largely Polish and Italian. "Still, there's an obvious pride when you have someone from the same nation." However, Msgr. Danna said other factors were more important, particularly since the previous pope was also non-Italian. "I think it signals to most people that the church is truly becoming universal."

"It's a matter of pride that the pope would come from Germany," said Randall Ratje, a Lutheran and the national director of the Steuben-American Society. "I think the greater impact will be seen in Germany itself. Let's hope he has the same positive effect in Germany and on the world's perspective on Germans that the last pope had on Poland."

Politicians from Florida and Maryland who represented the United States at the Mass inaugurating Pope Benedict XVI's papal ministry were impressed with the pageantry of the ceremony and with the new pope's views. "It was a stunning moment for any Catholic to confront your faith like that and see the majesty of it and see the power the faith has over you," said Lt. Gov. Michael S. Steele of Maryland. "You really do feel a part of the universal church."

Florida Gov. Jeb Bush was selected by his brother, President George W. Bush, to lead the official U.S. delegation. In an e-mail interview with the *Florida Catholic*, he wrote that he was "impressed with the rich tradition, pageantry, beauty and symbolism of the inaugural Mass."

"I was also moved by how thousands of faithful came from all across the globe to join the pope as he began his journey," added Bush, who became a Catholic in 1996.

Other delegation members were Steele, a former Augustinian seminarian; Carl A. Anderson, supreme knight of the Knights of Columbus; Helen Alvare, associate professor of law at The Catholic University of America in Washington; and Frank Hanley, president emeritus of the International Union of Operating Engineers.

"We went to represent all Americans, particularly those of the Roman Catholic faith," said Bush, who had an opportunity to meet the new pontiff in a receiving line of dignitaries.

The Republican governor also said he believes the College of Cardinals made a good choice in selecting Cardinal Joseph Ratzinger as the new pope, calling Benedict XVI "a true theologian (who) offers moral clarity in an era of ambivalence."

Steele, also a Republican, said he believes Pope Benedict will be a "teaching pope" who will challenge Catholics and non-Catholics alike to resist the "dictatorship of relativism."

"John Paul II wrapped his arms around us and said, 'Be not afraid,'" he said. "Pope Benedict takes us by the hand and says, 'Learn, listen, understand.' It's what parents do every day, particularly when their children fall and hurt themselves." Steele said the new pope would "help us understand what our faith means to us" by calling Catholics to the "classroom of our faith." The lieutenant governor said he was impressed with the way then-Cardinal Ratzinger responded to criticisms several years ago from those who pushed for the church to "keep up with the times" by relaxing its teachings on such issues as contraception and abortion. "Cardinal Ratzinger told us to look at the churches that have done that," Steele said. "Where are they today? They continue to struggle."

U.S. cardinals said the pope brought his own charisma and contribution to the papacy. "This pontificate is totally new, the pope has chosen a new name, but at the same time he has indicated a real desire to be in continuity" with the legacy of Popes John Paul II and Benedict XV, said Cardinal Justin Rigali of Philadelphia. The cardinal said the new pope is dedicated to the teachings of the Second Vatican Council and interested in collegiality, or how the local bishops share responsibility and decision making with the pope and the Roman Curia. Pope Benedict will approach these issues in "his own way, but in faithful collegiality to John Paul II and Benedict XV," Cardinal Rigali said.

Cardinal Adam J. Maida of Detroit said the new pope will be "his own man" and "a spiritual guide." "God will use him as an instrument of grace," he said. "God has picked the most unusual people and put them in places of authority. Even with (the pope's) gifts, talents and shortcomings," ultimately "it will be the grace of God" that leads the church, Cardinal Maida said.

"He's a very loving, lovely person, very unassuming, and shortly you will see this," Cardinal Edward M. Egan of New York said following the election. Asked by a reporter how the new pope might fare with U.S. Catholics given his sometimes negative portrayal in the press, Cardinal Egan said: "I think he'll play very well as soon as people get to know him. You need to be slow in making judgments. Sometimes it's good to watch for a while and see if what you've heard is true."

Cardinal Roger M. Mahony of Los Angeles said one must be careful not to make judgments about a person based on "labels" and "caricatures." He cautioned that people who think they know the new pope from having read about his defense of church teaching and his disciplining of theologians do not know Pope Benedict. "His job was preserving the doctrine of the church against dilution or errors," he said. Now, he said, "I think you will see emerge his far more spiritual and pastoral sides."

Questioned about the new pope's lack of pastoral experience, Cardinal Rigali pointed to the new pope's 1977–82 tenure as archbishop of Munich and Freising, Germany. "It was precisely because he had been a pastor, precisely because he had been involved with the people," that Pope John Paul II chose him in 1981 to come to Rome and be in the service of the universal church, Cardinal Rigali said.

Cardinals Rigali and Egan praised Pope Benedict for his theological sophistication and ability to speak several languages. The new pope speaks German, English, Italian, French and Spanish, they said, adding that they had heard he also speaks Portuguese. Cardinal Rigali said the pope's interest in languages showed a "desire to reach out to people. The reason he wants to speak languages is because he's interested in the people who speak those languages."

Cardinal Theodore E. McCarrick of Washington said Cardinal Ratzinger was the right man to be elected pope because he has "a sense of the church at this time after the long pontificate of John Paul II as we move into other challenges."

Jewish leaders voiced hope that the new pope would advance Catholic-Jewish relations. They said they expected him to continue his predecessor's commitment to advancing Catholic-Jewish relations and hoped he would reaffirm the church's teaching on Judaism even more forcefully. Israeli President Moshe Katsav, the Anti-Defamation League and the European Jewish Congress all released congratulatory statements, encouraging the new pontiff to follow Pope John Paul II's path of dialogue and reconciliation.

Based on personal encounters with Pope Benedict, the Israeli ambassador to the Holy See, Oded Ben-Hur, said the pontiff "understands the bond between us, the common roots, and we are looking forward to working with him." In late 2003, Ben-Hur asked then-Cardinal Joseph Ratzinger if the abridged *Catechism of the Catholic Church*, expected in late 2005, could include an entire page on *Nostra Aetate*, the 1965 Second Vatican Council declaration that reshaped Catholic attitudes toward Jews and Judaism." He looked me straight in the eye and said, 'I will do it,'" Ben-Hur said.

The major challenge facing Catholic-Jewish relations remains spreading Pope John Paul's teachings to the faithful, said Rabbi

David Rosen, the American Jewish Committee's head of interfaith relations. "There are a lot of sections of the Catholic Church, especially places where there is no living Jewish community, like parts of Latin America, where preconciliar attitudes still prevail," he said. "What I would like to see is a continued commitment that seeks the active implementation of the new theology into a grass-roots education," Rabbi Rosen said.

Rabbi Michael A. Signer, director of the Holocaust Project at the University of Notre Dame and a guest professor at Rome's Gregorian University, said he hoped Pope Benedict would encourage more education on the church's relationship to Judaism. Rabbi Signer said he wanted "some reinforcement in terms of the Congregation for Catholic Education that the teaching of *Nostra Aetate* and interreligious dialogue is integral to the education of those who catechize the church."

"The ingredients of a deeper understanding and positive teaching about Judaism are all present in Benedict XVI's writings," said Rabbi Signer, who uses one of the new pope's books in his class at Gregorian University. "The question will be how will he embody them and teach them in his new office."

In the political realm, Pope Benedict's keynote address at a 1994 religious conference in Jerusalem showed his support of the relationship between the Vatican and Israel, Rabbi Rosen said. A member of the negotiating team that established diplomatic relations between Israel and the Holy See in 1993, the rabbi said the future pope called the history of Catholic-Jewish relations "full of blood and tears" and referred to the "shadow of Auschwitz," which the rabbi said were "factors that must serve as an imperative to the Catholic Church to change its relationship with the Jewish people."

One worrisome issue for the Jewish community is the possible beatification of Pope Pius XII, whom some critics believe could have done more to save Jews during the Holocaust. "That would certainly have a souring effect on Catholic-Jewish relations," Rabbi Rosen said.

Some African church officials expressed concern that the new pope might not accurately reflect the needs of southern Africa, where AIDS and abject poverty are devastating the region.

Bishop Louis Ndlovu of Manzini, Swaziland, former president of the Southern African Catholic Bishops' Conference, last met with

Cardinal Ratzinger in February 2005 to arrange the visits of southern African bishops for later in the year. He said it is unlikely that southern Africa will be high on the new pope's list of priorities. "He is a bit reserved and is not a man who loves traveling," Bishop Ndlovu said. "But you never know, he may want to follow in the steps of his predecessor."

Bishop Kevin Dowling of Rustenburg, South Africa, said Pope Benedict's reputation as a hard-line traditionalist means "there will be little opportunity for openness of debate on issues, including the possible use of condoms as part of prevention strategies in the face of the AIDS pandemic." Bishop Dowling said he fears insufficient attention will be paid to Third World countries' "huge concerns," such as poverty and structural injustice. "We have to allow for the Holy Spirit to work and the possibility that he may change through the different experiences a pope might be exposed to," Bishop Dowling said. The pope's views could shift if "his visits to poor countries were done in such a way that he could sit in a shack and see a young mother dying of AIDS with her baby, as I have been doing for so many years," he said.

Archbishop Raphael Ndingi Mwana'a Nzeki of Nairobi, Kenya, said he believed Pope Benedict would "continue to (be a) champion for the poor in society" and would work to fight "the raging poverty and suffering of Africans." Archbishop John Onaiyekan of Abuja said, "Pope Benedict XVI has been there with the late pope, and he will toe the same line on the issues of female ordination, gay priests and the use of contraception. He has been against female ordination, homosexuality, use of contraceptive devices . . . and there is no way he will change overnight. There is no cause for alarm. The Holy Spirit has chosen his candidate, and he is infallible," the archbishop said.

Latin American church leaders welcomed the election of Cardinal Joseph Ratzinger as Pope Benedict XVI, but some theologians expressed concern about the possible impact of the man who played a role in the investigation of the theology of several of their colleagues in the 1980s. "He is a man with a very good grasp of the reality of today's world, of the relativism and moral subjectivity that dominate the world," said Bishop Andres Stanovnik of Reconquista, Argentina, secretary-general of the Latin American bishops' council, known as CELAM. Bishop Luis Stockler of Quilmes, Argentina, who studied with the cardinal in Germany in the 1950s, characterized the new pope as "a man of God, intelligent and very humble," according to the Buenos Aires daily *La Nacion.*

Some theologians, however, worried that an overly intellectual approach could open a gulf between church leadership and Latin America's 330 million Catholics. Several also expressed concern that the cardinal's homily at the Mass before the conclave reflected more concern with European secularism than with poverty and other problems afflicting much of the world's population.

The gap between the rich and poor is an increasing concern in Latin America, the region of the world with the largest percentage of Catholics. In Brazil and Colombia, the richest 20 percent of the population receives about 60 percent of the income, while the poorest 10 percent accounts for less than 1 percent. One-third of Peruvians and Guatemalans live on $2 a day. "The hot-button issues for Latin America are not stem-cell research or abortion, but things like social justice and corruption," said Dominican Father Edward Cleary, who has worked in Bolivia and now directs the Latin American Studies Program at Providence College in Rhode Island. The question, he said, is: Will this pope learn something from the church in Latin America?

The bloc of Latin American cardinals at 21 was second only to Europe at 58 at the conclave. Some observers said they hoped the new pope would not pay more attention to revitalizing the European church than to addressing problems in Latin America, where about one-third of the world's Catholics live.

"The church has become a Third World church, but (the new pope's) agenda is a European agenda," said Brazilian theologian Jose Oscar Beozzo. The choice of the name of a saint who evangelized Europe, Beozzo said, implies "that the central task of the church and his pontificate is the re-evangelization of Europe."

In his remarks to the cardinals at the end of the conclave, Benedict XVI pledged to "pursue the commitment to enact the Second Vatican Council," and Chilean Holy Cross Father Diego Irarrazaval, international coordinator of the Ecumenical Association of Third World Theologians, said he hoped that a "renewing spirit" would persist.

"Joseph Ratzinger promoted that renewal at the council, and he can do the same now as universal pastor," Father Irarrazaval said. "I would like to see more faithfulness to the Gospel that opts for the poor and less adulation of human beings."

In his closing comments at the end of a Mass with the cardinals April 20, Cardinal Ratzinger also mentioned other issues—including ecumenical and interreligious dialogue and "social development . . . that respects the dignity of all human beings"—that Latin American theologians are watching closely. In Argentina, Archbishop Domingo Castagna of Corrientes said, "We expect the new pope to be a pastor of the church and a pastor to all, just like John Paul II and John XXIII."

Even Animal Rights' Activists Responded

EVEN animal rights' activists issued statements applauding the election of Benedict XVI, a reputed cat lover. The Humane Society of the United States and People for the Ethical Treatment of Animals, known as PETA, gave the pope high marks for his previous comments about the care of animals. In an April 20 news release the Humane Society noted that then-Cardinal Joseph Ratzinger had said in a German press interview in 2004 that animals must be respected as "companions in creation." He said that while it is licit to use animals as food, "we cannot just do whatever we want with them. . . . Certainly, a sort of industrial use of creatures, so that geese are fed in such a way as to produce as large a liver as possible, or hens live so packed together that they become just caricatures of birds," seems "in fact to contradict the relationship of mutuality that comes across in the Bible."

"It is extremely significant that the new leader of the Roman Catholic Church has stressed the importance of treating animals with mercy and kindness," said Humane Society president and CEO Wayne Pacelle in a statement. PETA director Bruce Friedrich asked Pope Benedict to "lead the way into a new era of compassion and respect for all beings, regardless of species."

CHAPTER 14

Reaching Out to Other Religions

THE DAY after his installation, the pope met with the 70 Christian representatives, 7 Muslim delegates and 17 Buddhist representatives who had attended his installation the day before. Jewish representatives missed the meeting because it was held during their Passover observance.

Introducing the delegates, Cardinal Walter Kasper, president of the Pontifical Council for Promoting Christian Unity, told Pope Benedict that they all offered prayers for his ministry, which includes "a special responsibility for the promotion of unity among all Christians (and) for the advancement of understanding and friendship among the followers of the world religions for the building of peace among all peoples."

In this first meeting with representatives of other Christian communities and of other religions, Pope Benedict XVI pledged his pontificate would be marked by dialogue to promote truth and serve humanity. "I assure you that the church wants to continue building bridges of friendship with the followers of all religions, in order to seek the true good of every person and of society as a whole," he said.

In remarks to the Orthodox, Oriental Orthodox, Anglican and Protestant delegates, Pope Benedict said their prayers and presence at the funeral of Pope John Paul II was a "tribute of sympathy and affection" that "went well beyond a simple act of ecclesial courtesy."

"Much progress was made during the years of his pontificate, and your participation in the mourning of the Catholic Church over his death demonstrated how true and great is the common passion for unity," he said.

Pope Benedict said the Lord has made divided Christians increasingly aware of the importance of unity among them. "We all feel urged and encouraged to proclaim Christ and his message to the world, which often appears today to be troubled and restless, unthinking and indifferent," he said.

The pope told the Christian delegates, "I strongly feel the need to reaffirm the irreversible commitment" of the Catholic Church to pursuing the search for Christian unity. "The path toward the full communion desired by Jesus for his disciples requires a concrete docility to that which the Spirit is saying to the churches," he said, as well as "courage, sweetness, strength and hope."

The search for unity must be founded in prayer, Pope Benedict said. Christians must recognize that Christ is at work among them, sowing feelings of friendship, healing past wounds and "teaching us to live with a greater attitude of dialogue in harmony with the commitment that belongs to those who carry his name."

Pope Benedict offered special thanks to the Muslim delegates from Gambia, Iran and Italy and said, "I express my appreciation for the growth of dialogue between Muslims and Christians, both at the local and international level."

"The world in which we live," he said, "is often marked by conflicts, violence and war, but it earnestly longs for peace, peace which is above all a gift from God, peace for which we must pray without ceasing." Pope Benedict told the Muslim and Buddhist leaders that all who profess a religious faith must be committed to peacemaking. "It is therefore imperative to engage in authentic and sincere dialogue, build on respect for the dignity of every human person, created, as we Christians firmly believe, in the image and likeness of God," he said.

The pope asked members of all religions and "all who seek the truth with a sincere heart" to work together and to commit themselves to promoting "understanding, respect and love" among all peoples.

In his first foray outside the Vatican, Benedict XVI visited the Basilica of St. Paul Outside the Walls to pray at the tomb of the apostle and pay homage to his legacy of spreading the Gospel. "The church is by its nature missionary; its primary task is evangelization," the pope said in his homily. "At the beginning of the third millennium, the church feels with renewed strength that Christ's missionary mandate is more pressing than ever," he said.

Several thousand people attended the 30-minute service, which expressed the "inseparable tie" between the church of Rome and St. Paul. As Pope Benedict entered the basilica to applause, people stood on chairs to get a better look, and some chanted his name in Italian. He grasped several outstretched hands, stopping to bless the foreheads of those in wheelchairs and a few infants.

Pope Benedict said Pope John Paul II's many trips abroad were inspired by the same love of Christ that transformed St. Paul on the way to Damascus, and he asked God to nourish that love in him in order to meet the "urgency of the evangelical announcement in today's world."

He recalled St. Benedict's motto to "prefer absolutely nothing to the love of Christ," saying that St. Paul, too, made Christ the center of his life. "Passion for Christ led him to preach the Gospel not only with words but with his life," Pope Benedict said. The blood of the martyred Sts. Peter and Paul, as well as the many 20th-century martyrs Pope John Paul beatified and canonized during his pontificate, fertilized the church, the pope said. "If then the blood of martyrs is the seed of new Christians, one can expect a renewed blossoming for the church at the beginning of the third millennium."

CHAPTER 15

Pope Benedict XVI's Challenges

BENEDICT XVI faces many challenges in the new church. Among them are the changing role of the Catholic laity, the effects of globalization and the world economy and the needs of the Third World.

Lay people are playing an increasingly important role in the church that Pope Benedict XVI inherits. A growing shortage of priests coupled with increasing numbers of lay ecclesial ministers—lay people in ministry who formally work in the church's name and under its hierarchy—is an integral part of the current church scene.

Another is the extensive replacement of priests and nuns by lay teachers, and increasingly by lay administrators as well, in Catholic education. Catholic hospitals and other welfare institutions have become more and more the province of lay expertise and leadership. Parishes, the heart of Catholic life, abound with volunteer and sometimes paid lay ministries—catechetical, liturgical, youth and social service.

The 1983 Code of Canon Law extended lay consultative roles in church institutions and opened to lay people a number of official church positions or responsibilities once reserved to clergy, including the pastoral coordination of parishes where there is a lack of priests. Church experience with the new code and the possibilities it opens is still evolving.

Zeni Fox, a professor of pastoral theology at Seton Hall University in New Jersey who has written extensively on lay ministry, said Pope John Paul's apostolic exhortation on the laity focused mainly on the laity's mission to the world and exhibited "an almost begrudging acceptance of ministry in the church by lay people." She said the growing lay involvement in the church is "an unfolding reality that grows out of the (Second Vatican) Council but has not been incorporated fully into the structural and theological life of the church." As a result of the council's teachings on the laity, "things were set in motion that go beyond what was envisioned when the documents were written and go beyond where we quite know what to do with them," she said.

She said a document the U.S. bishops are working on concerning lay ecclesial ministries is an example of the church coming to grips with new issues that have arisen such as the defining of lay ecclesial ministry, spelling out formation and education requirements and saying what the church needs to do to receive and support lay ecclesial ministers. As head of the world church, "it's unrealistic to expect that Pope Benedict would acknowledge in any way the lay ecclesial ministries in the United States. I think it's too soon to expect that," she said. "But I would hope that the pope would be affirming of the role of the laity in the church as well as in the world, and not be fearful of it."

Sheila Garcia, assistant director of the Secretariat for Family, Laity, Women and Youth for the U.S. Conference of Catholic Bishops (USCCB), said during Pope John Paul's 26-year pontificate there had been a steady trend "toward increased lay participation in the church at all levels."

"In parishes we see this in terms of lay ministers as well as laity in the pews who are much more involved in running parish programs. We see it in dioceses with the increased number of lay employees, again at all levels including chancellor. And in lay movements, of course, which have really revitalized the church," she said. A major issue, too, is the laity's role in consultative structures, she said, adding, "That's going to be a major challenge for the foreseeable future." Garcia said the growing trend toward certification, assuring that lay people assigned to church ministries have the necessary training and skills to minister effectively, raises issues of what financial responsibility the church has for their formation.

Lay people generally have to pay for their own training and certification, she said, and one side effect is that the financial burden makes it difficult to recruit younger people for such ministries. "The bulk of people studying in lay ministry programs are over 40," she said. Because we have fewer priests, there are going to be issues around relationships with the ordained. I don't mean to posit that as a problem, but those are things that are going to have to be worked out," she said. "The fact that most of the lay ministers in parishes are women is another issue. Collaboration is a major concern that you hear women talk about all the time," she added. "How do lay ministers and the ordained collaborate?"

Daniel Lizarraga, former executive director of the USCCB Secretariat for the Church in Latin America, said laity have taken important leadership roles as delegates of the Word in many priestless communities in Central America and Brazil. They lead the Liturgy of the Word on the Sundays when no priest can come and conduct catechetical programs and sacramental formation.

Elsewhere in Latin America as well, lay involvement in church ministries and activities "is greater than it has been, not to the extent that it is in the United States," he said. "It's more limited, but it's increasing out of necessity."

Dolores Leckey, a senior fellow at the Woodstock Theological Center and first director of the USCCB office for the laity, said Pope John Paul "did a lot to advance the laity. He genuinely believed in the power of baptism." His 1989 apostolic exhortation on the laity "was a true call to the laity to participate" in the life and mission of the church, she said, "but words take you just so far."

"How all this got enacted is very spotty, I mean how it gets translated into where people live their lives," she said. "I think what he did was to provide the church with the documentation to continue promoting the role of the laity. . . . If we have a crisis, it may be a crisis of the will to follow through."

The growth in the church during Pope John Paul's 26-year pontificate indicates the challenges Pope Benedict will face. Worldwide there were 749 million Catholics in 1978, according to the statistical yearbook of the church. In 2003, the last year for which global figures are available, there were 1.08 billion Catholics—a 44 percent increase in a quarter-century.

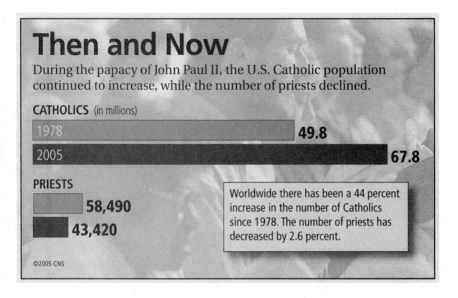

Then and Now

During the papacy of John Paul II, the U.S. Catholic population continued to increase, while the number of priests declined.

CATHOLICS (in millions)

| 1978 | 49.8 |
| 2005 | 67.8 |

PRIESTS

58,490

43,420

Worldwide there has been a 44 percent increase in the number of Catholics since 1978. The number of priests has decreased by 2.6 percent.

©2005 CNS

In that time the number of priests worldwide dropped from 416,329 priests to 405,450, a net loss of 2.6 percent. Globally, there were 1,800 Catholics per priest in 1978. In 2003 there were 2,664.

In that same time period the number of lay catechists grew exponentially, from 174,000 to some 2.8 million. Lay missionaries, not even listed as a category in 1978, now number more than 140,000.

In 1978, only 1,046 of the nearly 203,000 parishes or quasi-parishes, or about 0.5 percent, were administered by someone who was not a priest. In 2002, the latest year for which those figures have been published, there were 3.5 times as many not administered by a priest—3,575 out of some 217,000 parishes. The United States is among those places where deacons, sisters, brothers and lay men and women are coordinating the parish life of parishes where there is no resident priest. In the past 12 years their numbers have more than doubled, from 268 in 1993 to 566 last year. In the United States the Catholic population grew from just under 50 million in 1978 to more than 67 million in 2004, a 34 percent increase, while the number of diocesan and religious priests dropped from 58,485 to 44,212. Among the nearly 30,000 diocesan priests, more than one-quarter are now retired.

A 1997 study showed that the number of paid lay ministers in U.S. parishes was nearly 30,000 and had been growing at a rate of more than 5 percent a year over the previous five years. Similarly, the permanent diaconate in the United States rapidly expanded during the last pontificate, from about 2,500 in 1978 to some 15,000 today. Priests in U.S. parishes today are outnumbered by permanent deacons and paid lay ministers by more than a 2–1 ratio.

Fox said that as lay people take up leadership positions in parishes and dioceses "they do expect to have a voice." Unfortunately, she said, that "can be seen as a power struggle" between laity and clergy. "The way I experience it," she said, "is that they are looking for a place at the table, not a place on top."

Commentators noted that the pope elected to lead the world's 1.1 billion Catholics will face challenges from an increasingly globalized church and economy. Church experts said that this involves reframing Catholic social teachings to deal with the ever-widening economic gulf between rich and poor now that capitalism reigns supreme, and retooling a church that has become globalized through its rapid growth in Africa, Asia and Latin America.

While a new pope can directly retool the institutional church to meet new needs, experts said that he will have little ability to change the world economy as the church does not carry enough clout with world political and governmental leaders. Influencing economic globalization will require a pope who speaks out clearly against flaws in the system, makes influencing economic globalization a high church priority and encourages church alliances with other like-minded civic groups, they said. Globalization of the church is linked to globalization of the economy, with a new pope having the task of reassessing what it means to be the church and a Catholic in the modern world, said Fernando Segovia, theology professor at Vanderbilt University in Nashville, Tenn., and past president of the Academy of Catholic Hispanic Theologians of the United States.

Segovia and other experts said meeting both challenges involves giving local bishops and national bishops' conferences more power to address issues as they apply to their countries. Needed is a reemphasis of the Second Vatican Council teaching on collegiality, the sharing of authority between the papacy and the world's bishops, Segovia said. "How much leeway is the Vatican going to allow after a pontificate that hadn't allowed much" local authority, asked Segovia. The tremendous expansion of the church in non-Western parts of the world means dealing with different ways of understanding what belief is, he said. This includes such issues as liturgical practice, the role of women in the church and the church's relationship to native religions and Islam, he said. "For a church so thoroughly Western, this will be a challenge," he said.

Other experts added that evangelizing and promoting economic development need to go hand in hand as the church tries to adapt and adjust to new realities. The world is divided between the "have-nots" and the "have-lots," said Holy Cross Father Daniel Groody, assistant theology professor and director of the Center for Latino Spirituality and Culture at the University of Notre Dame. While being a moral voice for social change in favor of the poor, the new pope also has "to cultivate spiritual development as part and parcel of physical development," said Father Groody. Pope John Paul II was good at emphasizing the primacy of the spirit and integrating this with the need for material development, said Father Groody. A new pope "needs to build bridges across denominational and political lines, build a common vision based on the momentum that is already there" to influence economic globalization.

Other experts said that the new pope would have to reframe Catholic social teachings to encompass the specific problems of economic globalization just as Pope Leo XIII reframed social teachings at the end of the 19th century to meet the challenges of the Industrial Revolution and the call for workers' rights. This reframing has to be done "not by condemning capitalism. It's the only show in town," said Holy Cross Father Ernest Bartell, retired Notre Dame economics professor who specializes in international issues. Criticisms have to be fine-tuned to zero in on specific aspects of economic globalization, he said. "Capitalism does generate wealth," Father Bartell said. "The church needs to help create vehicles that will incorporate more people into the world of economic opportunity," he said. It also has to stress fighting corruption and protecting the environment as the market economic model does not provide correctives for these, he said.

"The market allows for pollution. This is only resolved outside the market through national legislation and international treaties," he said. The church has to empower people through its preaching and teaching and its initiatives to bring people together, said Father Bartell. "Bishops' conferences have to cooperate with other religions on these issues."

Influencing economic changes in favor of poor countries is an up-hill battle, said Father Bartell. The will by world leaders to promote meaningful development has weakened, he said.

Decades ago leaders were speaking of earmarking 1 percent of the yearly gross national product of each developed country for foreign aid and now the target is 0.5 percent, he said.

Daniel Finn, who is a professor of both theology and economics at St. John's University in Collegeville, Minn., said free trade agreements promoted by the United States in the underdeveloped world are an example of how the church must divide the good from the bad on concrete issues. "In general, trade and the foreign investment that comes with it are helpful," he said. "But underdeveloped countries are at a disadvantage in trade agreements. They don't have as many cards to play," said Finn. "The church is called to make clear how the United States uses its narrow self-interests in promoting trade agreements," he said. A new pope has to encourage national bishops' conferences to become active on economic globalization issues because specific situations change from country to country. "There has been a discouraging of local bishops' conferences taking on issues. It would be a good thing for the church and its social doctrine if local bishops are allowed to take on the application of church teachings to local situations," he said.

Vanderbilt's Segovia said that efforts to reframe church social teachings should take a lesson from liberation theology by taking seriously the current economic situation and incorporating it in its theological analysis of problems. Liberation theology was a response to the economic dependency theory, which held that underdeveloped countries remained that way because of policies in the developed capitalist world, he said. "Liberation theology included an economic component in its fight for liberation from dependency," he said. Today, a "reformulated theology" also needs a "critical analysis of the global reality in economic terms."

Father Gerald O'Collins, a Jesuit theologian in Rome, said the pope needs to seek new ways to answer the world's spiritual needs. The "enormous and dramatic" changes that have swept across the world since Pope John Paul II was elected demand that Pope Benedict XVI seek a fresh way to answer the world's spiritual needs, said the Australian priest, who is a professor emeritus at Rome's Gregorian University.

"Faith is seeking; it's an ongoing process that needs a newness and freshness in a world that's changing so fast," said Father O'Collins. He said "the rise of Islam," a globalized economy and powerful mass media "are all new factors" that need to be taken into consideration when proclaiming the Gospel message. "We are in touch with many more people, many more cultures, the world is hugely changed. We can't just live in a library and pull books from a shelf" to answer the world's needs, he said. The church cannot "just repeat the language of 100 years ago," because to do so "is not facing reality," he said.

Father O'Collins served as an advocate for Belgian Jesuit Father Jacques Dupuis when Father Dupuis' book *Toward a Christian Theology of Religious Pluralism* was being investigated by the Vatican's doctrinal congregation. Pope Benedict was head of the congregation at the time the 1998–2001 investigation was under way. The congregation concluded that the book contained no doctrinal errors but had "ambiguities and difficulties on important points which could lead a reader to erroneous or harmful opinions."

Father O'Collins said, "Everyone in theology is trying to understand" what faith is all about, and "they're trying to translate it into contemporary language."

"Innovation (in theology) is needed. It's not about repeating the past, but seeking a new way forward," he said. The diverse challenges around the world range from killer diseases like the outbreak of the Marburg virus in Africa, to free trade agreements in Latin America, to severe poverty in Asia, to a growing Muslim population and decreasing number of Catholics in Europe.

"Asia is absolutely not Latin America, and Latin America is not Africa. Lumping them together is a very simplistic way of looking at things," said Msgr. Felix Machado, undersecretary of the Pontifical Council for Interreligious Dialogue. In Asia, where only 2.9 percent of the population is Catholic, according to the Congregation for the Evangelization of Peoples, "one of the challenges is that Christianity has always been perceived as a foreign religion. The church must win credibility and truly make itself Asian," Msgr. Machado said.

With Catholics representing a large percentage of the population in only East Timor and the Philippines, interreligious dialogue is an important issue for the church in most of Asia. Much of the population also struggles with "scandalizing poverty," despite the shift of high-technology industry to countries such as India, Msgr. Machado said.

The poverty affecting 43 percent of Latin America's 534 million people is of particular concern to the church in that region, where conferences of bishops have spoken on human trafficking and on the impact of free trade agreements on poor merchants and farmers. An estimated 20 million Latin Americans have emigrated from the region in search of jobs, according to the U.N. Economic Commission for Latin America and the Caribbean.

Other challenges are posed by a return to democratic governance in many countries in the past two decades and the inroads made by evangelical and Pentecostal movements, according to Bishop Andres Stanovnik of Reconquista, Argentina, secretary-general of the Latin American bishops' council, or CELAM. "In Latin America, we must deepen our faith and commit ourselves to the consequences of the encounter with Jesus Christ. This must be manifested in concrete gestures of solidarity," Bishop Stanovnik said.

Poverty and disease are among the greatest challenges faced by the church in Africa, where more than 25 million people are living with HIV or AIDS and 12 million children have been orphaned by the disease. Other illnesses, such as malaria, also threaten to "undermine very quickly any educational or health progress that has been made," said Father Kieran O'Reilly, superior general of the Society of African Missions. The challenges facing the church in Africa vary from country to country, according to Cardinal Peter Turkson of Cape Coast, Ghana. "The African church is on the increase, and membership and vocations are growing," Cardinal Turkson said. Challenges, however, include political and tribal strife, government corruption and the need for interreligious dialogue. The election as pope of an African—such as Nigerian Cardinal Francis Arinze— would have had an impact not just on the church, but on the entire region, Father O'Reilly said, "because no matter where you look in the world Africa really doesn't matter to most people who make decisions."

In Europe, meanwhile, the Catholic population has decreased in recent years, posing a challenge to church leaders not only there, but also in other regions. Because the African church was built up by European missionaries, "if the image of the church in Europe is of a dying church, it gives us an orphaned feeling," Cardinal Turkson said. "It is important that the church in Europe come back alive." The decline of European Catholicism also poses an obstacle to dialogue with non-Christians in Asia, said Msgr. Machado. "People of other religions, especially Muslims, are saying why are you practicing (Catholicism)" when it is in decline in Europe, he said. "The church in Europe does need to revitalize, because otherwise it is held up in our parts of the world as a failure of Christianity."

"Suddenly it would become the real universal church," Father O'Reilly said, "and maybe Europe will rediscover its Christian identity and roots, led by somebody who can show us a vision of the risen Christ as they have expressed it in their culture, whether it is South America, Central America, Africa or Asia."

A key challenge for Pope Benedict is to continue building on the outreach to Islam established by his predecessor, a number of American experts noted. Pope John Paul II "built up a relationship of trust and opened a lot of gates," said Sheikh Muhammad Nur Abdullah, president of the Islamic Society of North America. He said he hoped the new pope would "continue this heritage and build on this trust . . . to enrich what we already have." Sheikh Abdullah said the fears and suspicions of Muslims evidenced in U.S. homeland security policies and actions have become a major obstacle to improved Christian-Muslim understanding globally, as the former tide of students from Muslim countries attending U.S. colleges and experiencing Christian-Muslim tolerance has dropped significantly. He hoped U.S. Christian and Muslim leaders could work together to change that atmosphere.

John Borelli of Georgetown University, who played a central role in developing the three official regional Catholic-Muslim dialogues in the United States, said that "a whole variety of issues come into play" in assessing the current state of Catholic-Muslim relations and the challenges for the future. On the diplomatic and political level, Borelli cited a need to address concerns of religious freedom and pastoral care for Christian minorities in some Islamic countries that deny religious rights to non-Muslims. He noted that Pope John Paul's outreach through visits to Morocco, Syria, Egypt, Jordan and other Muslim countries and his numerous meetings with Muslims in Jerusalem and other places have contributed to an atmosphere of greater trust. He added that Muslims were among the leaders of world religions who participated in the interreligious gatherings for peace that Pope John Paul convened in Assisi, Italy, and many Muslim leaders publicly expressed their admiration for the pope and condolences on his death. Borelli said local dialogues, like those cosponsored by the bishops in the United States, have also been established in various other countries and the Holy See now has an ongoing international dialogue cosponsored by Egypt's Al-Azhar University, the oldest and most prestigious learning center in the Muslim world.

Christian Brother David Carroll, undersecretary general of the Catholic Near East Welfare Association, said Catholic-Muslim relations today are marked by a mixture of very serious problems and hopeful openings that could augur major changes. Brother Carroll said Catholic schools and charitable works in predominantly Muslim countries are among the best hopes for long-term changes in Muslim attitudes toward Christians. When Muslims come into contact with Christians and Christian beliefs, especially in their formative years, those experiences effectively contradict fundamentalist preaching they might hear, he said. As an example, he cited the Muslim dialogue with Catholics in the New York Archdiocese, in which he is a participant. Two of the Muslim partners in that dialogue were educated in Catholic schools in the predominantly Muslim countries where they grew up, he said.

Sayid M. Syeed, general secretary of the Islamic Society of North America, said Muslim-Catholic understanding in the United States is different from many parts of the world. U.S. Catholics understand the Muslim experiences of discrimination as a religious minority because they had the same experiences two or three generations ago, he said, and U.S. Muslims now "are going through a similar experience. . . . The cumulative experience of Catholics is a guiding light for us."

By contrast, he said, in many parts of the world the Catholic-Muslim history is one of 1,000 years of conflict, and it could take generations to overcome distrust and hostility. As a result of the late pope's actions and gestures toward the Muslim world, "we have jointly started to build a new mood," he said, and the new relationship has been institutionalized, so that it will continue "regardless of personalities."

"Ultimately Catholicism itself has taken a major stride," he said.

Borelli said Pope John Paul went beyond the Second Vatican Council in advancing Catholic-Muslim relations. He said Vatican II called on Christians and Muslims "to forget the past," but the pope spoke not of forgetting but of "purification of memory" by repentance and forgiveness. In the pope's approach, "there is no peace without justice and there is no justice without forgiveness," he said. "I think Muslims will expect this attitude to continue" in the Catholic community. While the world's Catholic and Muslim populations are the world's largest religious groups, each with more than 1 billion adherents, Borelli said it would be a mistake to think of them "like two tectonic plates." Catholic-Muslim relationships are different in the United States than they are even in Europe, he said, and in Europe the issues are different in France than they are in Italy or the Netherlands. The issues in secular states that allow religious pluralism are different from those in countries where Christians find their religious freedom restricted by Islamic governments, he added.

Brother Carroll's first response to a question about the challenges the next pope will face in Catholic-Muslim relations was unusual and provocative. "In general, the overriding challenge is for all Christian churches: Why is Islam so successful in recruiting new members while we are not so successful?" He said he believes it is because "the process of becoming Christian is overcomplexified." While Christians are asked to go through a long period of formation before baptism, he said, people join Islam simply by "proclaiming their faith in one God."

While there are many positive developments in Catholic-Muslim relations that Pope John Paul's successor will be expected to build up, he said, one of the pope's chief concerns will be how to deal with "the negative realities" of lack of religious freedom for non-Muslims in some Islamic countries. "If you're looking at Shariah (Islamic religious law incorporated into civil law), for Christians this is a very difficult issue," he said.

Pope Benedict XVI faces bioethical challenges unforeseen 27 years ago. When Pope John Paul II was elected to the papacy in October 1978, the world's first test-tube baby was not yet 3 months old and a young woman named Karen Ann Quinlan remained in a New Jersey nursing home, breathing on her own two years after her parents won a court battle to remove her respirator. It would take three years for the first test-tube baby to be born in the United States and four more after that before Quinlan, fed through a nasal gastric tube, would die of pneumonia.

As complicated as those bioethical issues of life and death seemed at the time, Pope John Paul II's successor will face a vastly more complex series of questions and challenges, according to Catholic bioethical experts. Today, up to 1 million test-tube babies have been born worldwide, with questions just surfacing now about their long-term physical and emotional health. And the much publicized 2005 debate about the "right to die," in the case of the severely brain-damaged Terri Schindler Schiavo, involved withdrawing food and water, leading to her death from starvation and dehydration 13 days later.

"By the time (Pope John Paul II) became pope, we were already dealing with abortion, and euthanasia really took hold during his pontificate," said John Haas, president of the National Catholic Bioethics Center in Philadelphia. But the bioethical questions that confront Benedict XVI are much more scientific and technical, as stem-cell research involving human embryos gains greater acceptance in many parts of the world and various gene therapies permit the creation of "enhanced" human beings—children with characteristics desired by their parents, athletes able to perform unheard-of feats and seniors whose bodies defy the aging process. Haas said the issue of embryonic stem cells will present "a profound problem for Catholics in terms of doing molecular research." With research involving cell lines derived from embryos "happening everywhere," he added, "we might be blessed if no therapies develop from embryonic stem cells" and more scientists turn their attention to adult stem cells, which have achieved some therapeutic successes in humans.

Since Louise Brown, the first test-tube baby, was born in England in July 1975, the question of children's parentage has become increasingly murky. In 1976, Michigan attorney Noel Keane wrote the first contract between a couple and a surrogate mother. Ten years later, "Baby M" in New Jersey became the subject of a lengthy and emotional court battle between her surrogate mother and her father. These days, a baby might have five or more potential parents, as in the case of a divorcing California couple who no longer wanted the child created from a donor egg and donor sperm and carried by a surrogate mother. Or a child could have just one legal parent if, as one father of triplets has asked, a Tennessee court rules that his former girlfriend has no parental rights because the children she gave birth to were created from a donor egg and the father's sperm.

Helen Alvare, a law professor at the Catholic University of America in Washington and former spokeswoman for the U.S. bishops on pro-life matters, said Pope Benedict faces "a huge ethical question" on the topic of "enhancements—all the types of things that can enhance the human body or fix some problem." She said some couples' "desire for the best possible child" can result in a mind-set that sees human life along the same lines as "souped-up SUVs and Hummers."

"What does it mean when you can buy human beings?" Alvare asked, noting that laws against the sale of human body parts do not apply to the sale of sperm, eggs and embryos. Also of grave concern for Pope Benedict XVI is the question of ordinary and extraordinary medical treatment and the withdrawal of food and water, highlighted by the case of Schiavo, who died two days before the pope. Alvare recalled attending a symposium for Catholic lawyers in 1984 and planning a talk on the issues surrounding withdrawal of treatment. But a colleague told her then, she said, that her topic was "old hat" and the new ethical issue was withdrawal of food and water.

Haas, who sees an "increasing push for euthanasia" based strictly on medical views about quality of life and likelihood of survival, said he hoped Pope John Paul's own death would serve as a model for

Catholics worldwide on end-of-life decisions. The late pope's care-givers were "relatively modest in their interventions," but nothing was done to hasten the pope's death, he said.

On issues of life and death, Pope John Paul "has left such a tremendous legacy," Haas added. "It may take a generation for it to be fully understood."

CHAPTER 16

Media Coverage of Papal Transition

P EOPLE worldwide gathered in churches and in front of TVs as Pope John Paul II's funeral was celebrated in Vatican City.

From predominantly Buddhist Myanmar to predominantly Catholic Latin American countries, in chapels, cathedrals and outside mosques, Catholics and non-Catholics remembered the Polish pontiff. In the Middle East, the funeral was broadcast on Arab TV networks, including Christian, Muslim and secular stations. Many Arabic stations aired live coverage from the Vatican as well as studio discussions between Catholic and Islamic leaders.

Maronite Father Joseph Mouannes, general secretary of the Lebanese bishops' communications commission, said that when he left a TV studio April 8, throughout Beirut church "bells were ringing and the muezzin were echoing their Islamic prayers. I was shocked. I was asking myself, 'What is happening in Beirut now?' and then I remembered, 'It's the funeral of the pope.' You can't imagine, all the city, with all the bells ringing, and the muezzin praying. It was something unbelievable." In Bethlehem, West Bank, nearly 200 faculty members and students from Bethlehem University crowded into the small university chapel for a Mass; some students had to be turned away because there was no room. At one point in the Mass, three female students held aloft a placard with the words "*Santo Subito*" and "Immediately Saint" that intersected in a cross; the slogan was written again in Arabic atop the cross.

In their homes, many Israelis and Palestinians followed the funeral on their televisions. "I watched the pope on television when he was here five years ago, and he had such charisma and projected such warmth and love then that I realized that, even I, a secular Jew, also had warm feelings for him," said Mali Sorek, 53, who spent the morning viewing the pope's funeral Mass in her Jerusalem living room. "He was a very special man." In Pakistan, the national flag flew at half-staff on April 8 as a mark of respect for Pope John Paul. More than 40 police officers stood guard and mounted roadblocks outside Our Lady of Fatima Church in the capital, Islamabad, during a memorial Mass attended by diplomats and leaders of other faiths. The Mass was concelebrated by Archbishop Alessandro D'Errico, the Vatican's nuncio to Pakistan, and Bishop Andrew Francis of Multan.

In Mexico City, mourners stayed up all night at the Basilica of Our Lady of Guadalupe to watch the funeral, which was broadcast live on large screens and on television nationwide. Pope John Paul visited Mexico five times, and Mexicans left a sea of candles before a bronze statue of the pontiff in front of the basilica. President Vicente Fox, who attended the funeral, declared April 8 a national day of mourning and ordered flags flown at half-staff across the country.

In Haiti, some citizens recalled the first words the pope spoke as he stepped onto the tarmac at the Port-au-Prince airport in March 1983: "Things must change here."

"He was the first person to speak about change here," said Luc Mesadieu, presidential candidate for the Christian Movement for a New Haiti, a Protestant evangelical party, recalling the period three years before the fall of dictator Jean-Claude Duvalier. "At the time, no one dared to speak about change." In Casales, a community of descendants of the Polish army that fought with Napoleon against Haitian slave independence fighters, Pope John Paul was remembered with a special Mass. "We are proud to be descendants of the same ancestors as those of Karol Wojtyla," Massgoers told local media.

In Toronto, a city Pope John Paul visited in 1984 and again for World Youth Day in 2002, Polish-Canadians transformed the area around St. Casimir Church into an impromptu shrine to the pope. On April 8, the major thoroughfare on which the church is located was closed to allow Toronto's Polish community and others to attend a memorial Mass. That evening, the Toronto Archdiocese's Office of

Catholic Youth organized a memorial Mass at St. Basil Church in recognition of the pope's special love for young people.

In Moscow, some 1,000 people packed the city's Catholic cathedral to watch the funeral Mass televised live. The same day in neighboring Ukraine, Ukrainian Orthodox Patriarch Filaret of Kiev celebrated a memorial service at St. Volodomyr Orthodox Cathedral. "Prayers for Pope John Paul II today were the manifestation of Christian love, which is inherent in every Christian," said Patriarch Filaret, who met the pope during his 2001 visit to Ukraine.

In Myanmar, Catholics throughout the country began to pray in their perpetual adoration chapels for Pope John Paul, reported UCA News, an Asian church news agency based in Thailand. On April 8, some 3,000 Catholics jointed 140 priests and religious as well as leaders of other faiths at a special Mass in St. Mary's Cathedral in Yangon.

In Britain, screens were erected in London's Trafalgar Square, and some 200 mourners gathered in the rain to watch the ceremony. Most Masses throughout Britain on April 8 were suspended so Catholics could watch the funeral on television. The exception was Westminster Cathedral in London, which rang its bells to mark the start of a Mass for the pope at the time his funeral began at the Vatican.

In Wadowice, Poland, the pope's hometown, a giant TV screen was erected to allow residents to watch the pope's funeral. At the end of a two-and-a-half-hour Mass in the west Indian state of Goa, more than 4,000 people listened to a replay of a six-minute speech Pope John Paul delivered in the local Konkani language during a 1986 visit. After the service, most of the congregation remained to watch a live telecast of the funeral.

Preparation for this moment was lengthy and intense. It was standing room only in the Vatican press office as reporters arrived from around the world to cover Pope John Paul II's death. Vatican officials processed new accreditation requests at record speed and worked on expanding accreditation services and media work space to accommodate the flood of reporters.

Some journalists praised the Vatican information system for handling the days before the pope's death with unprecedented openness. Marcello Sorgi, director of the Italian national daily *La Stampa* said that compared to the past, information "has been very transparent." One reporter who has covered the Vatican for 25 years said it "used to be like pulling teeth" to get any official information at all. "Now we've gotten three briefings a day," he said. "They're sort of opening the doors. It's unusual."

From the time the pope fell gravely ill a few days before his death, the Vatican was unusually open about the pontiff's fading health and seemed to accept that his passing would be a major media event. The outpouring of prayers and affection was broadcast around the world.

Others were less positive. On April 1, some speculated that the pope was already dead and the news was being kept secret. For several days there was a shortage of chairs. Some reporters sat on the floors of the press office to write on their laptops. Others walked back and forth frantically in search of a place to sit, complaining into their cell phones while multiple television stations blasted news from sets around the offices. As the deathwatch continued overnight April 1 into April 2, reporters brought sheets, blankets, sleeping bags and carryout meals to keep the marathon going. As hours and days passed, relatives of reporters even showed up—including babies brought in to see their journalist moms, if only for a few minutes. The frenzied high-energy level of the press corps as reporters waited for the final word of Pope John Paul's death gave way at times to widespread tiredness. Sleep-deprived, haggard faces and eyes with dark circles were plentiful.

In the space between briefings and false alarms came time for reflection. Older and experienced Vatican reporters reminisced about previous papal deaths and conclaves. Other Vatican experts debated the meaning of the Bronze Gate entrance to the Apostolic Palace being left ajar the afternoon of April 1. Was it a signal that the pope had already died, as Roman folklore would have it, or just the shift change for the Swiss Guard?

Newcomers interviewed old-timers to get their bearings on the pope story and the intricacies of Vatican City. Amid moments of frenzy were a few of near-violence. Journalists pushed against and past each other to grab copies of the latest medical updates in crushes like those seen in soccer stadiums. Some reporters expressed disgust over the behavior of colleagues. "The TV people are the worst," one reporter said. "And somebody ought to count up how many times the networks declared him dead April 1 and then took it back."

Both planning and old fashioned fly-by-the-seat-of-your-pants journalism went into this story. Media outlets for years had been assembling lists of possible candidates, diagrams of the Vatican and the Sistine Chapel and studying the apostolic constitution *Universi Dominici Gregis*, written by John Paul II, which set new rules for a conclave. The media knew that the church would emphasize tradition but also looked at reality—the last papal funeral was 26 years before—before the Internet and before 24/7 TV coverage. Every media outlet looked for its own angle literally and figuratively.

Church property became valued real estate for media. NBC-TV not only joined a media compound at the head of Via della Conciliatione where cameras could get their head-on shot of St. Peter's Basilica, but also set up on a rooftop where they could feature the basilica dome in the background and capture the small smokestack above the Sistine Chapel. For that shot NBC-TV rented a section of the expansive Urban College, the Vatican's residence for missionary students studying in Rome. CNN took up residence on another section. Other networks found similar locations. Representatives of the news media had scouted the sites years before and negotiated and renegotiated contracts.

The networks also lined up commentators. NBC added to its staff Msgr. John Strynkowski, who had headed the U.S. Bishops' Secretariat for Doctrine and Pastoral Practice before becoming rector of the Cathedral-Basilica of St. James in the Diocese of Brooklyn, N.Y. The network put him under an exclusive retainer and made him one of its primary commentators. Msgr. Strynkowski flew to Rome with the NBC crew as the pope lay dying. CBS News relied on Father Brian Ferme, at the Catholic University's School of Canon Law, and he got significant airtime from the CBS Washington studio. The scramble for commentators was intense. CNN, based in Atlanta, scored a hit when it landed Archbishop Wilton D. Gregory of Atlanta as commentator for the pope's funeral. He was a two-fer "get"—a church notable and a liturgical scholar.

In Rome, the major networks—NBC, ABC, CBS and CNN—made steady trips to and from the North American College for the guests most in demand—Cardinals Egan, McCarrick, George, Keeler, Mahony, Maida and Rigali.

At the North American College where they resided until they had to move into the Vatican for the conclave, the churchmen gave interviews seemingly everywhere. They answered questions in the college courtyard, on the back lawn, in the front parlor, in the faculty lounge. They did telephone interviews from their rooms. They climbed rickety steps and tramped through weeds to give interviews in makeshift studios and on scaffolding at North American College.

Afterward a Nexis search revealed that during that April, the seven cardinals were cited in 3,441 media outlets, not including most church media. The previous month the total hits for the same cardinals was 418, about 12 percent of April's coverage. (The numbers did not include hits for Bishop William Skylstad, president of the United States Conference of Catholic Bishops, USCCB staff and others the USCCB promoted as qualified spokespersons.)

Such media coverage did not come without preparation by the church as well.

Remote preparation began in 2003, when the USCCB Department of Communications produced *John Paul II: A Light for the World*. The book marked the 25th anniversary of the papacy of John Paul II. The communications department produced it to give journalists what were called "essential resources," accurate information about that papacy. The book provided the backbone for a papal Web site, including useful materials on the conclave developed by senior media relations officer David Early, who put them on the Web the moment the pope died. Catholic News Service also posted materials which became key resources. The Web page was well used, and the U.S. bishops' Management Information Services found almost 41 million hits to the USCCB site in April, an increase of about 9 million over the month before.

After Pope John Paul II died, the bishops' conference set up a media office at North American College to facilitate cardinals' responses to reporters' voracious appetites for information. On April 9, the day after the pope's funeral, the cardinals agreed not to give interviews in order to concentrate more fully on prayer, reflection and private discussion before the start of the conclave April 18. Media became so desperate they became lurkers. Cardinal Keeler went to a concert at his titular church, Santa Maria Della Angeli, Phil Pullella from Reuters was there. "Hello, Phil," he said. "And that's off the record."

Many reporters who flew to Rome for the papal transition felt let down by the decision to become silent. "I'm disappointed as a journalist. And it's especially disconcerting because we know that the Americans are probably going to be the only ones who observe it," said Jesuit Father Thomas Reese, editor in chief of *America* magazine. He predicted that while the U.S. cardinals would "follow the rules" and end all press contact, Italian and other cardinals would continue to talk to their favorite journalists on background.

Many church officials in Rome said the pope's death and funeral offered a "teaching moment" like no other. Around the world, TV viewers saw hour after hour of live broadcasts that spotlighted the outpouring of affection for the late pope while explaining how the church works and what it believes. "We did the entire funeral Mass live, and we were allowed to catechize in the sense of explaining the different moments of the Mass. For a major network to do that was just fantastic for the church," said U.S. Father Thomas Williams, a member of the Legionaries of Christ who did commentary for NBC-TV.

For several days after the pope died, cardinals in Rome—especially those from the United States—were available to the media for additional comment on Pope John Paul and for general insights into the coming Conclave. The abrupt halt in media contact had been in the cards for some time, however. Some cardinals pushed for a no-interview policy soon after their daily meetings began April 4. Judging by the rules Pope John Paul revised in 1996 for the next conclave, he would probably have agreed with the media ban. He mentioned the need for secrecy 17 times and provided that well before the conclave began each cardinal would take an oath promising not to divulge information about matters "in any way related to the election of the Roman pontiff."

After the conclave the churchmen understood the importance of getting the story out especially to their people back home. The Tuesday night of the election—which occurred in the evening in Rome and midday in the United States—Cardinals Egan, Rigali and Mahony returned to North American College from the conclave and supper with the new pope. They met with media from 10 p.m. until 11:30 p.m. At 11:30 p.m. Cardinal Rigali did *Nightline* with Ted Koppel. Earlier in the evening, a media horde that had assembled at the North American College had despaired that the cardinals would return, and most reporters and a TV truck left around 9:45 p.m. When some cardinals arrived shortly afterward media staff called around town and reporters returned breathless from restaurants, hotels and the streets. They wrote well into the night. AP's Rachel Zoll wrote and filed from an apartment at the North American College. It was old-fashioned journalism. Earlier that evening two reporters from the same U.S. city would not leave the college unless they left together. Someone walked them off the property. They headed to their hotels. When they split up, one hopped a cab back to the seminary college. She planned to sit on the steps until 2 a.m. if she had to in case the cardinals returned. They were just driving in when the cab let her off. She beat her competitor.

The next morning after Mass with Pope Benedict XVI in the Sistine Chapel all seven cardinals who head U.S. archdioceses met with the media at a press conference and then with their hometown outlets. Afterward the cardinals did the morning shows and individual interviews with local affiliates.

The media coverage would have pleased John Paul II. Whether appearing before television cameras, radio microphones or reporters scribbling away with a pen, Pope John Paul II "was a natural" when working with the media, said U.S. Archbishop John P. Foley.

Archbishop Foley, who was named head of the Pontifical Council for Social Communications under Pope John Paul, said that the pope "was completely at ease with the media, and they were welcome to cover everything he did." That included showing almost every side and season of the pope's life, from hiking and swimming to praying and coping with an aging body, and the tradition of welcoming the media was present even after the pope's death, the archbishop said.

Archbishop Foley said the pope had not made a specific request for the media to be present at the formal and private viewing of the pope's body in the Vatican's Clementine Hall, but he said the decision to let in reporters and cameras and provide live television coverage of the normally closed-door event was decided upon in "the same spirit" the pope had of openness toward journalists. "He sought out the media. He had been an actor, and he liked creative people; he liked being around them."

Archbishop Foley said that through the media coverage documenting the pope's life and achievements, the pope was "showing what even one priest can do, because after all he was a priest." His department tried to keep 5,000 communicators happy during April events at the Vatican. When Pope John Paul II died the archbishop was in the United States—between Philadelphia and Annapolis, Md.—but was hunted down in both places and did about 20 interviews, including *Meet the Press*. With the death of the Holy Father, he was out of office but returned to Rome "to work as a 'volunteer.'" His office had planned for the moment, but protocol dictated that it did not admit it had done so.

In making plans, Archbishop Foley's office realized that they could not have communicators coming to their office inside the Vatican, which is right next to the *Domus Sanctae Marthae*, the cardinals' residence during the conclave. In preparation, he asked to take over several rooms on the ground floor of a Vatican-owned building just off St. Peter's Square for the work of accreditation.

"We knew that we had to expand and make more professional our facilities for television commentators," Archbishop Foley said. "As one who has done English-language commentary for 21 years, I knew that a TV monitor on a wooden board supported by two sawhorses would not be adequate for a major occasion." Eventually he convinced the civil authorities of Vatican City State to prepare facilities adequate for 50 commentators, each one with his or her own booth with a monitor and headphones and a light—and with the technical facilities under this type of grandstand facility. "When an art exhibit threatened to take over all or part of that area, we successfully did battle to protect the area—and even to have repairs made of the damage caused by the art exhibit in its attempt to expand," he added.

He recalled that for previous events, the space outside St. Peter's Square was filled with satellite trucks. "While this area was not under Vatican jurisdiction, we—together with the Vatican TV Center—negotiated with the city of Rome, with the Italian state network,

RAI, and with the European Broadcast Union to construct a three-story stand and fiber-optic cables to satisfy about 26 different networks and to avoid clutter in the square and to preserve the sight lines for all in attendance," he said. "Other networks had already leased local rooftops and hillsides."

What were the results? In the period between April 1–24, the Pontifical Council for Social Communications provided accreditation and assistance to 4,843 communicators involved in television, radio and photography. The press office of the Holy See provided credentials to about 2,500 journalists. Obviously, for the TV people and photographers, they had to guarantee visual access through selected locations and rotating pools. For the major ceremonies, they also had to inform TV networks of the availability of the images from St. Peter's Basilica and Square—and it was necessary for them to start a Web site independent of the official Vatican site, which was overwhelmed with inquiries.

Through that Web site, Archbishop Foley's staff "were not only able to keep those in Rome informed but also to make it possible for 155 networks in 84 countries to receive the needed information and texts to bring a live telecast of the funeral of Pope John Paul II to what was certainly one of the largest audiences in the history of television," he said. Later, they were able to make available the Mass for the inauguration of the pastoral ministry of Pope Benedict XVI to 124 television networks in 75 countries. Obviously, there were other telecasts from Rome during those historic days—especially the "white smoke" and the first appearance of Pope Benedict XVI. All these telecasts were made available to networks around the world through the Vatican Television Center and through the Italian state broadcaster, RAI.

A number of "firsts" should be noted, said Archbishop Foley—two Israeli channels telecast the funeral of Pope John Paul II with commentary in Hebrew; nine channels in the Palestinian territories telecast the funeral with Arabic commentary reaching all of Israel and Jordan as well; the Republic of Congo (Brazzaville), formerly ruled by a Marxist regime, used a telecast from the Vatican for what was believed to be the first time; Greece and Cyprus televised the funeral—with commentary in Greek. Thus, the ecumenical and interreligious outreach of Pope John Paul II had a profound effect on the coverage of his funeral—and the references of Pope Benedict XVI to his commitment to similar ecumenical and interreligious outreach were providential. Archbishop Foley also noted that the last major document of Pope John Paul II, *Il Rapido Sviluppo*—"The Rapid Development" (of communications technologies)—was on the theme of communications, and one of the first audiences given by Pope Benedict XVI was to the communicators who has covered the funeral of Pope John Paul II and his own election and beginning days as pope.

John Thavis, Catholic News Service's Rome bureau chief, afterward admitted that despite intense preparation, not everything was anticipated. "As reporters, we had a few years to prepare for the papal transition, and we thought we were ready. But of course there were surprises," he said. "One surprise was the magnitude of the reaction to the pope's death, the outpouring of sympathy and respect. For us, it was a very tangible thing, because we suddenly had to maneuver around the massive numbers of people who showed up at the Vatican. No one had ever seen anything like it."

Another thing journalists did not expect was the openness shown by the Vatican in the final days of Pope John Paul's life. "As we all know, over the last 15 years the Vatican considered the pope's health so private that they didn't even confirm he had Parkinson's until the death certificate was issued. After the pope's two hospitalizations in February and March, that began to change," Thavis said.

"I think the Vatican recognized that because John Paul II had been a global pope, this was going to be a global event. And that as a spiritual father to the world, he belonged to the world. It was not like the old days, when a curtain was simply drawn. This time, the Vatican began to prepare everyone for the inevitable," Thavis said. When the pope took this last turn for the worse, reporters expected a closing in, a batten-down-the-hatches mentality from Vatican officials. They expected the Vatican to hold to the old saying that a pope is in good health until the day he dies. But something different happened.

"That first night the pope lay dying, St. Peter's Square was kept closed. But then wiser heads prevailed," Thavis said. "The square was opened the next day and the next night, and it filled up, in particular with young people. They sang, chanted, prayed under the pope's window. Occasionally, a guard quieted them. But for the most part, they let them be. Because he was their pope."

Also new was that by the end the Vatican began to speak openly about the pope preparing to take his final journey. "On the third night, Vatican officials came down and joined the scene in the square. Again the square was filled with tens of thousands of people. By then, the folks at the Vatican realized this was a great moment of popular prayer, and they wanted to help lead it: Cardinal Szoka, Cardinal Sodano, Archbishop Boccardo. And so, in the end, the pope died surrounded by his people. The announcement of his death was made in the square, amid all those folks praying, with the world watching. They gave him a send-off. It was one of the truly touching moments in the whole ordeal."

"Meanwhile," Thavis continued, "in the Vatican press office, the news of the pope's death arrived earlier, and in a very different way in the end. As his death drew near, the press office was being kept open day and night, so I had my son bring down a sleeping bag, and the night of April 1, I bunked out in our little CNS booth. The next day the pope was still alive. When evening rolled around, around 8 p.m. some of the reporters tried to get away for a meal and a shower. So strangely enough, the press office was not very full. The Vatican spokesman Joaquin Navarro-Valls was gone. I was in our booth, watching the prayers in St. Peter's Square on the Vatican feed. And then I heard a woman in the press office scream. I looked at our computer screen and saw that the Italian news agency ANSA had flashed a headline: *Il papa e morto*. But there was no attribution. No one at the Vatican had announced it. The day before a false report about the pope dying had gone around the world. Was this one true or false?

"I didn't really know the meaning of the word frenzy until I saw the press office in those moments. I was immediately on the phone with my CNS editors in Washington. We had to decide whether to put out a news alert based on ANSA. And at that moment, my phone beeped, and I knew it was true. For several years the Vatican press office has had an agreement with the main agencies to alert them whenever there's big news. The alert works like this: first the press office sends a text message to your cell phone, saying there is an important statement from the spokesman, Navarro-Valls, coming to your e-mail address. That's why my phone beeped. The e-mail had arrived.

"The problem is, although the e-mails are designed to arrive in everybody's inbox at the same time, they don't. I still don't understand why, but people can wait several minutes. On this particular night, I am sure by accident, I was among the first to receive Navarro-Valls' e-mail.

"It said simply that the pope had died at 9:37 p.m. I was still on the phone to Washington, so we put out an immediate alert to clients. Then other journalists came rushing into the CNS press booth: they had not received e-mails and were frantic. They came to see our e-mail, and when they did, they went with the story. Our booth was a very crowded place for those few minutes. More than an hour later, Navarro showed up to confirm in person what we all knew. But for the first time, the pope's death had been announced by e-mail.

"The Vatican's openness continued during the funeral period. The morning after the pope died, I was in a pool of eight journalists who were taken up to see the first private viewing of the pope's body. We didn't really know what to expect. We entered the Clementine Hall and were practically alone in the room with the pope. We had a TV crew with us, and their cameras were rolling, and it was being fed live to the world. These TV images continued throughout the funeral, as you know. There used to be great vigilance about protecting the image of a deceased pope. Suddenly that concern seemed to evaporate. When the pope's body was moved to St. Peter's Basilica for viewing, many people approached with their cell phone cameras on. Even that was tolerated."

The Vatican press office, which deals with print journalists, was overwhelmed. The Vatican had to set up two press centers, one for permanently accredited journalists and another for temporarily accredited, the newcomers. "In Italy, where everything is kind of related to soccer, that was immediately seen as Serie A and Serie B—the major league press office and the minor league press office," Thavis said. "Naturally, some folks tried to sneak into our major league press office, but the Vatican posted policemen to check everyone's credentials, and even managed to unmask a few infiltrators."

"The idea was that, whether you were working in the main or

auxiliary press office, we would all have contact among ourselves. After all, the two press offices were less than 200 yards apart. But that's
where the planning didn't go far enough: because after the pope's
body went on display in St. Peter's, in between the two press offices
now ran an endless river of people, hundreds of thousands, and it
made crossing the street almost impossible," Thavis said.

Every journalist was working very hard. During the papal transition period, the production of CNS, for example, more than doubled.
CNS published over 475 news and feature stories on the papacy, and
900 photos and graphics. The news agency deployed five additional
correspondents in Rome, bringing in people with skills that allowed
them to conduct interviews in seven languages. Visits to the CNS
Web site doubled during that period.

The distinctiveness and greatness of Pope John Paul II as a communicator lay in his ability to use the media effectively without suc-
cumbing to their dangers, Archbishop Celestino Migliore said in an
address May 14. He was known as a "showman of God" and called
pontifex massmediaticus, or mass media pontiff, the archbishop said.
But he said Pope John Paul operated as a mass communicator in the
service of a truth that "is not man-made" but "totally dependent
upon God."

The archbishop, who is Vatican nuncio to the United Nations,
spoke at a New York bookstore. He spoke on "John Paul II: A Great
Communicator of Our Times," and said that "never before him did a
pope use the media as effectively."

"The art of communicating seemed to have been written on his
DNA," the archbishop said. "He then put it to use in service of the
Gospel in terms of the Gospel, and not simply (for) pure social communications." Archbishop Migliore said Pope John Paul "knew well
the risks of sensationalism" and the danger that television's tendency
to turn to the spectacular could "overshadow the sense of mystery"
and the concept of the people of God as a mystical body. He was
aware "and not silent" about the fact that "the mass media could and
often does distort reality," the archbishop said. Pope John Paul "was a
firm point of reference" who "kept us focused on the subtle frontier
between the transcendent and the here and now."

Archbishop Migliore recalled that before he became the U.N.

nuncio he served seven years in the Vatican Secretariat of State, and there had weekly contact with the pope. "I never left an encounter with the pope the same way I went in," he said. "There was something mystical in his eyes that always brought me to another level." The archbishop also said Pope John Paul "had the sense of prophetic gesture." As examples, he cited the encounter "with his would-be assassin in prison," his embrace of the rabbi at the Rome synagogue, his insertion of the written prayer in the Jerusalem temple wall, his talk at a Syrian mosque and his participation in the interreligious prayer services at Assisi, Italy. Archbishop Migliore also spoke about Pope John Paul's use of the Internet, his communication through many languages, his extensive international travels and other forms of communication. However, it was not the specific forms that held most importance, but his use of all these forms to carry out his "clear vision as pontiff," whose job was to "build bridges between man and God," the archbishop said.

He also said Pope John Paul not only used the media but had an impact on them, an impact shown in their coverage of his death and funeral. The media "adopted a positive memory" of the pope's legacy that recognized the best in "all the dimensions of his works, including the transcendent," he said. In his weakened condition of his last days, when the pope could no longer "speak a clear and strong word," his continued communication of moral authority upset the media's criteria of usefulness, beauty and strength, he said.

Pope shared special relationship with reporters—and they with him.

JOHN THAVIS,
CATHOLIC NEWS SERVICE

FOR the small corps of journalists who cover the Vatican, Pope John Paul II's death marked the departure of a global protagonist and the end of an era. Many of them also felt a personal sense of loss. They had witnessed the many seasons of his papacy—from vigorous globe-trotter to feeble old man—and gradually had formed a bond of sympathy with their newsmaker. For those who had followed this pontificate from start to finish, the world suddenly seemed a dimmer place.

During the second papal conclave of 1978, I was working for a Rome newspaper when news came over the wire that white smoke was pouring out of the Sistine Chapel. I hopped on my bicycle and pedaled furiously to St. Peter's Square, in time to hear an elderly cardinal come out and proclaim, "*Habemus papam!*" (We have a pope!) When the cardinal announced that the new pontiff was Cardinal Karol Wojtyla, most of the Italians in the crowd didn't recognize the name. "An African?" they wondered out loud. No, a Pole. More to the point, a non-Italian. There was perceptible grumbling.

Then Pope John Paul came out on the balcony of St. Peter's Basilica. I stood right below because I wanted a good look at him, and I was amazed at his youthful and energetic countenance. When he began to speak in Italian, he quickly won over the crowd.

From the beginning, it was clear this would be a media-friendly pope. He spoke seven languages, thrilled the multitudes and spoke his mind. He wrote a lengthy encyclical in his first year, but always understood the value of a sound bite and photo op.

After two years away from Rome, I picked the pope up again in 1982. That was the year he went to Fatima to thank Mary for protecting him during the assassination attempt at the Vatican a year earlier.

Like most reporters who covered his papacy, I had the most direct access to Pope John Paul during his foreign trips. Until the mid-1990s, the pope would stroll back into coach class of his charter jet and run the journalistic gantlet, taking questions from the 50 or so reporters allowed on the plane. A good question—one that piqued his imagination—could keep the pontiff in front of you for a minute or more. He was courteous with reporters and clearly enjoyed the repartee. On rare occasions he showed his irritation, bristling at a question about birth control in India or telling one reporter in an aisle-clogging huddle to sit down.

On the world stage, he had an actor's sense of drama and timing and appreciated symbolic gestures. That made him a reporter's dream and left journalists with some indelible impressions: the pope dropping in on a slum-dwelling family in Latin America, visiting a Jewish synagogue or riding a "peace train" to Assisi with religious leaders from around the globe.

The pope's energy level in earlier days was amazing. I remember watching him enter a parish church in Africa at the end of a long day. His aides wanted to rush him through the ceremony, but the pope was having none of it: He went up and down the aisles, shaking the hands of parishioners, kissing babies and making them feel as if they were the center of the universal church.

Vatican reporters had marveled for years at the pope's ability to bounce back from dire health problems, including the 1981 shooting, a blood virus, a broken thigh bone, a dislocated shoulder, gallbladder removal, an appendectomy, and various fevers and falls. In 1992 in Angola, after watching the pope wince momentarily as he walked up a set of altar steps, I asked a papal aide if the pope was feeling all right. A month later, doctors removed a tumor the size of an orange from his colon. That prompted the first of many reports of imminent papal death; if the pope was bothered by what appeared in the papers, he never let on. The pope's secretary, Polish Archbishop Stanislaw Dziwisz, used to enjoy remarking—with a sense of black humor—that several journalists who predicted the pope's demise were no longer with us.

One of the hardest things for Vatican journalists to witness was the progress of the nervous system disorder that gradually immobilized the pope over the last 10 years of his life.

His once-expressive face became a mask; his spontaneous banter with reporters and others dried up; in the end, he couldn't even approach the crowds that had so energized him in earlier years.

Despite some frustration, the pope seemed to accept these debilitating changes with the serenity of faith, convinced it was a chapter of life that the world should witness. Not all journalists understood this.

On foreign trips, some reporters observed episodes that seemed unthinkable a few years earlier. After he could no longer walk, the pope had to be lifted and heaved into cars, thrones and lifts in undignified fashion. Many reporters were moved by these scenes and often chose not to write about them. The ailing pope probably would not have minded reading the details of his decline, however. He seemed to trust reporters, and journalists covering the Vatican cannot remember him ever complaining about a story or about his treatment in the press.

In 2002, he even asked 14 journalists—including some who had been critical of the Vatican—to write the meditations for his Way of the Cross liturgy on Good Friday. As one of those invited to contribute, it occurred to me that the pope had an unusual amount of faith in reporters: He was convinced that our knowledge and experience might actually shed new light on the episodes of Christ's passion.

As the pope's own *via crucis* ended, the same journalists were thinking about the many things that changed during John Paul's pontificate—the increasing frailty, the loss of speech and the faded smile—and what didn't change: his intense faith in a new life that gives meaning to human suffering.

INDEX